THE CAMBRIDGE
COMPANION TO

RALPH ELLISON

EDITED BY

ROSS POSNOCK

Columbia University

 CAMBRIDGE
UNIVERSITY PRESS

CAMBRIDGE UNIVERSITY PRESS
Cambridge, New York, Melbourne, Madrid, Cape Town, Singapore, São Paulo

CAMBRIDGE UNIVERSITY PRESS
The Edinburgh Building, Cambridge, CB2 2RU, UK
Published in the United States of America by Cambridge University Press, New York

www.cambridge.org
Information on this title: www.cambridge.org/9780521827817

First published 2005

Printed in the United Kingdom at the University Press, Cambridge

A catalogue record for this book is available from the British Library

ISBN-13 978-0-521-82781-2 hardback
ISBN-10 0-521-82781-7 hardback
ISBN-13 978-0-521-53506-9 paperback
ISBN-10 0-521-53506-9 paperback

The Cambridge Companion To Ralph Ellison

Ralph Ellison's classic 1952 novel *Invisible Man* is one of the most important and controversial novels in the American canon and remains widely read and studied. This Companion provides the most up-to-date introduction to this influential and significant novelist and critic and to his masterpiece. It features newly commissioned essays, a chronology and a guide to further reading. The essays reveal new dimensions of Ellison's art radiating out from *Invisible Man* into new domains – technology, political theory, law, photography, music, religion – and recover the compelling urgency and relevance of Ellison's political and artistic vision. Since Ellison's death his published oeuvre has been expanded by several major volumes – his collected essays, the fragment of a novel, *Juneteenth* (1999), letters and short stories – examined here in the context of his life and work. Students and scholars of Ellison and of American and African-American literature will find this an invaluable and accessible guide.

CONTENTS

FIGURES

CONTRIBUTORS

PAUL ALLEN ANDERSON in the Department of History and in the Program in American Culture at the University of Michigan, is the author of *Deep River: Music and Memory in Harlem Renaissance Thought* (2001).

SARA BLAIR is Associate Professor of English at the University of Michigan and author of *Henry James and the Writing of Race and Nation* (1996).

ANNE ANLIN CHENG is Associate Professor of English at the University of California, Berkeley and author of *The Melancholy of Race* (2000).

GREGG CRANE is Associate Professor of English at the University of Michigan and author of *Race, Citizenship and Law in American Literature* (2000).

SHELLY EVERSLEY is Assistant Professor of English at Baruch College, CUNY and has published essays in *American Literary History* and *Minnesota Review*.

LAWRENCE JACKSON is Associate Professor of English at Emory University and author of *Ralph Ellison: Emergence of Genius* (2002).

TIM PARRISH is Associate Professor of English at Texas Christian University, and author of *Walking Blues: Making Americans From Emerson to Elvis* (2001).

ROSS POSNOCK is Professor of English at Columbia University and author, most recently, of *Color and Culture: Black Writers and the Making of the Modern Intellectual* (1998).

LAURA SAUNDERS is an independent scholar living in New York, where she is a writer for *Forbes*.

ERIC SUNDQUIST is Professor of English at the University of California, Los Angeles and his most recent book is *To Wake the Nations: Race in the Making of American Literature* (1993).

KENNETH WARREN is Professor of English at the University of Chicago and author most recently of *So Black and Blue: Ralph Ellison and the Occasion of Criticism* (2003).

JOHN S. WRIGHT is Professor of African American & African Studies and English at the University of Minnesota, and author of *A Stronger Soul Within a Finer Frame: Portraying African-Americans in the Black Renaissance* (1990).

CHRONOLOGY

1913	Ralph Ellison born on March 1 in Oklahoma City to Lewis Ellison, a dealer in ice and coal, and Ida Millsap Ellison (b. *1884*), a literate daughter of Georgia sharecroppers.
1916	July 19 Lewis Ellison dies at age 39 from a perforated ulcer after an accident hauling ice. Ida now the sole support of her two sons, Ralph and Herbert, the latter born the month before her husband's death. She is employed as a domestic and hotel worker. Active in the African Methodist Episcopal Church.
1919	Ellison family moves into AME church parsonage and Ida works as a sexton. The church library becomes a favorite place for Ralph. He begins first grade at Frederick Douglass Elementary School, a segregated school in Oklahoma City.
1920–24	After leaving the parsonage, the Ellison family lives in a series of rented rooms and houses, with Ida struggling to make ends meet. July 8, 1924, she marries James Ammons, a literate common laborer. He dies a year later.
1927–30	As a member of the Douglass school band, Ellison becomes a trumpet player during the height of the Jazz Age; Oklahoma is a mecca of southwestern blues, jazz, and swing and the home of the Blue Devils band led by "Hot Lips" Page. Immersed in the music scene, Ellison also pursues his love of literature and writing. Ida Ellison marries John Bell.
1932	Graduates from Douglass High School where he achieves first chair as trumpeter in the school band.
1933	Wins a scholarship to the Music School of Tuskegee Institute, Alabama. Arrives at college with two head wounds after hoboing on freight trains to Alabama and being beaten by railway detectives.

1935	Switches allegiance from the Music School to the English Department. Tuskegee freshman Albert Murray, who becomes lifelong friend and influence, admires him from afar. Discovers Eliot's "The Waste Land" and begins to write poetry and study the major modernists intensively.
1936	Leaves Tuskegee for summer, planning to return to gain degree; heads to New York, arrives in Harlem on July 4. Meets Alain Locke and Langston Hughes on his second day in New York. Studies sculpture with Richmond Barthe, works as a receptionist and file clerk for the psychiatrist Harry Stack Sullivan. Friendship with Hughes introduces him to left-wing political and literary circles. Decides to remain in New York.
1937	Meets Richard Wright, who has moved to New York to head the Harlem bureau of the *Daily Worker* of the Communist Party. Wright, who also edits *New Challenge* with Dorothy West, invites Ellison's first book review, and will be the decisive figure in radicalizing Ellison's political and literary views. Ellison attends the Second League of American Writer's Congress, sponsored by the Party, and hears Kenneth Burke's controversial lecture on "The Rhetoric of Hitler's Battle"; Burke will become a crucial intellectual influence. Mother dies October 16 in Dayton, Ohio. Spends the winter in Ohio, supporting himself hunting and selling quail and harvesting pears and walnuts.
1938–41	Returns to New York in April. With Wright's help he is hired by New York City Federal Writers Project of the WPA to compile information on the history of blacks in New York and keeps the job until 1942. Marries Rose Poindexter, an actress and dancer, in 1938. Begins working as a reviewer for *The New Masses*, a major journal of US Communist left. Declines to become a member of the Party, remains a fellow traveler. May, 1940 attends the Third National Negro Congress, a proletarian movement that he calls "the first real basis for faith in our revolutionary potentialities," and his enthusiastic report becomes his first front-page piece in *New Masses*. Publishes short stories in New York literary magazines. Wright's *Native Son* published in 1940, sells 200,000 copies within three weeks. Ellison hails it in a review as the "first philosophical novel by an American Negro." Estranged from his wife by 1941.

1942	Works with Angelo Herndon as managing editor of *Negro Quarterly*, a journal of left-liberal independent critical thought. Lasts four issues. Increasingly at odds with *New Masses* and its Stalinist position. Wright withdraws his membership in the Party.
1943	Avoids service in the Jim Crow US Army by enlisting in the integrated Merchant Marines for two years, working as a sea cook. Continues publishing stories. Meets Kenneth Burke. Covers the Harlem Riot for the *New York Post*.
1944–45	Publishes "King of the Bingo Game" in *Tomorrow*; he regards it as his first mature piece of fiction. Meets Fanny McConnell, who works for the Urban League and had formerly been in theatre in Chicago. Returns from the war zone in Europe in April, 1945. Publishes "Richard Wright's Blues," his first major essay, in *Antioch Review*, which places Wright's new bestseller, his autobiography, *Black Boy*, in the context of a blues aesthetic. Divorced from Rose Poindexter. Awarded a fellowship from the Rosenwald Foundation to write a novel about a black pilot in a German POW camp. Soon evolves into *Invisible Man*.
1946–52	Marries Fanny McConnell, who becomes his indispensable partner in life and art. She supports him for the seven years he works on *Invisible Man*. Ellison gains additional income from freelance photography and installing high fidelity sound equipment.
1952	*Invisible Man* published by Random House on April 12. Reaches number 8 on the *New York Times* bestseller list.
1953	*Invisible Man* awarded National Book Award on January 27. Earlier that day meets William Faulkner for the first time.
1956–58	Awarded the Prix de Rome, funding a year's residency as a fellow at the American Academy in Rome. Fellowship renewed for a second year.
1958–61	Teaches American and Russian novel courses at Bard College. "And Hickman Arrives" published in *Noble Savage* (*1960*), an excerpt from his novel-in-progress that would remain unfinished at his death. Seven other excerpts would be published in various literary magazines over the next seventeen years.

1962–64	Teaches writing at Rutgers University. Publishes "The World and the Jug," a two-part rejoinder to Irving Howe that becomes his artistic credo and a classic statement of intellectual freedom. *Shadow and Act* published, gathering together more than two decades of his non-fiction prose. Fellow in American Studies at Yale.
1967	Loses much of the manuscript of his long-awaited second novel in a fire that destroys his summer home in the Berkshires.
1969	Awarded Medal of Freedom, America's highest civilian honor, by President Johnson at awards ceremony in the White House.
1970	Awarded the Chevalier de l'Ordre des Artes et Lettres by his longtime intellectual hero André Malraux, the French minister of cultural affairs.
1970–79	Albert Schweitzer Professor of the Humanities, New York University.
1978	*Invisible Man* ranked as the most important American novel published since World War II in a *Wilson Quarterly* poll of American literature professors.
1982	Thirtieth Anniversary Edition of *Invisible Man*, with new introduction by Ellison, a major summary of his ideas.
1985	National Medal of Arts.
1986	*Going to the Territory*, second collection of prose written or published from 1963 to 1986. The opening essay, "The Little Man at Chehaw Station," is one of Ellison's masterpieces.
1994	April 16, dies in Harlem where he lived for more than forty years on Riverside Drive.
1995	*Collected Essays of Ralph Ellison.*
1996	*"Flying Home" and Other Stories.*
1999	*Juneteenth,* a fragment of his unfinished novel assembled by his literary executor John Callahan.
2000	*Trading Twelves: The Selected Letters of Ralph Ellison and Albert Murray.*

ROSS POSNOCK

Introduction: Ellison's Joking

Writing of late 1990s Hollywood films (*Independence Day*, *Men In Black*) in which black men and white bond in the midst of the greater dangers represented by alien invasions and incipient cosmic disasters, Paul Gilroy in *Against Race* (2000) finds them expressing a "real and widespread hunger for a world that is undivided by the petty differences we retain and inflate by calling them racial." A few lines later his book concludes by posing a utopian challenge to bring visions of "planetary humanity from the future" into the present and reconnect them with "democratic and cosmopolitan traditions."[1] If in our global, transnational age the renewed promise of cosmopolitan democracy has emerged as an animating ideal of popular, political, and academic culture, this is a way of saying that we are only now beginning to catch up with Ralph Waldo Ellison (1913–94).[2]

Of all American writers, Ellison most forcefully took up the challenge of thinking beyond the imprisoning reductiveness of race and of liberating the cosmopolitan energies of democracy. It is apt that Ellison has long been ahead of us, for he found art and utopian thinking intimately aligned, describing the "true function" of both politics and fiction at their most serious as a "thrust toward a human ideal" which demands "negating the world of things as given."[3] Only then is the "potential" for effecting change possible. Gilroy leaves Ellison unacknowledged, an absence that perhaps suggests that the canonical (and simplistic) image of the novelist as a politically disengaged mandarin and high modernist still muffles the complicated actuality of Ellison's thinking, much of it devoted, in fact, to exploring how, in American democracy, aesthetics and politics are entangled.

The *Cambridge Companion* aims to be a timely corrective. This volume will recover the urgency of Ellison's vision for the contemporary moment and reveal new dimensions of Ellison's art as it radiates out from the epochal *Invisible Man* (1952) into new domains – technology, political theory, law, photography, music, religion – and new texts. Since his death several volumes have appeared, including the magisterial *Collected Essays* (1995), the compelling fragment *Juneteenth* (1999), and the raucous, wonderfully bracing exchange of letters between Ellison and Albert Murray published as *Trading Twelves* (2000). The *Collected Essays* of nearly 900 pages, reprinting Ellison's *Shadow and Act* (1964) and *Going to the Territory* (1986), includes eleven uncollected pieces and nine unpublished ones, and establishes definitively Ellison's stature as that rare figure – both a major novelist and literary/cultural critic. Ellison's achievement in criticism and in fiction is virtually unique among postwar American prose writers; for precedents one must turn to the creative and critical work of T. S. Eliot and Ezra Pound in the early decades of the century.

In enlarging the Ellison corpus, these posthumously published books will give new impetus to the effort to unsettle received wisdom, particularly the various static images affixed to Ellison over the decades. Lambasted by the Black Arts movement of the 1960s as apolitical, canonized by white liberals and neoconservatives as an icon of blandly affirmative Emersonian individualism, Ellison has suffered both caricatures. In an attempt to retire these simplifications, this introduction sketches the distinctive logic of Ellison's sensibility as it informs the entwined dimensions of his aesthetic, cultural and political thought. Like all great writers, Ellison has his own ground rules, so to speak, which implicitly ask that we set aside or at least defer familiar moorings, standards and assumptions, the better to enter his imaginative universe with a minimum defensiveness. This relaxing of defenses is particularly important for Ellison because, like Emerson, W. E. B. Du Bois and John Dewey before him, he conceives democracy and art not simply as doctrine, or knowledge, or contemplation, but as strenuous, risky ways of acting in the world.

Ellison's namesake Ralph Waldo Emerson noted in his journal that "flowing is the secret of things & no wonder the children love masks, & to trick themselves in endless costumes, & be a horse, a soldier, a parson, or a bear, and older delight in theatricals."[4] If "flowing is the secret of things"– of nature and of matter and of humans' mimetic faculty – it finds its apotheosis in Emerson's relentlessly expanding early nineteenth-century America. He looks around to observe that "new arts destroy the old. See the investment of capital in aqueducts, made useless by hydraulics; fortifications by gunpowder; roads and canals, by railways; sails, by steam; steam by electricity" (175). Emerson's insight into the ubiquity of metamorphic flowing in his country's natural, human, and social order echoes in Ellison's famous claim (apropos of the Boston tea party when Americans disguised as Indians dumped tea into Boston Harbor) that "when American life is most American it is apt to be most theatrical." Ever since, "the mobility of the society created in this limitless space has encouraged the use of the mask for good and evil." Masking, Ellison writes, is a joking "play upon possibility and ours is a society in which possibilities are many" (*Collected Essays* 107–8).

But if theatricality is second nature, Americans also deny it, famously insisting on a pristine Adamic innocence. Masking elicits denial perhaps because it shatters the cherished belief that governs the epistemology of American innocence – the transparent fit between appearance and reality. Recall, for instance, that impeccable individualist Isabel Archer at the start of *The Portrait of a Lady*; her fondest principle is that "she would be what she appeared, and she would appear what she was."[5] But with the advent of masking, as Ellison notes, at least two things intrude between "appearance and reality" – "ironic awareness of the joke," and "perhaps even an awareness of the joke that society is man's creation, not God's" (108). In other words, masking plays havoc with transparent self-identity, precipitating a fall into knowledge of and responsibility for complexity and history. In flight from both, in flight from the destabilizing, denaturalizing "joke" inscribed in their country's motley social and cultural order, Americans find refuge in fantasies of purism, of cloistered autonomy. These are ratified by absolute authority (God or Nature) that also sanctions as immutable truth the rule of invidious racial hierarchy and ethno-racial separatism.

Repressing self-division, we also have divided ourselves from each other and sapped the strengths of democracy. Fulfillment of democracy's dynamic possibilities is continually deferred to the future, while the present remains stunted in the obdurate reflexes of American racism, leaving the citizenry mired in disavowals and fears of black and white fraternity. As an antidote, Ellison would in effect reinvigorate the capacity for joking, for improvising new forms, so that Americans can begin to come alive to the fact that the nation's population and cultural life has always been a vibrantly miscegenated affair, mirroring the "fluid, pluralistic turbulence of the democratic process" (*Collected Essays* 500). What is required is psychic, social and political renovation. In making us aware of the urgent need for change, Ellison's art is desperately serious joking, nothing less than a demand to embrace the anarchic energies of freedom within the variegated American scene.

Ellison, like Emerson, has always regarded trust in certitude, in the fixed and permanent, as little more than surrender to ideological conformity of any stripe; as he says of efforts to define America, to do so "is to impose unity upon an experience that changes too rapidly for linguistic or political exactitude" (*Collected Essays* 511). Forgoing the illusory comforts of exactitude, Ellison's body of work from first to last solicits the power of the tentative and improvised especially as expressed in a nearly balletic suppleness that embodies "a slightly different sense of time," one in which "you're never quite on the beat ... Instead of the swift and imperceptible flowing of time, you are aware of its nodes ... and you slip into the breaks and look around."[6]

This famous passage from the prologue to *Invisible Man* should be read as a signature moment in Ellison's thought; focusing on action rather than identity, it summons the subtle poetry of invisibility as the stance of maximum power, be it aesthetic or athletic (the reefer smoking narrator is, after all, describing Louis Armstrong bending his trumpet into a "beam of lyrical sound" and recalling a memory of a prizefighter suddenly slipping inside his opponent's sense of time). What Philip Roth in *The Human Stain* (a novel that has been called a homage to *Invisible Man*) esteems as the capacity for "being game in the face of the worst. Not courageous. Not heroic. Just game," suggests something of the craftiness for slipping into the breaks and looking around.[7] To be game is also in effect the advice of the narrator's grandfather, the "odd old guy" and former slave who causes all "the trouble" by his deathbed whisper. He says: "keep up the good fight ... our life is a war and I've been a traitor all my born days ... Live with your head in the lion's mouth. I want you to overcome 'em with yeses, undermine 'em with grins ... "(16)

If Ellison could be said to have a creed (though this would seem to require the surrender to exactitude against which I have been arguing) both of these gnomic passages might be said to distill it. But it is a self-consuming creed for it imparts not a portable summary of beliefs but instead unsettling riddles that demand of their recipients an imperative to be game, to remain in agile off-balance alertness. The effect on the narrator is to keep him perpetually "running," as his anxious dream discloses at the end of Chapter One. The demand to keep running, to keep weaving in and out of time, and to keep your head in the lion's mouth, encourage the discipline needed for living in wartime, as does Ellison's favorite oxymoron of "antagonistic cooperation." All are modes of survival in a baffling world of transition where nothing solid is its solid self. This world is better known as American democracy, replete with "mysteries and pathologies"; but even the invisible can negotiate them and act politically, as grandfather's advice implicitly insists.[8] "Play the game but don't believe in it," counsels the brilliant, deranged Vet from the Golden Day. Or, as Ellison said years later, "grasp the mysterious possibilities generated by ... our freedom within unfreedom" (*Collected Essays* 531).

Because they are never quite on the beat, these teasingly paradoxical statements spark thought in the reader, and the exertions of thinking are especially vital to uphold against "the feverish industry dedicated to telling Negroes who and what they are" (*Collected Essays* 57). Ellison turns his back on the industry (he has the social sciences, particularly sociology, in mind) which works overtime to make the production of racial and ethnic identity a basic instrument in keeping US culture stratified and atomized, a permanent Jim Crow regime of segregation in effect. He opts for an alternative outlook whose impatience with "separate but equal" derives from the unassailable recognition that America comprises "motley mixtures of people": "In this particular country even the most homogenous gatherings of people are mixed and pluralistic" (*Collected Essays* 500). And not only mongrel, but masked: "the declaration of an American identity meant the assumption of a mask" (107). Once one grants the American reality of masking, of impurity, of motley mixtures, once one grants, that is, the fact that "whatever the efficiency of segregation as a sociopolitical arrangement, it has been far from absolute on the level of *culture*," then the repressive demands of identity enforced by hierarchies grounded in the fetish of blood, ownership and origin become stymied and precarious (163). What emerges is the primacy of practice which entails improvising evolving strategies of stylish being in the world. As his close friend Albert Murray once said, "anytime you're talking about conduct, you're talking about culture," and cultural conduct is above all "a process of stylization; and what it stylizes is experience … It is a way of sizing up the world, and so, ultimately, and beyond all else, a mode and medium of survival"[9] (qtd Posnock 201).

Keeping in mind Ellison's fascination with practice, particularly with what he calls "the American compulsion to improvise upon the given," will help loosen the grip of the received critical wisdom regarding *Invisible Man* – its (alleged) devotion to that familiar old chestnut American identity, be it expressed in the existential anguish of invisibility, or the narrator's quest for self-discovery. The identity theme, however venerable, is ultimately too flat and static, too pacific, to engage Ellison's passion for art's joking, recalcitrant vigor: "it is in the very *spirit* of art to be defiant of categories" he says (*Collected Essays* 514). And he inscribes defiance at the start of his novel, in grandfather's deathbed riddle which henceforward will itch at the narrator's ears and the reader's, and in overlaying urban realism with the surreal, disorienting prologue's bending of time and space.

Instead of affirming the preordained or familiar, be it in regards to literary genre or anything else, Ellison pursues the incalculable "futuristic drama of American democracy" (*Collected Essays* 851). This drama conditions American art and identity, an inextricability that explains why the existential or "identity" reading of *Invisible Man* is inadequate: biased to the inward and psychological, this reading ignores the political, thus sundering what Ellison entangles. To represent a "society caught in the process of being improvised out of the democratic ideal" requires that the artist cultivate a certain disposition, that he/she "hang loose and try to be as receptive, resourceful and as encompassing in capturing truth as his larger subject is in evading it"(*Collected Essays* 466).

The writer's stance of alert flexibility encourages him or her to fashion prose supple and eloquent enough to take the approximate measure of the "experience of human beings living in a world of turbulent transition" and thereby train readers to become "conscious, articulate citizens" (*Collected Essays* 444, 482). Like Whitman before him, Ellison makes reading a "gymnast's struggle" (the poet's phrase) to sharpen minds for civic responsibility. Coming to learn to live in this world, the narrator of *Invisible Man* discovers, is to learn "to give pattern to the chaos which lives within the pattern of your certainties" (580). Joining author and reader are characters endowed with eloquence – Ellison names Henry James's "'super subtle fry'" as exemplars of "ideal creatures" who were "unlikely to turn up in the world" but whose powers of articulation project a community of "human possibility." Here "the interests of art and democracy converge" (*Collected Essays* 482). Fiction, says Ellison, is a "mere game of 'as if,' therein lies its true function and its potential for effecting change." The community brought into being by literary experience is a "fictional *vision* of an ideal democracy" because it scrambles hierarchy and authority by, for instance, letting young boys and escaped slaves who are afloat together on a raft disclose "transcendent truth and possibilities" (482).

The aesthetic community, wherein is cultivated the requisite dexterity to negotiate the democratic "whirlpool," stands in utopian rebuke of the fact that the "rich possibilities of democracy" are stunted by "glaring inequities" and "unfulfilled promises" (504). Compounding these problems is the resurgence, beginning in the 1970s, of the "feverish industry" of identity with its "heady evocations of European, African and Asian backgrounds accompanied by chants proclaiming the inviolability of ancestral blood. Today [Ellison is writing in the late 1970s] blood magic and blood thinking, never really dormant in American society, are rampant among us" (505). These are the kinds of remarks that earned Ellison the ire of black nationalists and, later, proponents of multiculturalism. But it is important to specify precisely what Ellison is criticizing. His target is not the familiar conservative one that decries ethnic consciousness as a violation of the sanctity of American unity.

Rather, Ellison's complaint is that blood thinking is an anxious, defensive response to the radical challenge of American democracy. In the face of its demands American citizens are often overwhelmed, so they "seek psychic security from within" their "inherited divisions" (503). "We cling desperately to our own familiar fragment of the democratic rock, and from such fragments we confront our fellow Americans" (500). The result is that "deep down, the American condition is a state of unease" (504). We "shy from confronting our cultural wholeness," says Ellison in the crucial essay "The Little Man at Chehaw Station" from which I have been quoting, "because it offers no easily recognizable points of rest, no facile certainties as to who, what, or where (culturally or historically) we are. Instead the whole is always in cacaphonic motion" (504). Before this spectacle of barely controlled chaos which "eludes accepted formulations," (512), proponents of ethnic and racial identity stand flatfooted, refusing to enter into the cacaphonic rhythm, or slip into the breaks and look around. To do so, to relish rather than retreat from the American "vortex," requires a psychic elasticity equivalent to the reefer induced bending of time and space that the narrator experiences in the prologue. Perhaps those who advocate blood magic and blood thinking would loosen up after a bit of reefer. Then they would be ready to set aside their tribal armor and play the "appropriation game," enter into the volatile mix of clashing styles and become "American joker[s]" (511, 507).

The ludic element in Ellison's thought comes to the fore as a mimetic response to the volatile, motley mess of American culture, what he calls our chaotic "unity-within-diversity." To enter into this mess produces "comedy," says Ellison, both conscious and unconscious, and makes the American a joker. He gives us an exemplary instance: recalling the sight of a dashiki-clad blue-eyed mulatto in English riding boots and "fawn-colored riding breeches," with a homburg on his "huge Afro-coiffed head," who has just climbed out of a new Volkswagen Beetle "decked out with a gleaming Rolls-Royce radiator," Ellison comments: "whatever his politics, sources of income, hierarchal status and such, he revealed his essential 'Americanness' in his freewheeling assault upon traditional forms of the Western aesthetic. Whatever identity he presumed to project, he was exercising an American freedom ... Culturally he was an American joker," playing "irreverently upon symbolism of status, property and authority" (506–7). In other words, the Americanness of this "American joker" is found not in a prior affirmation of essence, a fact of descent, but instead is *derived* from his playful act of assemblage. The joker achieves identity through his improvised pastiche. Decades before hip-hop, Ellison was asserting the centrality of its formal exuberance, if not its regressive content.

Blood magic and blood thinking abruptly short-circuit the game of impro-visation with a party-pooping purism that is a symptom, says Ellison, of "the current form of an abiding American self-distrust ... a gesture of democracy-weary resignation" (508). Against the exhaustion and unease of those who subscribe to various ideologies of American purity – be it Adamic innocence, "nature's nation," American exceptionalism, Jim Crow racism and Jim Crow (separatist) multiculturalism – Ellison sets the vitality of American impurity embodied in the motor of the culture – "the appropriation game." Everyone played it. Pilgrims played it with Indians, Africans with the Hebrew Bible, whites with African-Americans and vice-versa, all busy taking over useful elements from the other and remaking them for their own purposes:

> It is here, if we would but recognize it, that elements of the many available tastes, traditions, ways of life, and values that make up the total culture have been ceaselessly appropriated and made their own ... by groups and individuals to whose own background they are historically alien. Indeed, it was through this process of cultural appropriation (and misappropriation) that Englishmen, Europeans, Africans, and Asians *became* Americans. (510)

To view American culture as an "appropriation game," an approach pioneered in the 1930s by Constance Rourke, is to expose the myth of American innocence and its romance of autogenesis. Instead of an innocent, Ellison was a "blues-toned laugher-at-wounds who included himself in his indictment of the human condition," as he once described the poised and stoical voice whose cadences he sought to render in the prose of his novel (481). In accepting complicity, Ellison means to break the spell of innocence, much as Philip Roth would do in his insistence that the human stain is indwelling, in everyone: "there's no other way to be here. Nothing to do with disobedience ... it's why all the cleansing is a joke. A barbaric joke at that. The fantasy of purity is appalling. It's insane."[10] It also tends to foment violence because purists tend to preserve their purity by producing difference as degraded, dangerous otherness, a stigmatizing that often leads to scapegoating of sacrificial victims to fortify the boundary of self and other. This is one reason Nietzsche said that the only idea of culture that is not deadly understands culture as a "certain 'style' of life, not given by nature or destined by history but formed of an assemblage of living institutions." Commenting on this, Geoffrey Hartman observes that Nietzsche's (and Ellison's we could add) notion of culture as assemblage and style is a "beneficial and peaceable rather than militant concept [that] has become rare in modernity."[11]

The fact that cultures are made and sustained by ongoing acts of cosmopolitan thievery, as the black minister and thinker Alexander Crummell noted in the late nineteenth century, has always been a scandal in a culture of romantic individualism with its passion for personal authenticity and genuineness. Emerson, the supposed prophet of that culture but more accurately its subtlest critic, said "every man is a quotation from all his ancestors" and "every house is a quotation out of all forests and mines and stone-quarries" (Emerson 319). And he goes on in the same essay, "Quotation and Originality," to quote Goethe's remark: "'What would remain to me if this art of appropriation were derogatory to genius?'" (329). *This* Emerson, who finds "flowing [is] the secret of things," and who says "there is no pure originality," groups with Ellison and with Crummell and with Henry James. In 1867 the novelist noted that "to be an American is a great preparation for culture . . . we can deal freely with forms of civilization not our own, can pick and choose and assimilate and in short (aesthetically etc.) claim our property wherever we find it."[12] Together this appropriately motley crew forms a counter tradition of cosmopolitan, anti-romantic cultural theory whose motto might be borrowed from Ellison's remark that "it is very difficult in this country to find a pure situation. Usually when you find some assertion of purity, you are dealing with historical, if not cultural ignorance"(443).

He said this in a tribute essay on Alain Locke, the black philosopher and "cultural mid-wife" to the Harlem Renaissance, a self-described cosmopolitan whose iconoclastic theories of the relation of race and culture powerfully influenced Ellison and his friend the critic and novelist Albert Murray. For Locke, cosmopolitanism means, above all, that "culture has no color." Nor do individuals, groups or nations possess "special proprietary rights" to culture.[13] To end "the vicious practice" of exclusionary ownership of "various forms of culture" would be to abandon a practice that undergirds imperialism and that "has been responsible for the tragedies of history." Deracializing culture leaves us free to "face the natural fact of the limitless interchangeableness of culture goods" (203). Locke's vision tallies with a better known one – the "kingdom of culture" – a realm beyond the reach of Jim Crow segregation, entrance to which, says W. E. B. Du Bois in *The Souls of Black Folk* (1903), is the goal of black striving.

In his essay on Locke, Ellison understands the very notion of "human enterprise" as conditioned by the fact that "we live one upon the other; we follow, we climb upon the shoulders of those who have gone before" (*Collected Essays* 446). This acute sense of embeddedness issues not in a melancholy recognition of belatedness but rather inspires the playful spirit of appropriation and reinvention, a riffing that *Invisible Man* achieves in regards to Hawthorne, Melville, Stephen Crane, Booker T. Washington, James Weldon Johnson, Frederick Douglass, among others. These figures remain not static touchstones but become fluid, metamorphic presences. In short, *Invisible Man* puts in practice its author's theory of cultural renewal.

Arguably, the virtuoso performance of appropriation in the novel is Ellison's turning of "Emerson" into a figure of protean significances in excess of received wisdom. In naming two characters "Emerson," one a wealthy pillar of the establishment, the other his angry, deviant offspring, Ellison sets the canonical figure of sovereign selfhood spinning, as it collides with its subversive kin. The tensions generated by the two "Emersons" – one stolidly familiar, the other secretly "flowing" – not only testify to the wit and audacity of Ellison's reworking of a crucial precursor, but also constitute one of the most searching acts of cultural criticism to be found *within* a novel. By taking Ellison at his joking and strenuous word, *The Cambridge Companion* aims to bring forward a fuller sense of the breadth and depth and vibrancy of Ellison's cultural witnessing, artistic making, and "freewheeling appropriations."

Notes

1. Paul Gilroy, *Against Race* (Cambridge: Harvard University Press, 2000), p. 356.
2. Until Lawrence Jackson's research Ellison's date of birth was listed as 1914. I have corrected it to 1913. See Chapter One of this volume.
3. Ralph Ellison, *The Collected Essays of Ralph Ellison*. Ed. John F. Callahan (New York: Random House, 1995), p. 482. Hereafter cited in the text as *Collected Essays*.
4. Ralph Waldo Emerson, *Emerson's Prose and Poetry*. Norton Critical Edition. Ed. Joel Porte and Saundra Morris (New York: Norton, 2001), p. 523. Hereafter cited in the text as Emerson.
5. Henry James, *The Portrait of a Lady*. Norton Critical Edition. Ed. Robert Bamberg (New York: Norton, 1975), p. 54.
6. Ralph Ellison, *Invisible Man* (New York: Vintage, 1982), p. 8.
7. Philip Roth, *The Human Stain* (Boston: Houghton Mifflin, 2000), p. 340.
8. See Danielle Allen, "Law's Necessary Forcefulness: Ralph Ellison vs. Hannah Arendt on the Battle of Little Rock." *Oklahoma City University Law Review*, Fall, 2001 (857–95).
9. Quoted in Ross Posnock, *Color and Culture: Black Writers and the Making of the Modern Intellectual* (Cambridge: Harvard University Press, 1998), p. 201.
10. Roth, *Human Stain*, p. 242.
11. Geoffrey Hartman, *The Fateful Question of Culture* (New York: Columbia University Press, 1997), p. 6.
12. Henry James, *Letters: 1843–1875* (Cambridge: Harvard University Press, 1974), p. 77.
13. Alain Locke, *The Philosophy of Alain Locke: Harlem Renaissance and Beyond*. Ed. Leonard Harris (Philadelphia: Temple University Press, 1989), p. 233.

I

LAWRENCE JACKSON

Ralph Ellison's invented life: a meeting with the ancestors

Jerry Watts's 1994 book *Heroism and the Black Intellectual* was the first to treat at length throughout the contradictions of Ralph Ellison's cultural and political position. Watts saw Ellison's hesitation to support vigorously the 1960s struggle for racial and social justice in America as a kind of truancy, an abandonment of an earlier principle. In Watts's view, Ellison endorsed a fairly conservative idea called black exceptionalism – the hero's triumph against the odds – as a means of outwitting the peril of racism. In order to strengthen his claim that Ellison became isolated from the civil rights movement and even broader shifts in American society, Watts offered a critique of Ellison's psychological make-up, picking up the controversy over Ellison's career where it had been left in the early 1970s, when Ellison faced boos when he ventured to make a speech.

> As a heroic individualist, Ellison appears to be tormented by his ambitions. The Achilles' heel of heroic individualism is unrealistic, almost obsessive-compulsive, artistic ambition. In such a mental state, one not only strives for perfection but also perceives anything less as defeat or weakness. Certainly, there is something tragically obsessive-compulsive about Ellison spending forty years writing a second novel.[1]

Watts believes Ellison's failure to publish more than one novel no less tragic than his absence as a high-profile representative for the Negro people. The critic supports his argument by pointing to the comparatively productive careers of Langston Hughes and Richard Wright. Though Ellison did and did not spend forty years writing a single piece of fiction – part of it was posthumously published as *Juneteenth* (1999) and the whole was outlined and plotted around 1951 and drafted, except for its final chapter, by 1958 – Watts' conclusion seems hasty for two reasons. First, the condemnation of Ellison has the danger of ignoring the extraordinary social and cultural impact of *Invisible Man*. The novel has had considerable influence in shaping the habits and mores of Americans, particularly the college-educated elites, and more generally in shifting the process of canon-formation in literature departments in the United States, than Watts may readily acknowledge.[2] Also dubious is the tendency to see Ellison as a neoconservative of the Norman Podhoretz school. This misstep erases Ellison's radical years with the Communist Party, *New Masses* magazine, the League of American Writers, *New Republic*, and *Negro Quarterly*, experiences crucial to Ellison's perspective as he crafted *Invisible Man,* the achievement for which he will be remembered.[3]

But Watts' interest in Ellison's entry into the canon and how Ellison maintained his position after arrival is important. Ellison's incorporation into the upper echelons of US literary circles in turn makes the issue of Ellison's political trajectory and outlook of considerable importance to African-American artistic and intellectual life. J. Saunders Redding wrote in his 1939 book *To Make a Poet Black* that African-American writers have had "two faces. If they wished to succeed they have been obliged to satisfy two different (and opposed when not opposite) audiences, the black and the white."[4] Ellison seemed to emerge unaccountably and fully formed at the peak of the modern American literary tradition. How artificial was Ellison's crafting of his literary arrival and durability? How strategic were his moves in the public sphere?

Ellison's career combines the dynamics of both alienation and acceptance and his life's journey indicates the sacrifices and rewards available even in the face of steeled opposition. Part of the difficulty in establishing convincing arguments about Ellison's influence in post-World War II America occurs because of the haze that frequently surrounds Ellison's literary influences, and the historical pressures he faced while writing his novel. A comparison of nuggets from Ellison's autobiographical works with documents from the historical record yields an incomplete yet fascinating psychological profile that sheds light on his judgments about allegiances, his definition and construction of community, and also offers an explanation regarding what Watts terms his "obsessive compulsiveness," Ellison's determination to write with power and style that compared favorably with the work of the most esteemed writers in American literature.

A biographical approach to Ellison's social, artistic, and political evolution during the late 1930s and 1940s, combined with an effort to understand Ellison's life relative to the patterns he established as a child, and paying close attention to the relationships he maintained throughout the rest of his life, can begin to provide more concrete evidence to determine how Ellison arrived at various artistic and political stances. An examination of key moments in the formation of Ellison's personality needs to be concerned with some of Ellison's reactions to white racism and his sense of ancestry, two areas where he is most regularly criticized and regarded with suspicion. Typically, the central works revealing Ellison's life in detail conceal his privacy.[5] Ellison wrote widely of his own life and then collected some of the essays into a volume called *Shadow and Act* published in 1964. Ellison published a final collection of essays in 1986 called *Going to the Territory* that extended his thesis that American identity is fundamentally mulatto, and where he more eloquently rendered and placed renewed significance on his early years, bringing to the page many of the figures from his Oklahoma youth like Jefferson Davis Randolph, Inman Page, and Roscoe Dunjee. Since Ellison is chiefly upbraided for failing both to crusade against white racism and to validate the suffering of African Americans, of especial interest are his experiences and comments concerning the nature of racial oppression in his own life. Another component of his reputation that relates directly to the controversy is Ellison's construction of artistic lineage, a lineage that has piqued scholars, writers, and critics for four decades.

Ellison made his most enduring comments on lineage in the essay "The World and the Jug" in 1964, but to some degree he was sating a public with tantalizing views in the place of the novel that they anticipated. To some degree, the essay of 1964 and the collection that followed it a few months later were a kind of artistic swan song. Critics have speculated on the reason for Ellison's inability to publish another full-length work of fiction, imagining a decisive moment following the publication of *Invisible Man* that would illuminate the specter plaguing Ellison's later career. But suppose Ellison's most significant struggles had taken place earlier, and he spent a great portion of his career protecting his image rather than generating new fiction? I suspect that the unknotting of the mystery of his life, and the events that prevented him from writing another major work of fiction are grounded in his earlier years, when he was producing *Invisible Man*.

Ellison's contemporary reputation rides high in part because he is thought to have pulled himself up by his own bootstraps and to have been self-reliant – Americans' fondest idea of themselves. Ellison is understood as the chief architect of his individual identity and he devoted considerable energies to that image of himself. In writing the first biography of Ellison, I was determined to be skeptical regarding Ellison's status as a saint and an icon, the romantic individual who stands alone.

A reinterpretation of Ellison's inner life and social milieu benefits from the relatively new notion in the history of biography of the multifaceted, contingent, relational human personality. Leon Edel, the well-known biographer of Henry James, recommended as a model André Maurois's *Aspects of Biography* (1929) as one of the twentieth century's more formidable reflections on the nature of the biographical enterprise. Maurois lauded

Lytton Strachey's *Lives of the Eminent Victorians*, the book that strove to relieve English language biographies from "ill-digested masses of material, slipshod style, tone of tedious panegyric, lamentable lack of selection, of detachment, of design" (viii).[6] Maurois noted a shift in biographical effort from hagiography to close examinations of the variegated life, warts and all. Maurois reminds us that whereas the classical world believed in fixed types of man, and bent the details of the life to fit into the model, modern-day biographies begin with a spirit of open intellectual inquiry, aided by the tools of psychology and ethics. The researcher begins his task by refusing to "shrink from any of the intellectual consequences to which his researches may lead him" (14). Maurois's approach employed an innovative assumption about the human personality – that people behave and internally organize themselves in a variety of ways, from scattered complexity to coherent unity. This fluid process which is the personality ranges from disparate elements to signs of homogeneity, from multiplicity to singularity. And, importantly, there are sometimes observable rhythms to this fluid movement. For black Americans, as well as for Americans from the South, the pull of history and the nation's historical record during the last century have encouraged an awareness of this reconstitution of the self, a dynamism that reflects the emotional and historical tendencies ongoing in the nation.

Maurois concludes by shifting our attention from the writer to the reader. Biographies are consumed in the twentieth century for vastly different reasons than before, mainly having to do with the fact that "modern man is more restless" and "longs, in the course of his reading of fiction or of history . . . to believe that others have known the struggles which he endures, the long and painful meditations in which he himself has indulged. So he is grateful to those more human biographies for showing him that even the hero is a divided being" (34–5). This emphasis points to the contemporary expectations of the audience for and the writer of biography and suggests that the biographical enterprise is always historically contingent, always constructed by the psychological needs of its audience. Writing a biography of Frederick Douglass in 1866, after the Civil War and the Emancipation, a writer would be in the perfect position to write a panegyric. A biographical work on Ellison emerging in 1955, before the Montgomery boycott, but following *Brown v. Board of Education* and Ellison's National Book Award (1953), might appear as a panegyric as well. But a biography published decades after awaiting Ellison's second novel and at a pivotal moment in American history that seeks an inclusive national identity must ask different and sobering questions.

Maurois' general insights animate the spirit of contemporary biography.[7] In the specific terms of African-American biography, there are additional scholarly imperatives. Arnold Rampersad, the biographer of Langston

Hughes, suggests that the complexity of metaphor for black biography must shift from Du Bois's 1903 idea of "double consciousness" to the 1940 image in his autobiography *Dusk of Dawn*.[8] Du Bois shows African-Americans trapped in a cave that is covered by a glass wall, allowing them to look upon the world of whites; a few manage to escape, mangling themselves in the process. The self-brutalization necessary to overcome the invisible wall of white supremacy turns the black folks into maniacs. In other words, Rampersad encourages the application of psychoanalytic techniques in order to examine the psychic devastation of racism. Life writing that engages African-American figures must have as a guiding imperative a sensitivity to weighing the psychic cost of African-American life.

The question of psychological pain in Ellison's life is one of the great mysteries in American literary history. What precisely were the wounds of a leading artist from a tradition of writers most committed to the themes of slavery, lynching, discrimination, and inferiority? Ellison always refused an answer. In his 1963–64 essay "The World and the Jug," Ellison mounted a large-scale critical defense and counterattack against Irving Howe, the author of "Black Boys and Native Sons," an essay designed to raise the critical reputation of Richard Wright and to chastise James Baldwin. In a famous statement on the nature of black American identity, Ellison suggested that African-Americans had not suffered unduly during slavery and years of public degradation.

> [M]y view of "Negroness" is neither his [Irving Howe's] nor that of the exponents of *negritude*. It is not skin color which makes a Negro American but cultural heritage as shaped by the American experience, the social and political predicament, a sharing of that "concord of sensibilities" which the group expresses through historical circumstances and through which it has come to constitute a subdivision of the larger American culture ... More important, perhaps, being a Negro American involves a *willed* (who wills to be a Negro? *I* do!) affirmation of self against all outside pressure – an identification with the group as extended through the individual self which rejects all possibilities of escape that do not involve the basic resuscitation of the original American ideals of social and political justice.[9]

Ellison's work critiqued the "culture of poverty" school of thought, the idea that black culture was inferior and promoted self-defeat, a view promulgated in the influential studies of historian Stanley Elkins and the sociologists Abram Kardiner and Lionel Ovesey. Elkins's book *Slavery* (1959) and Kardiner and Ovesey's *The Mark of Oppression* (1951) offered elaborate arguments designed to show the severe damage done to the black American during slavery and Jim Crow.[10] The academic arguments for pathology in African-American life continued to thrive in the 1960s and contributed to influential public policy analyses such as the famous 1965 Moynihan Report. Ellison became the black anchor for positions of resistance. In the 1970s, the historian Herbert Guttman suggested that there was no irrefutable evidence substantiating black pathology or family disorganization in the antebellum or postbellum eras.[11] Guttman's corrective made full use of Ellison's premise: African-Americans were proud and had endured slavery and its aftermath with dignity and intelligence.

Particularly during the second half of the 1960s and 1970s, years that saw a revival of Richard Wright's works and an emphasis on the ravages of segregation and slavery, Ellison strove in his autobiographical writings to portray the character and ambition of the black pioneers who left the old South for the Western territories. The majority of Ellison's essays devoted to his own memory struggle valiantly to overcome not racism, but instead, the powerful grip of liberal scholarship and racial bromides from fellow blacks who, to advance their individual goals, spread the fire and brimstone myth of a depraved and destitute African America.

Ellison's impatience with fellow black writers and the black literary critics had a long history. Apart from his formative experiences, Ellison had no real professional reasons for devotion to the black publishing community. When the novel *Invisible Man* was published, few African-American writers and critics wholeheartedly supported the book. The African-American press hedged their praise of the novel (save Langston Hughes, a life-long Ellison supporter). This tendency was best expressed by J. Saunders Redding, the literary heir to Alain Locke and Sterling Brown, a critic who obviously had the training to see what Ellison was doing symbolically and structurally in the novel. While Redding conceded that Ellison was a writer of power, in his review he said that the novel failed to provide a subject matter of epic proportion.[12] In a famous metaphor, he compared the novel to digging a compost pit for a backyard garden with a steam shovel. Other black newspapers followed in a similar vein, not objecting to the novel's Aristotelian scope of proportion, but rather, looking a bit askance at Ellison's discoveries: incestuous farmers, bitter and cynical college presidents, and young men blindly aping Booker T. For them, the novel was hardly optimistic enough, and whereas Richard Wright had unveiled the depravity of black life with a kind of moral fervor, Ellison seemed ready to laugh at and to ridicule the evidence of sadness that he had uncovered.

His most bitter rejections came from New York's still vibrant black Left. Abner Berry of the *Daily Worker*, Lloyd Brown, writing for Ellison's old journal, now renamed *Masses and Mainstream*, and John O. Killens of Paul Robeson's *Freedom* all condemned the novel as antithetical to the interests of black working people. They claimed to have no use for Ellison and accused him of willfully writing about perversity in black life for the titillation of his chic New York-based and Freud-quoting audience. To his black reviewers, Ellison was engaging in a game of literary symbol and allusion to Western classics in order to guarantee a major success. This argument, apparently, went even beyond the reviewers from ideologically determined journals. According to Richard Wright's 1960 lecture on black intellectual life, Ellison and Chester Himes nearly came to blows in 1953 after Himes persisted in the accusation that, far from a rare burst of talent, Ellison had merely taken advantage of a well-worn literary formula that would appeal to white elites.[13]

In *Phylon*, perhaps the leading black academic journal of the day, Alain Locke recognized the unusual distinction of the novel and called it one of three artistic peaks produced by black writers, the others being Toomer's *Cane* and Wright's *Native Son*. Ellison had produced a great novel, though one Locke thought at first "[s]mothered with verbosity and hyperbole."[14] Like George Mayberry, who reviewed the novel for *New Republic*, Alain Locke looked hopefully to the future promise Ellison held, though Locke's plaintive command became a haunting curse: "For once, too, here is a Negro writer capable of real and sustained irony. *Invisible Man*, evidently years in the making, must not be Ralph Ellison's last novel." Again and again, critics thought the work distinguished for a first novel and decided that Ellison would certainly improve his technique with age.

In 1954, that watershed moment in the history of racial segregation, Morgan State University critic Nick Aaron Ford published in *Phylon* an essay that compared Wright, Willard Motley, Frank Yerby, and Ellison, and he voiced serious reservations about *Invisible Man*: "[T]he only avenue open to the Negro who wants to keep his self-respect is complete withdrawal. This seems to be the meaning of the final episode."[15] Ford thought that the novel was uneven, and the tension between comedy and tragedy, and realism and surrealism quite strained. "Another fault in the book, as I see it, is the very noticeable unevenness of style, which may be due to the author's inability to decide whether he wanted to be serious or comical in his personal attitude toward his material" (36). Ford, like Ellison's other black peers working in the South, did not have enough distance to enjoy fully a wayward picaresque; they wanted heroic epics, narrated in mythic realism.

Ellison's insight and aesthetic sensibility greatly differed from the majority of black Americans in the segregated college system, a difference that was confirmed for him in 1954 when he went on a tour of black colleges. He wrote to Albert Murray on April 12, 1954, about his findings. At Southern University he found a confrontation with the black middle class that was nearly a miniature epic: "[O]ne night at a party at the dean's home the

Negroes started needling me and I started asking questions and soon had everybody yelling at me, defending the right to be second-rate! Naturally it was the Mose doctor and physicist who yelled the loudest. One Negro even drew his Caddy on me!" (74). At Howard University Ellison found the scene "depressing." "[Sterling] Brown, [E. Franklin] Frazier, [Arthur P.] Davis, Lovel and others were there but none of them would say a mumbling word – not even when I attacked some of their assumptions concerning Mose and America and culture" (75). His frustration was turning him into an antagonist. In a quiet moment at Howard, one of his old friends told him he should act more like Matthew Arnold; Ellison was disgusted by the complacency of the black intelligentsia, an opinion that he had held, it is worth noting, as early as 1942.[16]

Ellison's disputes with his black critics in the first years following the publication of *Invisible Man* provide the downbeat for an alternate biographical rhythm to his public image. A pattern of difference, resistance, or even studied evasiveness developed as soon as the details of his life were subjected to scrutiny, beginning with the year that Ellison claimed to have been born. Apparently no work on Ellison since the publication of *Invisible Man* has offered any other year for his birth date than 1914. However, several documents make the birth date of 1913 a much better choice; in fact, prior to about 1942, there seem to be none with a birth date of 1914. Ellison's high school and college records carry the 1913 birth date, and that date corresponds with the 1916 death certificate of his father Lewis Ellison, a tragedy which Ellison repeatedly claimed to have occurred when he was three years old. Finally, when he got married for the first time in September of 1938 to Rose Poindexter, he listed his age as twenty-five. Ellison went on to be considered a celebrant of the "extreme fluidity" of society; the birth date could represent an example of his freedom to choose as he embarked upon a career. This element of mystery and the apparent example of self-created identity uncorked the world of boldness and self-confidence, the life without racial injury that Ellison seemed to have stopped up in a jug.

The exposure of multiple birth dates refocuses our attention towards Ellison's remarks, particularly his statements about his ancestry and origins. Malcolm Little became Malcolm X in the late 1940s and, just a few years earlier, Ralph Ellison decided that he was going to be born in 1914 instead of 1913. The phenomenon drove home the point for me that we are always dealing with two Ralph Ellisons: one, the man born in 1913, and limited by that temporal marker; the other, the man who changed his birth date and engaged in a different sense of possibility. Giving himself an extra year enabled him to find his balance when he slept outdoors in New York after his mother died in 1937. If he was a bit younger it was less unseemly for him to accept charity, even in the form of warmly extended mentorships from people like Richmond Barthé, Langston Hughes, or Richard Wright. The rejected birth date is significant in terms of his decision to abandon his career as a trumpeter/music conductor, in favor of becoming a professional writer. Ellison may have also changed his birth date in an effort to evade military service in the Jim Crow US Army. As late as 1938, he was still using the 1913 birth date on official documents, but by 1942, he was passing as a year younger, during the year he became one of the League of American Writers, most sought after literary analysts, public speakers, and editors. Clearly the adoption of the new birth date is an important moment in the arrangement of the writer's life and in the construction of precisely what Ellison supposed a writer in New York City would be: urbane, avant garde, sapiently literate and, importantly, unintimidated by the terror of white malice.

It seems reasonable to suspect that Ellison had a kind of home-improvement approach to his own past and history. Ellison's personal life was something that he tended to tidy up or to make as pleasant as he could; for Ralph Waldo Ellison, the man whom he became as early as 1942 and fully embraced as he neared the publication of *Invisible Man*, 1914 was a more optimistic year. Ellison's revision was not, after all, on the scale of amendment of a writer like Zora Neal Hurston, who seems to have moved the clock forward from 1891 to 1901. Certainly one of the things that Ellison always suffered some embarrassment over was the fact that he hadn't graduated from Tuskegee. Ellison was upfront about leaving college without a degree; his status probably addled him most when talking literature and politics with white City College graduates on the New York Writer's Project who would have been inclined to think Tuskegee an academic backwater. Whatever the issues surrounding his 1936 departure from Tuskegee, it was a moot point by 1938, when the Music School in which he had enrolled was discontinued. It had become impossible for him to finish his education in Alabama, even if he had been on track to win a degree, which he was not.

Ellison's anxieties about college didn't have much significance because his was not an era of college; even a couple of years at college were a distinction in the 1930s, when only a small percentage of Americans earned degrees. If he made himself younger, it perhaps had more to do with the year that he graduated from high school, the Frederick Douglass School of Oklahoma City, where he was enrolled in the upper school course for five years, from 1927 until 1932. Ellison started high school in 1927 but did not graduate with his class of 1931, which included several powerhouses: a judge, the future head of Atlanta's school system, and several concert musicians. In fact, one of Ellison's early heroes, a newspaper editor named Roscoe Dunjee, championed Hiliard Bowen, the boy who was Douglass's valedictorian and, one might imagine,

Ellison's rival. Due to poor grades in Latin and algebra and probably due to his absence from school for about six months in 1922–23, Ellison graduated in 1932, then tried, unsuccessfully, to enroll at Langston University, or as it was then called, the Colored Agricultural and Normal Institute at Langston. In the late spring of 1933, he received an extraordinary opportunity to attend Tuskegee and the twenty-year-old accepted. Shifting the birth date made him seem more legitimate, relative to his graduation year from high school. It gave him another year to approach the boys coming out of homes with two parents, the guys who excelled at football and were devoted to jazz, unlike Ellison, who played on the teams and in the groups, but wasn't considered one of the elite.

Ellison's act of natal revision seems to have occurred when he was a staff worker at *New Masses* magazine and actively participating in an unpopular struggle for racial and social justice. By making himself younger, he gained a psychological advantage with the young left-oriented critics in and around New York City, especially one group that thought well of themselves, those who published in *Partisan Review*. Ellison was a man keenly aware of his competitors and he entered the writers' trade at a time when several of the best American writers of the second half of the twentieth century were coming out of the gate. Delmore Schwartz, Saul Bellow, Stanley Edgar Hyman, and Norman Mailer are four people who on any given occasion during the 1940s, Ellison might have run into at a literary event. Obviously, a competitive camaraderie with American Jews, who at that time suffered social rejection at the hands of the Anglo-Saxons, was quite natural for an African-American like Ellison. Certainly he saw their work being published in the early and mid-1940s, sometimes alongside his. Yet these men were recognized as elite prodigies who gained fame and recognition at very young ages. Ellison had washed out from Tuskegee, and limped through Douglass High. Schwartz and Mailer had Harvard under their belts; Bellow Northwestern; and Hyman was a professor at Bennington College. Also, around the time the age shifted, between 1937 and 1943, Ellison understood his life as racially determined more than at any other point; this period coincides with his greatest communion and friendship with Richard Wright, whose entire corpus of work revealed the power of race in determining identity. Ellison had intense personal desires to see himself, an American Negro, competing on identical terms with whites. Even though he only became a year younger, this symbolic rejuvenation put him in closer striking distance.

If Ellison required his ego to be salved, he had distinctly less need after the conferral of the National Book Award in 1953. However, his later self-revision had less to do with his own lived past than with the issue of precisely who had been his artistic forebears, the creation of his literal and figurative genealogy. The scope of his achievement was such that readers and critics became obsessed by precisely how he had evolved. In "The World and the Jug" (1964) Ellison declared that Richard Wright and Langston Hughes, men who had started his career, were his literary relatives, which is to say that they were influential in his development but, like a father, uncle, or brother, he did not choose them, they were a part of his environment. On the other hand, Faulkner, Eliot, and Hemingway – who in their writing had achieved a universal statement of unquestionable artistic value – were his ancestors, the progenitors of literary forms and stylistic originality whom he hoped to join at the table of high culture.

> But perhaps you will understand when I say he [Richard Wright] did not influence me if I point out that while one can do nothing about choosing one's relatives, one can, as artist, choose one's "ancestors." Wright was, in this sense, a "relative," Hemingway an "ancestor." Langston Hughes, whose work I knew in grade school and whom I knew before I knew Wright, was a "relative"' Eliot, whom I was to meet only many years later, and Malraux and Dostoievsky and Faulkner, were "ancestors" – if you please or don't please!   (140)

In February of 1964 Ellison symbolically allied himself with the icons of Anglo-American literature over the beloved black journeyman (Wright had become more dear after his death). The timing of his statement for artistic freedom was inauspicious; five months earlier bombs had exploded in Birmingham, killing black children. His choice of influences may have been honest and principled but it struck a painful note of assimilation and seemed to demand that Negroes vault yet another brook of fire, and this time in the face of terrorists. Irving Howe was one of the last of the still radical New York intelligentsia surviving the McCarthy era, credentials he touted with crusading essays like "Black Boys and Native Sons." So Ellison's rebuttal of the "Left" literati and his refusal to valorize loudly the best-known writers of his race made him suspicious to many blacks while his restraint endeared him to powerful whites. Ellison was apparently in no mood for highhanded treatment either by white liberals or by black militants, with some of whom he had old scores to settle that extended back to the 1930s. Every time a self-appointed race-counselor requested a defiant slogan from Ellison on the racial situation of the country, he seems to have drifted further into the welcoming world of the academy and genteel society: the American Academy of Arts and Sciences; the Century Club (he was successfully nominated by Robert Penn Warren in 1964); and his professorship at Rutgers.

For some of his critics, Ellison's movement away from participation in radical social struggle to the American academy atrophied his art. Ellison's choice of lineages and his support of civil society had more than a little to do with selecting an association with strength, with siding with what his college president Robert Russa Moton had called "The Force That Wins." Decidedly, the public questions of identity in the 1960s emotionally challenged the mature man (especially considering the interview of Henry T. Wingate on the PBS documentary *Ralph Ellison: An American Journey*)[17] and were remarkably similar to one that he faced in his earliest years, when he had to choose his father.

In "The World and the Jug" Ellison diminished his relationship with Wright and chose the most celebrated elite writers as his ancestors in a fashion similar to the way that he had taken a new birth date, and also in the way he elected the best father for his own personal life. Once he made that decision about which artists meant the most to him, suited his artistic purposes and fit his emotional needs, he appropriately heroicized the winners of the contest and vanquished the losers, as he had done with his biological father Lewis Ellison. After he confirmed his choice, he imbued it with significance throughout the remainder of his lifetime.

In his interviews and essays, Ralph Ellison liked to mention his father. Ordinarily he anchored his stories around Lewis Ellison's illustrious career as a soldier. For example, in a 1974 interview with John Hersey, Ellison talked about his father as having served in Cuba, the Philippines, and China.[18] In fact, his father served in New Mexico with the 25th US Infantry (where he probably took a liking to the Southwest which may have prompted his move to Oklahoma ten years later) and he served in the Philippines, where he caught malaria and began to have severe gastrointestinal problems and where on April 9, 1901, he was court-martialed and sent to the stockade.[19] Yet, Ellison always propped up the myth of his father's successful and bright military career. Here we have an example of cleaning up a personal life so that it is worthy to stand with competition. Ellison's strategic omission is also a tactic to defeat the soothsayers predicting blasted black lives under white domination.

Ralph Ellison's father, Lewis Ellison, died of a perforated ulcer in Oklahoma City in July of 1916. Ellison generally chose to admit to his interlocutors that he had grown up poor, but when pushed, he reveled in the strength of his mother and the matriarchal tradition in black families. (Chester Himes recorded Ellison's philosophy of black lower-class matriarchy in all of its glory in his 1947 book *Lonely Crusade*.) Obviously, growing up poor was hard, but it also suggested that he had made his own way, without any help. In some regard, Ellison wanted his role to be heroic like the one he gave his father. We can get a sense of his imagination by looking at the 1937 short story "Hymie's Bull," depicting a young man's flight on the railroad:

I thought of my mother whom I had left two weeks before, (this was 1934) not even knowing that I would ever hop freights. Poor mom, she had tried hard to keep my brother and me at home but she fed us too long and we were getting much too grown up to let her do it any longer so we had left home looking for jobs.[20]

This spartan image of home, sacrifice, and loyalty was the heroic past that Ellison wanted to exist; but the truth is a bit more complex.

To begin with, it is curious that Ellison had any direct memory of his biological father at all. They lived in the same household from Ellison's infancy through Ellison's third year. The family moved every year. Lewis Ellison worked the long and exhausting hours of a laborer. But most disruptive to the memory, eight years after Lewis Ellison's death, Ida Ellison married John Ammons, who was either 29 or 59 – the Oklahoma City records are inconclusive. Ammons taught the adolescent Ellison how to hunt, an episode recorded in great detail and with apparent pleasure in Ellison's unpublished monograph "Slick," written in 1939. In fact, Ellison regularly refers to the art of hunting as a bridge that enabled him to find significance in the short essays of Ernest Hemingway. But Ammons died in 1925 and comes into the public record only in a 1976 Ellison interview for *Massachusetts Review* with Robert Stepto and Michael Harper.[21] Four years later, Ida Ellison Ammons, by all accounts an uncommonly attractive woman, married her third husband, a man named John Bell, who is even more vaguely represented in the historical record than either Ammons or Lewis Ellison. However, it appears that Bell (who when he was courting Ida Ellison Ammons lived next door to a certain gentleman named Mr. Bledsoe) lived with the family until Ida's death in 1937, when the group moved to Ohio to escape, in part, the racial violence of Oklahoma.

Oklahoma City at the time had to deal with rambunctious Negroes moving across the real estate red lines, and causing the equally rambunctious Governor "Alphalpha" Bill Murray to call out the National Guard to create a "Negro Zone" in order to stave off the kind of racial riots that had claimed hundreds of black lives in Tulsa in 1921. Whatever the case, Ellison certainly "knew" John Bell better than Lewis Ellison. And he chose to erase Bell. Ida Ellison's remarriages may have been difficult for the prideful boy. The attractive woman's reputation was a topic of conversation in the tightly woven black community, and Ralph Ellison, as the oldest son, felt deeply inclined to guard the sanctity of his father's name, to decorate and to embellish it. One of Ellison's most perplexing adolescent crises came when Hattie Randolph, the wife of Ralph's mentor, the successful dentist T. J. Randolph, accused her husband of being Ralph's biological father. Ellison deflected this episode by constructing Hattie Randolph in an interview as a well-known community half-wit.[22] But the publicly voiced doubts regarding his paternal ancestry deeply and enduringly affected him. Part of what he gained by bringing his birth date up a year is a more comfortable sense of actually being his father's son, or perhaps at least born to his father and mother in marriage. It is possible to see the impact of his father's absence on Ellison's mind many years later. He maintained this formidable imaginary relationship with his biological father when writing to his mother in the months before her death, projecting his emotions onto the mythical image of the father. "Daddy no doubt felt the same way when he ran off to the army" he wrote to Ida Bell in April of 1937.[23] Ida Bell was sensitive to her son's need for a father of his own, as well as Ralph's considerable feelings of neglect. Ellison used his mother as a sounding board to recreate a past for a man he did not know.

By examining Ellison's mythical postulation of the father that he wanted to have, we can illuminate several of Ellison's disappointing relationships with men in positions of authority. When very young children lose the figure to whom they have attributed godlike powers (such as a parent), they suffer a deep injury to their personality or narcissistic self. The children go on to replace this figure in their lives, but the transference is often unsatisfactory, in part because of the central and unresolved tragedy. Ellison sought to escape limiting and painful day-to-day psychological and social realities by imagining many things – such as himself as a symphonic conductor – but also by recapturing an idyllic father. When confronted with the figures responsible for instructing him in the specific details of his craft, inevitably he went through a process of inflating them as symbols of authority, then disparaging them as he gained strength and autonomy. He seems to have experienced this process repeatedly with his own stepfathers. And here also we see a combination of tendencies and circumstances, where Ellison was unable to reveal the pain of his own personal life because it would be perceived as conforming to facile ideas about black degradation. His era conspired to prevent him from seriously expressing pain and so did his self-appointed ancestors. After Richard Wright published *Black Boy*, William Faulkner sent him salutations but with a significant caveat. Faulkner thought that Wright had slipped even from the qualified artistry he showed in *Native Son*. "I am speaking now from the point of view of one who believes that the man who wrote *Native Son* is potentially an artist."[24] Faulkner warned Wright off from writing from "the memory of his own grief"; with proper control, Wright might someday toe the mark of the artist. Ellison, who, when he met Faulkner in 1953 at the Random House offices, acknowledged his literary debt, took this kind of admonition for artistic achievement quite seriously. One's grief was taboo.

Knowledge of some elements of Ellison's psychobiographical drama and his milieu seems necessary to understand his later insistence on choosing his literary ancestors. Although Harold Bloom's anxiety of influence thesis offers an overarching condition through which Ellison struggled to achieve his reputation, Ellison seems free of an enormous subconscious drive to incorporate and surpass the achievements of the local "father" figures Richard Wright and Langston Hughes. In fact, Ellison's intellectual point is precisely that he did not have to engage in an Oedipal struggle with his intimates, because there were already writers of global significance to battle against for his writer's identity. Perhaps Ellison's 1960s refusal to respond to cries of black artistic militancy, which he felt were overstated, indicates his reluctance to put himself in the vulnerable position of cultural prophet, as did Eliot and Pound, and frequently to dangerous excess. It appears that Ellison had no single figure to overthrow in his development as an artist; rather, he repudiated his teachers systematically, regardless of their racial background. Also, part of the section of his life cut away that seemed to include Wright and Hughes was a much broader repudiation of the South and southern black communitarian identity. Ellison ultimately rejected this form of group psychology. He thought that despite the outer appearance of unity, altruistic concern, and love, there lay hidden in the black group-identification an underlying demand for conformity, a reliance upon feudalistic-era "pre-individual values."[25] Ellison's artistic struggle for self-definition significantly centered upon the attainment of "individual" values and autonomy.

In terms of American literary history, the critical figure repudiated in this drama is obviously Richard Wright. Ellison started to write, as he was quick to admit, because of an invitation extended by Richard Wright in June or July of 1937. Langston Hughes had not yet lent him his first typewriter. In his essays like "The World and the Jug" (1963–64) and in "Remembering Richard Wright" (1971), an extended prose elegy to Wright in Ellison's beatific style, Ellison tends to obscure the extent of the relationship. It needs to be stated simply that at the height of their intimacy, about 1940, Richard Wright and Ralph Ellison were close in the way that Hemingway and Fitzgerald were close; in the way that Robert Penn Warren and Allen Tate were close; and in the way that Eliot and Pound were close. In other words, the two men were sharing the same artistic, intellectual, and social atmosphere and they supported and sustained each other's mythical visions of the world. It would be difficult to exaggerate the importance of the relationship, which would appear even more significantly in their literary correspondence if they had not avidly visited each other and talked on the telephone at least every couple of days when Wright lived in New York City during the late 1930s and 1940s. I think that this literary friendship is vital to understand, while we simultaneously accept that they were very different writers, of different backgrounds, and with different interests. Although it is apparent that Wright influenced Ellison, questions regarding the degree of the influence will always be debated. The relationship is also especially important because it unites two areas about which Ellison later expressed some anxiety – literary ancestry and racial attitudes.

In a most poignant and eloquent letter, Ellison expresses his feelings about Wright's *12 Million Black Voices*.

> After reading your history – I knew it all already, all in my blood, bones, flesh; deepest memories, and thoughts; those which are sacred and those which bring the bitterest agonies and most poignant remembrances and regrets. Part of my life, Dick, has been a lacerating experience and I have my share of bitterness. But I have learned to keep the bitterness submerged so that my vision might be kept clear; so that those passions which would so easily be criminal might be socially useful. I know those emotions which tear the insides to be free and memories which must be kept underground, caged by rigid discipline lest they destroy ... Usually we Negroes refuse to talk of these things; the fact that I mention them now is an indication of the effect which your book has had upon me. You write of the numbness which our experience has produced in most of us, and I must say that while I was never completely numbed myself, I have had to rigidly control my thawing, allowing the liquid emotion to escape drop by drop through the trap doors of the things I write, lest I lose control; lest I be rendered incapable of warming our frozen brother. Of this, however, I am sure now more than ever: That you and I are brothers. Back when I first knew you, remember, I often speculated as to what it was that made the difference between us and others who shot up from the same region. Well, now, (and it is this which makes us brothers), I think it is because this past which filters through your book has always been tender and alive and aching within us. We are the ones who had no comforting amnesia of childhood, and for whom the trauma of passing from the country to the city of destruction brought no anesthesia of unconsciousness, but left our nerves peeled and quivering. We are not the numbed, but the seething. God! It makes you want to write and write and write, or murder.[26]

This letter is written in rich, emotionally charged language, joining Ellison to Wright's project of redemption and vindication, but most startling is the insistence on channeling rage. Ellison was in his late twenties here, and pulling out of his first marriage and his close links to the Communists. It was the eve of American participation in the war. He was slowly regaining Wright's intimacy after several months of strained contact. But the letter also acknowledges rage on the interior of the dense layers of Ellison's personality. How successful was Ellison in transcending his feelings of pain and anger and transmuting these feelings of rage and despair into other arenas? How do the other areas of his life reflect this process of transmuting rage? It seems likely that in Ellison's conception of adult manhood, racial abuse was on a par with childhood sexual abuse: one did not admit to it in public, and sometimes not even in memoir. Apparently Ellison experienced a "seething" kind of emotion more frequently than he let on, an emotional disposition, which led James Baldwin to call him the angriest man alive, and still breathing. The energy of anger was available to other perceptive writers as well. In *Advertisements for Myself* Norman Mailer described Ellison's genius as essentially "hateful."[27] But "seething" is an important self-description, because it connotes the image of a boiling point repressed, capped off. I think that Ellison entombed his emotional anger with the mortar and bricks of formal manners, conspicuous literary standards, and favored relationships with elite writers. But the heat behind the dungeon wall could not be hidden from all and sometimes threatened to scald him.

Occasions of vulnerability tested his skill at concealment of the festering anguish. In the winter of 1945 Ellison was on the verge of being drafted by the US army. He told Richard Wright of his father's terrible experience in the military and swore to Wright that he would spend the mandatory five years in prison before he would put on khaki. Wright fit this revelation about his comrade into an overall pattern. In accord with his views of the world (and a frequently commented upon gift of exaggeration), Wright thought that Ellison's whole life was dominated by race. Wright found it pathetic that Lewis Ellison had been destroyed by the military and that his son seemed destined for a similar fate. During the winter of 1945 Wright confided to his diary:

> Pending Ralph's visit, I keep thinking of him and of the fact that almost every act of a Negro is partly or wholly conditioned by his being a Negro. Ralph did not want to join the army because it is a Jim Crow army and he went into the merchant marine. He writes because he is a Negro; he really wanted to be a sculpture[sic], but he found he could not say what was hotly in him to say with stone and marble. Now again he [is] making decisions based solely on his racial identity. He has no choice.[28]

Here we have the analytical strength and limitation of Ellison's close friend, a Manichean tendency in Wright that Ellison would not have missed. The passage suggests that by submitting to his polar racial logic, Wright was dismissive and capable of looking at Ellison as less an individual than a statistical entry. And yet, it asserts clearly that in Wright's view, at least during the mid-1940s when Ellison began writing *Invisible Man*, his life was dominated by the punitive and deadly logic of race.

The description of Ellison's bitter relationship with the military appears in Constance Webb's biography of Wright, but Ellison was successful in having some of it suppressed. After hearing of the existence of Wright's diary from Wright biographers, he acknowledged his anger and fear about the entries and what they threatened: the literal confirmation of the man born in 1913. Ellison's decision in 1941 to make himself into Wright's "brother" and then later to distance himself from Wright suggests a pattern that we can observe with others: William Dawson, his music instructor, whom Ellison both revered and thought a fraud; Hughes, whom Ellison did not take seriously, but who influenced him decisively; Stanley Edgar Hyman, Ellison's close friend who helped him with publishers and magazines after the war and with whom he parted; and then, towards the end of his life, Ellison distanced himself from Albert Murray, Tuskegean and fellow chronicler of the Negro blues idiom. In all of these relationships was the dynamic of "brotherhood," occasionally filiation or patronage, and then, an extended bitter quarrel.

The quarrel with Hyman wandered into print and offered the other closed fist that Ellison could swing at people who demanded his militancy; Hyman represented the white liberal dilettante of black culture. Ellison's junior by about six years, Hyman helped Ellison as he turned towards the academy in the late 1950s, when his career as a fiction writer slowed. As the editor of *Negro Quarterly* in the 1940s, Ellison had courted Hyman's essays and reviews; at one point he even asked for Hyman's notes. Hyman, an up-and-coming staff writer for the *New Yorker,* invited Ellison to lecture in a Bennington speaker series in 1945. And while the men were very close friends (Hyman was one of the final readers of Ellison's typescript of *Invisible Man*), Ellison launched some of his strongest criticisms about the nature of black culture and black folklore against Hyman. One of the essays, the well-known rebuttal called "Change the Joke and Slip the Yoke," rejected the ubiquity of the symbol of the Negro as a masking trickster figure or smart-man-playing-dumb, in favor of the notion of a weak man who knows the nature of his opponents' weakness. In a personal letter to Hyman shortly before his death in 1970, Ellison again strongly reasserted his belief that Hyman misunderstood black culture in ways nearly identical to his 1958 essay. Psychic fulfillment for Ellison seems closely linked to vanquishing personal friends. The regularity of this maneuver, of achieving intimacy and then dismissing it, perhaps draws off the existence of an unresolved narcissistic injury suffered at the death of his father. Ellison maintained a consistent need to puncture persons he had placed in roles of authority. Here, too, the altered birth year has particular significance. Ellison used the changed birthday in fashioning a stronger self, one less susceptible to the infamous rabbit punch of white America: it is a small way to slip the yoke of fixed, predetermined, racialized identity. But as a part of changing the joke, in other words turning the tragic joke of black life into a joke on white life, Ellison felt compelled to reject manifestations of tragedy in his own personal circumstance.

Richard Wright became internationally known for his portraits of the raw and terrible nature of black life, stating it most furiously in *Black Boy*. Ellison countered Wright's bleak hard-boiled perception many years later in an address at the Library of Congress published under the title "Hidden Name and Complex Fate." He challenged Wright's ideas about the aridity of black culture and the knee-jerk scorn of whites with lyrical Whitmanesque catalogs testifying to the existence of pastoral, romantic scenes in the post-World War I Southwest. Ellison told the world that he saw writing as an artistic pursuit that he came to by way of the verse of Eliot, not Mencken's journalistic barbs which had introduced Richard Wright to his craft. And, as with his birthday, Ellison had his eye towards brightening a stark picture. When we look at his private life we glimpse another facet of Ellison's repressed tragedy, and understand that less of the yoke has been slipped.

Ellison wrote fondly, in the short stories "Hymie's Bull" and "I Did Not Learn Their Names," about hoboing down to Alabama. Neither of these stories was published in his lifetime and in them he admitted how rough it could be on the train. In 1933, when Ellison rode the rails down to Tuskegee, Haywood Patterson, one of the Scottsboro Boys, was being retried in Decatur, Alabama. Ellison mentioned run-ins with the police to Michael Harper and Robert Stepto, and in the short story "I Did Not Learn Their Names," his character spends a night in jail before making it to music school. It is apparent from the fictional evidence he left behind that hoboing to Tuskegee left a sustained impression on him and, also, like his father's experience in the military, the trip was violent and punishing. Somewhere on his ride down to Alabama, Ellison gained a contusion as well as a deep laceration close to his eye, wounds that left prominent scars that he wore for the rest of his life. Yet, he held his silence about the origin of the scars. Here is the kind of personal experience that, indeed, Ellison had written of in the letter to Wright in 1941, precisely the kind of episode that he subjected to "rigidly controlled thawing." And yet, if Ellison became, had to become, proficient at suppressing crucial episodes in his own life, there is at least the possibility that this mechanism of freezing overtook his capacity to thaw and rendered him mute in the process.

The train-ride episode lurks as the underside of Ellison's invention of 1914 as his birth year. He left the man of 1913 in the Decatur freight-yard. In his rebuke of Irving Howe, Ellison revealed that the world knew very little of his intimate life and that it was conceivable that he was more inclined to and had suffered more violence than Richard Wright. The classic dichotomies of the two men have endured: Ellison, the brown-skinned aristocrat who eschewed tales of racial brutality in favor of nuanced depictions of American life; and Wright, the bloody crusader, swinging the cudgel of black nationalism.

Ellison's sharp rejoinder was designed to give Howe pause. He struggled to escape being defined completely as a victim of white brutality. But the man who presented the cagey and aloof persona was not necessarily the privileged voice of Ellison's consciousness. In fact, Ellison strove to create enormous differences between himself and the other writers of his generation, precisely in terms of violence. In another episode at odds with his public persona, Ellison recorded on tape with Horace Cayton, the sociologist, an experience with Wright:

> I was going to the Gotham book mart one afternoon with Dick and a taxi driver almost ran us down. I walked around and tried to get the fellow out of the cab. Dick didn't say a word and I was ready to slug it out with this fellow because he was wrong. We didn't discuss it. I didn't feel that he was afraid, like a primitive fear of white folks or something, but this [idea of Wright as fearless and confrontational foe of racism] just strikes me as absolutely wrong and is consistent with some of the things in Constance Webb's book.[29]

The Ellison chasing down taxi drivers story is not widely known, and is perhaps even a bit unsettling. But more than once Ellison was prepared to take the heads off his friends: a drunken Himes in 1952; Hyman when he gave out Ellison's telephone number in 1945; and the reputation of Wright's family when he realized that Wright had recorded Ellison's moment of vulnerability in his diary.

Ellison left us a rationalization for holding the pain inside (and one might think, by extension, violence as well) in an extended quote from "The World and the Jug":

> But there is also an American Negro tradition which teaches one to deflect racial provocation and to master and contain pain. It is a tradition which abhors as obscene any trading on one's anguish for gain or sympathy; which springs not from desire to deny the harshness of existence but from the will to deal with it as men at their best have always done. (111)

Ellison modified the natural expression of violence into socially acceptable avenues, such as art, when it suited the pursuit of his constructed ideal. In private Ellison was quite capable of and perhaps even enjoyed getting rough. But the dynamic of his self-presentation is ironic because, while he avoided conforming to the handy notions of black depravity championed by Wright, he still found himself getting "black" by reacting swiftly to critics attempting to control his image. In a final letter to Hyman concerning an essay on Wright that wanted to attribute universal rage to blacks, Ellison snorted:

> You allow us no contempt – a quite different emotion than hate – no irony, no forebearance, no indifference, no charity, no mockery, no compassion, no condescension – not to mention that ambivalence of emotion and attitude which you so readily see in the blues.[30]

Clearly Ellison continued to respond to the prescriptions voiced by Howe that demanded that black life be one of unending psychological torture. Ellison wanted to assert a fuller spectrum of black humanity, a spectrum that especially went beyond ordinary poles of racialist logic. However, he found that feat difficult to accomplish without reconstructing his own life and arranging the intensity of his influences.

Ellison's stylized representation of himself, the man from 1914, both accounted for and painfully limited his expression. If we take him to be speaking for himself in the longer passages on black American identity in "The World and the Jug," his metaphor for black attitudes toward life has a prescience concerning his life as a writer.

> Negro American consciousness is not a product (as so often seems true of so many American groups) of a will to historical forgetfulness. It is a product of our memory, sustained and constantly reinforced by events, by our watchful waiting, and by our hopeful suspension of final judgments as to the meaning of our grievances. (124)

Here he privileges black consciousness as a product of "memory" as opposed to an accommodationist sort of lack – "historical forgetfulness." In other words, black people have not merely forgotten the historical record of injustice and maltreatment, they have cultivated their "memory." But it is also abundantly clear from the passage that Ellison perceives a remarkable tension in this process. For one thing, in terms of the public discourse, Negro Americans are commonly considered ignorant of the nature of their own historical narrative. Ellison places hope for Negro well-being with personalized memory, that singular, biased, subjective chronicler of a life, a memory reinforced, upheld, by our "watchful waiting." Ralph Ellison believed in watchful waiting. He constructed a mythic sense of himself, the man born in 1914, and he appropriated an image of a vibrant ancestor – his father Lewis Ellison – so that he might more comfortably anticipate the moment of final judgment. Certainly the narrator of *Invisible Man* chooses this strategy. Both men, real and fictive, hibernate in the interiors of the story of their own lives, grasping life in the hidden textures and crevices of their own memories, a mechanism of coping that makes covetous and restrained the force and generativity of their art.

Notes

1. Jerry Watts, *Heroism and the Black Intellectual: Ralph Ellison, Politics and Afro-American Intellectual Life* (Chapel Hill: University of North Carolina Press, 1994), p. 114.

2. Ellison's canonical status should not be underestimated nor should its political effects be dismissed. The popularity of the novel is evidence of important ideological shifts (and of course corresponding counter adjustments), most decidedly in the construction of values and reference points for the intellectual elite. In "Ralph Ellison, Race and American Culture" *Raritan* (Spring 1999), Morris Dickstein has written: "After steering us through every kind of emotional and ideological excess, Ellison's work represents the triumph of the center. Ellison wrote a great ideological novel, perhaps the single best novel of the postwar era, at once his own inner history and the complex paradigm of the whole culture" (50). Ellison's work has generated a miniature academic industry, and as Dickstein suspects, provided a "vigorous alternative to both black nationalism and Marxism" (49) for a generation of writers and academics.

3. Ellison's work on the far Left during the 1930s and 1940s has been decently documented by Barbara Foley, "Ralph Ellison as Proletarian Journalist," *Science and Society* 62 (Winter 1998–99): 537–56; Also see Ellison's formative work with the Negro Publication Society and the *Negro Quarterly* journal during 1942–43.

4. Quoted from Ulysses Lee, "Criticism at Mid-Century," *Phylon* 11 (Fall 1950): 336.

5. Jervis Anderson, "Going to the Territory," *New Yorker*, September 1977; Robert O'Meally, *The Craft of Ralph Ellison* (Cambridge: Harvard University Press, 1980); Lawrence Jackson, *Ralph Ellison: Emergence of Genius* (New York: John Wiley, 2002). In 1976 the writer Jervis Anderson completed a long interview-essay with Ellison, a key source for biographically rich details of Ellison's life. Robert O'Meally wrote the first monograph on Ellison, and his book covered the academic ground: a bibliography of Ellison's works; brief biographical snippets based upon Ellison's published essays; and finally, extended readings of Ellison's early fiction, *Invisible Man*, and finishing with examinations of Ellison's later works. I wrote a biography of the first forty years of Ellison's life, but several years after his death, his literary executor and legal estate were guarded and determined to protect Ellison's privacy and to conceal any evidence that complicated his reputation.

6. André Maurois, *Aspects of Biography* (New York: Ungar, 1929).

7. See Leon Edel, *Literary Biography* (Bloomington: Indiana University Press, 1973).

8. Arnold Rampersad, "Biography and Afro-American Culture," *Afro-American Literary Study in the 1990s*, ed. Houston Baker, Jr. and Patricia Redmond (University of Chicago Press, 1989), pp. 194–208.

9. Ralph Ellison, "The World and the Jug," *Shadow and Act* (New York: Random House, 1964), p. 131.

10. Stanley Elkins, *Slavery* (University of Chicago Press, 1959). Abram Kardiner and Lionel Ovesey, *The Mark of Oppression: A Psychosocial Study of the American Negro* (New York: Norton, 1951). Elkins's work depicted the stereotype "Sambo" of southern folklore – the carefree, indolent, and clownlike slave – as a veritable type that came into existence as a psychological response to severe trauma. Kardiner and Ovesey's book showed the enduring and measurable psychological damage to blacks as a result of slavery and racial segregation, particularly in terms of their ability to have healthy sexual relationships.

11. Herbert Guttman, *The Black Family in Slavery and Freedom, 1750–1925* (New York: Random House, 1976). In this watershed history, Guttman argues that enslaved Africans and their descendants successfully formed family units in slavery and during the Reconstruction and post-Reconstruction eras.

12. Saunders Redding, "Invisible Man," *Baltimore African American*, 10 May 1952:10.

13. Richard Wright, "The Position of the Negro Artist and Intellectual in American Society," Richard Wright Papers, Box 3 Folder 41, James Weldon Johnson Collection, Beinecke Rare Book and Manuscript Library, Yale University.

14. Alain Locke, "From *Native Son* to *Invisible Man*: A Review of Literature of the Negro for 1952," *Phylon* 14.1 (Winter 1953): 34–5.

15. Nick Aaron Ford, "Four Negro Novelists," *Phylon* 15.1 (WI 1954): 35.

16. Ralph Ellison, draft letter to Horace Cayton, ca. May 1942, Ralph Ellison Papers, Box 10, *Negro Quarterly* Folder, Library of Congress Manuscripts and Archives Division.

17. *Ralph Ellison: An American Journey*. Dir. Avon Kirkland (New Images Productions: 2002). In a concluding segment of the documentary, Judge Henry T. Wingate recalls that after a confrontation with a militant black student in the late 1960s, Ellison wept and said "I am not an Uncle Tom."

18. Ralph Ellison and John Hersey, "A Completion of Personality: A Talk with Ralph Ellison," *Conversations with Ralph Ellison* (Jackson: University Press of Mississippi, 1995), p. 273; Ellison, "Introduction to the Thirtieth-Anniversary Edition of *Invisible Man*," *Collected Essays of Ralph Ellison*, ed. John Callahan (New York: Random House, 1995), p. 476.

19. Lawrence Jackson, *Ralph Ellison: Emergence of Genius* (New York: Wiley, 2002), pp. 9–10.

20. Ralph Ellison, "Hymie's Bull," Dorothy West Papers, Box 3 Folder 58, Schlesinger Library, Radcliffe Institute for Advanced Study, Harvard University. When this story was first published in 1996 in *Flying Home and Other Stories* (New York: Random House), Ellison's literary executor chose a version of the story that deleted the word "alone" from the text. In the original version, Ellison used "alone" to describe the mother.

21. Ralph Ellison, Michael Harper, and Robert Stepto, "Study and Experience: An Interview with Ralph Ellison," *Conversations with Ralph Ellison*, pp. 319–41.

22. Ellison and Hersey, "'A Completion of Personality,'" p. 274.

23. Ralph Ellison, "'American Culture Is of a Whole': From the Letters of Ralph Ellison," *New Republic*, March 1, 1999, 36.

24. William Faulkner, letter to Richard Wright n.d. [ca. summer 1945], Richard Wright Papers, Box 97 Folder 1328, James Weldon Johnson Collection, Beinecke Rare Book and Manuscript Library, Yale University.

25. The rejection of and impatience with the black southern communitarian identity is the inevitable conclusion from the essay that initially crafted Ellison's literary reputation, "Richard Wright's Blues," *Antioch Review* (Summer 1945): 198–211.

26. Ralph Ellison, letter to Richard Wright, November, 3 1941, quoted in Michel Fabre, "From *Native* Son to *Invisible* Man: Some Notes on Ralph Ellison's

Evolution in the 1950s," *Speaking for You: The Vision of Ralph Ellison,* ed. Kimberly Bentson (Washington, D.C.: Howard University Press, 1987) pp. 210–12.

27. Norman Mailer, "Comments on the Talent in the Room," *Advertisements for Myself* (New York: Putnam, 1959), p. 433.

28. Richard Wright, "Diary," January 22, 1945, *Ralph Ellison: Emergence of Genius* by Lawrence Jackson (New York: Wiley, 2002), pp. 307–8.

29. Ralph Ellison and Horace Cayton, "Interview Notes," September 8, 1968, Horace Cayton Papers, Southside Branch, Chicago Public Library.

30. Ralph Ellison, letter to Stanley Edgar Hyman, May 29, 1970, " 'American Culture Is of a Whole': From the Letters of Ralph Ellison," *New Republic,* March 1, 1999, 40.

2

LAURA SAUNDERS

Ellison and the black Church: the gospel according to Ralph

"The point is, that like yourself, I existed in a *field* of influences ... "[1] Three decades after a furious Ralph Ellison wrote this to his friend, the well-known critic Stanley Edgar Hyman in 1970, it's evident that this view has prevailed. Ellison's "field of influences" – which for Hyman consisted only of racial oppression and other African-American writers – is now furrowed with discussions of his debts not only to Richard Wright but also to Kenneth Burke, Hemingway, Dostoyevsky, and others. Yet one extraordinary influence remains overlooked: it is the debt Ellison owes what may loosely be called the "black Church," and its role in the vision he at times fiercely opposed to that of Hyman and others. With the 1999 publication of *Juneteenth* this debt can no longer be ignored. Although *Juneteenth* is not, strictly speaking, Ellison's own second novel – he died in 1994, leaving it unfinished after forty years of effort – it is nevertheless his work, fashioned by his literary executor from Ellison's highly-polished narrative nuggets, some of which he published during his life. While we can't know how he would have assembled his own novel, its hero is clearly A. Z. Hickman, a Negro preacher who takes the Gospel as seriously as Ellison means readers to take Hickman himself. It is also clear that a pivotal chapter, both of Ellison's work-in-progress and *Juneteenth*, depicts Hickman's Christian conversion.

The bare facts surrounding this transformation are incredible: Hickman changes from a high-living, profane jazzman into a celibate preacher of the Christian gospel while he assists the delivery of a child to a white woman whose lies about her pregnancy have caused the murders of his own brother and mother. He then accepts the woman's (unrelated, possibly wholly white) infant as his own. This conversion sequence may be Ellison's most powerful piece of writing. It is certainly his most audacious, a high-wire performance few writers would dare: in a climactic scene he takes on the forbidding subject of conversion for an audience he knew to be largely "without religion" (as he put it), either skeptical or oblivious.[2]

Juneteenth is not unique in exhibiting this debt. There is abundant evidence of it throughout Ellison's work, although readers may not notice it given the secularization of American culture in recent decades. In addition to making hundreds of Biblical allusions, Ellison often uses theological words like "communion," "temptation," and "sin," in ways that – if not quite orthodox – are never ironic. He said there was "a prayer involved" in his choice of an epigraph from "Benito Cereno" for *Invisible Man*, because he hoped readers would pay it the same "quality of attention" they gave Melville's writing. Elsewhere he insists that Mahalia Jackson is a religious singer whose proper venue is church.[3] At times he even sounds like a preacher thundering from the pulpit, charging that "the founding fathers committed the sin of racial pride" or some such.[4] And whenever Ellison inserts a sermon in his text – whether it's on "the blackness of blackness," African-American history, or even "the letter A" – he is underscoring the subject's importance.

Yet Ellison's debt to the Church is complex, as is often the case with his influences. He was skittish about owning it, just as he was his debt to Wright. As an adult he claimed not to be a believer and told one interviewer that he didn't pray and hadn't been to church in years.[5] He didn't cherish his churchboy memories as he did others: there are no extended tributes to ministers like those he wrote for his music teacher William L. Dawson and former principal Inman Page. A striking example of this divided stance appears in the stirring final lines of his 1971 speech honoring Dawson:

> If there were a choir here, I would say let us sing "Let Us Break Bread Together."
> I am not particularly religious, but I am claimed by music, and I was claimed by
> William L. Dawson.   (*Essays* 438)

Here Ellison makes three assertions about himself: he says he isn't religious, and that he was "claimed" by music and by Dawson.

It is "claimed" that gives him away. The underlying idea is that Ellison is not the agent, but that music and Dawson have chosen him. In putting it this way, he is drawing on a Judeo-Christian conception of sacred encounters. According to this understanding – which the Biblical writers stress because it reverses the common assumption – it is not human beings who approach God but rather God who approaches them. (This is why Jews are called the "*chosen* people.") This idea is reiterated throughout the New Testament, as when Jesus says, "You have not chosen me, but I have chosen you"(John 15:16).[6] So in the space of two sentences we find Ellison denying that he is religious, yet turning to an idea drawn from the Church to describe the sacred role he feels that music and Dawson have played in his life. *And* he wishes a choir could sing a spiritual. Why is there this conflict in his relation to religion?

Background

Recalling his youth in Oklahoma City, Ralph Ellison said that the Church was "one of our two main institutions" (*Collected Essays* 275). (The other was school, with jazz an informal but welcome third.) As a youth he was drenched in it every way but literally: his family's African-Methodist-Episcopal denomination preferred the more sophisticated "sprinkling" of baptismal candidates to the full-body immersion practiced by the Baptists and others. Known by its initials, the AME church was (and is) a black mainstream denomination. It was founded in Philadelphia in 1793 by ex-slave Richard Allen and others after a notorious incident in which white ushers at St. George's Methodist Church forced a group of kneeling black worshipers to move to the back of the church during a prayer.[7] The sect borrowed much theology and practice from white Methodism; in the nineteenth century, membership expanded from northern urban roots to include Southern rural freedmen. AME politics were typically progressive and non-accommodationist, which attracted Ellison's mother, Ida Millsap Ellison.[8]

Her faith was Ida Ellison's mainstay after Lewis Ellison's death from an accident left her the sole support of Ralph, age three, and Herbert, still an infant. In a letter to his mother written in his twenties, Ellison recalled, "You've lived these years since Dad died ... toiling and praying from morning to night" (*Letters* 36). At the Avery Chapel on North Geary Street, Ida held the honored position of steward; dressed in a white uniform and nurse's cap, she sat in the Amen corner and shouted during services. At one point when she was in desperate straits church leaders hired her as sexton (janitor) and allowed the family to live in the church's then-vacant rectory, next door to the church. (It was the nicest house the young Ellison lived in, and he recalled spending delightful hours in its library as a six-year-old, reading novels and adventure stories left by former occupants [*Conversations* 276]). Ellison attended Avery's kindergarten when he was five, and his strict mother saw to it that he went to church and joined the junior fellowship. He was both "pleased and puzzled" when she loosened the reins a bit and allowed him, as a teenager, to leave Christmas sunrise services early for breakfast dances (*Collected Essays* 679; Jackson 25, 27–8, 74).

But Ellison's immersion in Christian ideas, language, and traditions went far beyond Avery Chapel's doors, in part because the boundary between church and state was far less distinct then than it is now. There was daily chapel at Douglass, the segregated public school he attended for twelve years, and its graduation was usually held in the largest black church in town. Of its principal Inman Page, Ellison said, "His voice and images are still evoked by certain passages of the Bible ... I can still hear him reading from St. Paul's Letter to the Corinthians." Chapel was also mandatory at Tuskegee; on Sundays students went twice, in the morning and later for vespers. Tent revivals, with their drama and high-pitched emotion, served as popular entertainment in the days before access to movies and television (*Collected Essays* 70, 585, 588; Jackson 3l, 101).

In all these experiences Ellison encountered facets of a highly-evolved, deeply-rooted verbal tradition that later comments show he was aware of. This tradition began when, contrary to what might have been expected, many slaves embraced Christianity. (Ellison agrees with Faulkner that they often took it more seriously than their masters [*Collected Essays* 55]). Slaves combined this faith with what Henry Mitchell, a scholar of black homiletics, terms African "love of oratory and meaningful narrative in which the whole community took part" to excel at preaching, despite little or no formal training and in many cases, illiteracy. Mitchell gives examples of self-taught slaves renowned for their preaching, among them Harry Hoosier, a carriage driver for Bishop Francis Asbury, the leader of American Methodism. Benjamin Rush, a signer of the Declaration of Independence, called Hoosier "the greatest orator in America." Some Negro preachers even managed to learn Greek and Hebrew.[9] Ellison nods to this strand of the tradition when Hickman recalls that at the Juneteenth revival, there was "that little Negro Murray ... who could preach the pure Greek and original Hebrew and could still make our uneducated folks swing along with him."[10]

Such rhetorical excellence wasn't rare. In *Slave Religion*, Albert Raboteau quotes a "traveler who listened to ex-slave preachers shortly after the Civil War: 'Some of the most vivid reproductions of Scripture narrative I have ever listened to were from the lips of such men, who might with proper training have become orators.'"[11] Ellison himself notes that some Negro preaching echoes with the "lingering accents" of an otherwise moribund tradition (*Collected Essays* 668):

> It's not too unusual that the rhetoric of a Negro sermon, for instance, can be traced back to Shakespeare, if you know where to look, or to the metaphysical poets. I'm not saying that ... unlettered ministers have read John Donne, but ... they are possessors of a living tradition ... Actually, the great tradition of nineteenth-century eloquence in oratory is most alive within the Negro community. We don't find it so much in Congress anymore, but you find it among Negroes, especially in the churches ... It is more oral than literary, but it would be a mistake to look upon it as primitive.   (*Conversations* 92)

The rhetoric was further enriched by the actual Biblical language, because preachers always took their texts from the 1611 "King James" (Authorized)

Version of the Bible, a translation contemporary with Shakespeare's plays and unsurpassed in beauty and majesty.

Sitting in church or a tent revival, Ellison also received lessons in technique. Dolan Hubbard has argued that the jazz-like "riffs" in his writing derive from sermons rather than music.[12] (In a letter, Albert Murray agrees: "The revs ... were the original riffers, anyway"[*Trading* 120].) For black preachers, narrative was also a vehicle for expressing ideas, as Ellison acknowledged:

> For a people lacking a class with broad formal education, narrative played a special role ... the Negro American's conception of himself was seldom supported by an articulate philosophy, or by conscious theology, or by any of the specifically analytic forms of the mind. (*Letters* 41)

And the preacher had to deliver his freight of ideas so as to engage listeners' imaginations. Otherwise they risked the jibe, "Your preacher can't preach" (Hubbard 16).

Perhaps most important, Ellison encountered a tradition that laid strong emphasis on two ideas: the authority of personal experience and the power of language. Both are hallmarks of Protestant Christianity, and he noted that the "spiritual outlook" of American Negroes is "basically Protestant" (*Collected Essays* 292). (Roman Catholicism doesn't reject either idea, but accords them a different emphasis.) The Reformation occurred in part because Martin Luther insisted on relying on the authority of his own conscience instead of that of the Pope and Holy Roman Emperor. "I do not accept the authority of the popes and councils ... I cannot and I will not recant anything," he told the Imperial Diet at Worms in 1521, "for to go against my conscience is neither right nor safe."[13] This emphasis has persisted in Protestantism, leaving critics to charge that it is too individualistic and prone to fissure. But others have found exhilarating its stress on the ability and even duty of each individual to strive for self-definition.

The Protestant emphasis on the transforming power of language also derives from Luther.[14] Whereas Roman Catholics looked to the sacraments to impart transforming grace, Luther radically raised the status of encounters with the "*Word* of God" – reading the Bible, and especially, listening to the Word expounded and proclaimed by preachers. "Preaching," he insisted, "continues the battle begun by the saving event [i.e. Christ's death and resurrection] *and is itself the saving event* [emphasis added]."[15] So preaching is not just teaching, but can itself be the medium of transformation. (This is why in many Protestant churches the pulpit is as prominent as the altar, sometimes more so.)

Mitchell notes that the African-American Protestant tradition stressed "the Word" as transforming. Sermons were "imaginative, narrative, and prone to generate experiential encounter ... in opposition to the Euro-American tradition of cognitive, essay-type sermons." Because of this focus on emotions "and the whole person ... African-American preaching has survived amazingly well and served to empower an oppressed people" (Mitchell 3, 4). Hubbard says that preaching became the chief way "African-Americans attempted to redefine themselves and their history through speech acts(4)." Attempted and succeeded, as that redefinition spurred the civil rights movement led by Dr. Martin Luther King, Jr. and others, many of whom were preachers. Ellison noticed their leading role – as opposed to that of educators – in a letter to Murray during the Montgomery bus boycott. "The crackers," he says, tried to:

> bribe schools like Tuskegee into staying third class, but hell, they forgot to bribe the preachers! I saw some photos of those brothers and some of them look like the old, steady, mush-mouthed chicken-hawk variety; real wrinkle-headed Bible-pounders! ... But they're talking sense and acting!   (*Trading* 116)

Ellison was talking sense and acting in a different sphere, drawing on the same heritage.

Ellison's own gospel

The black Church's most important influence on Ralph Ellison's writing consists not of language or technique but rather ideas that deeply inform and even generate it. In a sense Ellison composed and preached his own gospel, and he borrowed many of its elements from the New Testament Gospel (which incorporates the Old Testament) and its theology. Though some of his ideas aren't exclusive to Christian tradition, they are present in it, and he nearly always couches them in terms that link his gospel with the original.

Begin at the beginning: Ellison often mentions an almost primal "chaos" that resembles what was "without form, and void" before the Creation (Genesis 1:2). According to the Biblical writers, God subdued this void when he made the world, but he didn't dispel it. So chaos is always potentially present and often appears symbolically as water, especially the sea. When Noah's flood engulfs the world or Jonah is tossed in the raging sea, chaos is come again; when Jesus walks on water or calms a storm, the Gospel writers are asserting his power over it. In Ellison's dozens of uses of the word "chaos" there is a parallel understanding of it as a threatening formlessness ever present beneath what he calls the "fragile floor of civilized humanity." Unlike others – such as John Dewey, who embraced the "absolute opportunity which chaos affords" – Ellison finds nothing creative in chaos and rarely uses the word with a positive connotation.[16] While he contends that chaos cannot be denied – "We cannot live without an awareness of chaos" – he believes that it must be subdued through disciplined effort, often artistic effort. So he praises "the novel's ability to forge images which would strengthen man's will to say no to chaos and affirm him in his task of humanizing himself." In the music of Duke Ellington and Louis Armstrong he finds "a rejection of that chaos and license which characterized the so-called Jazz Age . . ." (*Collected Essays* 645, 700, 384). But he calls Rinehart, the hypocritical preacher in *Invisible Man*, " the personification of chaos . . . he has lived so long with chaos that he knows how to manipulate it" (*Conversations* 19).

Ellison's gospel also borrows from his Judeo-Christian heritage the notion of a Chosen People, a Promised Land, and Sacred Writ – Americans, the United States, and the Declaration of Independence and Constitution, respectively. Here he is in part echoing Melville, who had called Americans "the peculiar, chosen people – the Israel of our time."[17] But Ellison extends Melville's metaphor by identifying a fatal flaw incorporated into the country at its beginning – either racism or slavery, according to different essays. In his words:

> Thus the new edenic political scene incorporated a flaw . . . [that] embodied a serpent-like malignancy that would tempt government and individual alike to a constantly-recurring fall from democratic innocence . . . racism took on the force of an original American sin (*Collected Essays* 775, 778).

For Ellison, as for the Biblical writers, this original sin was not only evil, but also ramifying: "Slavery was a crass violation of the ideal democratic compact upon which this republic was founded, and *all else flows* from that initial fall from a transcendent ideal [emphasis added]"(*Letters* 46). He believes the taint affects art as well as politics, and that American literature founders unless it addresses moral issues – of which the most important is slavery and its heritage. He insisted to Murray that it must, in fact, "smuggle the black man into its machinery in some form, otherwise it can't function."(*Trading* 223) This is why Ellison at one point faults Hemingway, for substituting an inward-looking "morality of craftsmanship" for engagement with moral issues (*Collected Essays* 708).

And what of redemption from sin? In both the original Gospel and Ellison's, it comes through the undeserved suffering of a sacrificial victim. Ellison's engagement with the idea of the redemptive power of unmerited suffering is so profound that it seems generative, as though the work itself were Ellison's response to persistent questions that occurred to him as a child in church. Given his place on the lowest social and economic rung, it is easy to imagine him wondering, "How? Just how can it be true that the last can become first, or the downtrodden exalted? How exactly would it happen?"

To recapitulate: in the Gospel that Ellison heard preached week in and week out in his youth, the original sin that enters the world through Adam requires an extraordinary act of expiation. It is accomplished through the undeserved degradation, agony, and sacrifice of God in the form of his son, Jesus, and extends salvation beyond the Jews to all human beings. In Christian theology, Christ's unmerited suffering is the central, subversive fact that transforms established order and challenges the "wisdom of the world," the one that destroys the power of death and enables the resurrection. This makes it a paradox, and it underlies and gives authority to the other paradoxical, subversive statements made by Jesus, such as "the last shall be first" and "blessed are the meek," both of which Ellison loved to quote. Surely this idea caught his imagination for several reasons. It was the cornerstone of the faith of his mother and others he loved, ambient in the atmosphere he grew up in. For him as for them, it served as a way for the powerless to seize agency from the powerful, or at least to redefine their suffering. It gave those who embraced it the privilege – with no change in circumstance – of reversing the roles of victor and victim. At worst this redefinition provided comfort; at best it imparted strength to persevere and even, in the words of a popular theme of Negro sermons, "make a way out of no way."

But Ellison was also a close reader of his close friend the critic Kenneth Burke. So he must have recognized that the Gospel's provision of an alternate meaning for unmerited suffering supplies it with powerful and fruitful ambiguity. (Ambiguity in the sense of multiple meanings, not indeterminate ones.) As Burke noted, " ... it is in the areas of ambiguity that transformations take place; in fact, without such areas, transformations would be impossible ... [They are necessary] *so that A may become non-A*" – or hatred, love; or oppression, triumph.[18] Where there is transformation, there is drama, and Ellison found that the paradoxes asserted by the Gospel he heard as a boy could be put to rich use in his writing.

In Ellison's gospel it is the Negro who assumes Christ's role as scapegoat in American history: "The founding fathers ... designated one section of the American people to be the sacrificial victims for the benefit of the rest ... As a symbol of guilt and redemption, the Negro entered the deepest recesses of the American psyche ... " (*Collected Essays* 777–8). This assertion becomes his good news – the literal meaning of gospel – because it takes the fact of officially-imposed African-American degradation and finds another, positive meaning in it. Precisely because of this pain and suffering, he says, the last can become first in showing a needful nation how to live in the world. Or, as the protagonist puts it in the epilogue of *Invisible Man*:

> Was it that we of all, we, most of all, had to affirm the principle, the plan in whose name we had been brutalized and sacrificed, not because we would always be weak, not because we were afraid and opportunistic, but because we were older

than they in the sense of what it took to live in the world with others and because they had exhausted in us some – not much, but some – of the human greed and smallness, and yes, the fear and superstition that had kept them running.[19]

In *Juneteenth* this idea is both more explicit and more embedded, as I will show.

Once suffering has been redefined, however, how can victims find agency despite powerlessness? Ellison's answer to this question is "discipline," which is another element of his gospel. It is a quality he finds abundant and ingrained in many African-Americans – especially in the South, where generations learned from bitter experience how dangerous it could be to act on one's natural impulses and, say, strike back after being kicked. He told one young man, "The need to control and transcend mere anger has been our lot throughout our history, and for many years failing to do so, as the saying goes, got you dead." Ellison is saying that instead of striking back, the black man (or woman) who was kicked learned to save his (or her) own neck by controlling the impulse to counter violence with violence. Discipline preserved "maximum freedom . . . in selecting the moment" for retaliation, he notes. But he adds that

such emotional control [also] springs from our will to humanize a hostile society in our own terms and to convert that control into a source of pleasure and affirmation by transforming the threat of social existence into forms of self-definition and triumph. (*Letters* 40–3)

In other words, discipline is not only the means by which the oppressed assert agency, it is also the means by which oppression is resurrected as triumph.

Nowhere is this clearer than with jazz, one of the most important American contributions to the arts. Ellison says that what began as survival tactics – the "determined will to control violent emotion" as an unnatural but necessary "life-preserving discipline," i.e. the restraint of the impulse to hit back – developed into "the control-cum-flexibility that is characteristic of Negro expression at its best." And it is precisely this "control-cum-flexibility" that became both the wellspring and the defining characteristic of jazz. (It is also the quality Ellison sought in his own work.) Thus the triumph of jazz itself is a paradox, a living example of how the last can be first or the meek inherit the earth; the fact of its existence helps explain why Invisible Man's grandfather could call meekness a "dangerous activity" (*Invisible* 16). Ellison's faith in the value of discipline underlies his anger with some (black) activist students at Amherst: "No ideological catchwords could blind me to the fact that they were wasting a valuable opportunity for learning how to convert their anger into forms of conscious thought and creative action" (*Letters* 43).

To be sure, there are differences as well as congruities between Ellison's gospel and the original. Whereas the Biblical writers' vision is meant to be a universal one that transcends boundaries, Ellison limits his own to the United States and the African-American role in it. His vision is also earthbound, conceiving of redemption in terms of human beings and their essential relations; unlike many in the culture they come from, Ellison's fictional characters don't look to "pie in the sky" as a reward for earthly privation. Despite Hickman's references to God, Ellison shows little interest in the notion of a supernatural, transcendent deity who has created the world and is somehow at work in it. The disregard extends to Satan – though Ellison fiercely believes in sin. His focus is on what he describes time and again as "the human condition." "It is human will, human hope and human effort which make the difference," he insists. (*Collected Essays* 738)

But if Ellison doesn't focus on God as Author, he does think of the author as God. More precisely, he implies that the artist can – by disciplined mastery of craft – assume something of God's role on earth: he contends that the artist's mission is to find "abiding truths . . . by reducing the chaos of human experience to artistic form."(*Conversations* 97) Ellison isn't the first to ascribe quasi-Godlike powers to the artist, nor is this idea exclusive to Christian tradition, but he links the two with the word "abiding," a word that always has a religious connotation. At best the artist can "create or reveal hidden realities," an activity he calls "sacred," and finds liberating:

> Most of all, it is not only the images of art or the sound of music that give pleasure and inspiration; it is in the very spirit of art to be defiant of categories and obstacles. They are, as transcendent forms of symbolic expression, agencies of human freedom. (*Collected Essays* 120, 514)

Underlying these claims is a verse Ellison often heard as a child: "Ye shall know the truth and the truth shall make you free" (John 8:32).

Ellison chose words as the medium for his art, and his understanding of the nature of language is also Biblical. He often quoted the opening of John's gospel, especially the phrases "In the beginning was the Word . . . " and "the Word made flesh" (John 1:1, 14). As it happens, John's author was also quoting, consciously opening his own narrative with the first words of Genesis: "In the beginning . . ." Both of these Biblical writers thought of language as the defining gift God gave his human creation, as one interpreter says, the "activity proper to the creature man in direct imitation of Jahveh [God] who created him." This is because language can "give sense to what otherwise makes no sense, to bring light to what otherwise is darkness."[20] The Biblical writers underscore this idea when they show God giving Adam the power to name the animals in Genesis 2. (In an interesting allusion, Ellison says that analyzing American culture is "a matter of Adamic wordplay" because it involves "trying . . . to impose unity upon an experience that changes too rapidly for linguistic or political exactitude" [*Collected Essays* 511]).

Like the Biblical writers – and the Protestant tradition he was raised in – Ellison embraces the idea of the transforming power of language, in fact grounds his work in it. As Hickman tells Bliss: "Words are your business, boy. Not just the Word. Words are everything. The key to the Rock, the answer to the Question." But this power makes language a double-edged sword, "for if the word has the potency to revive and make us free, it has also the power to blind, and imprison, and destroy" (*Collected Essays* 81). One place Ellison first found the liberating power of language was in the Oklahoma City *Black Dispatch* editor Roscoe Dunjee's crusading journalism:

> As a constitutionalist, Dunjee understood the possiblility of words made sacred . . .
> In [the campaign for desegregation] the word was made flesh by a man who understood what America was about better than most . . .
>
> (*Collected Essays* 455–6).

He locates its evil power in the ways words were used to establish or enforce racial inferiority, including laws, court opinions, theological tracts, scientific studies and even fiction. In fact, he says, "Perhaps the most insidious, least understood form of segregation [is] the word" (*Collected Essays* 81).

If Ellison's religious heritage informs the core of his work, it also marks the surface by supplying an abundance of characters, stories, and images he draws upon so often that these allusions are a characteristic of his prose: it is a rare Ellison essay that doesn't have one, and *Invisible Man* and the stories have scores. In *Juneteenth*, they appear on nearly every page, but then the main character is a preacher. Though wonderfully apt, Ellison's use of them is not idiosyncratic: it ties him to "that vanished tribe" of "American Negroes" he dedicated *Juneteenth* to. Other members would not only easily grasp his references to Adam, Joseph, Samson, Job, Elijah, Ezekiel, Lazarus, Paul, and Jesus and an assortment of Bible images and verses, but find it natural to think in the same terms.

It is worth pausing over these references because current readers may miss them. Some are elaborate, others as brief as the ironic insertion of the words "like unto" into a comparison made by a character.[21] Often they are funny: one unfortunate Harlem character struts around in a "dashy dashiki . . . as bright and many-colored as the coat that initiated poor Joseph's troubles in biblical times" (*Collected Essays* 506). But Ellison's humor is usually driving home a serious point. Nowhere is this truer than in Hickman's wonderful reference when, after his mother's and brother's murders, he finds himself helping the woman whose lies caused those murders. His mind turns to Job, the paradigm of a man who tried to fathom the unfathomable:

> I guess it couldn't have been stranger than if one of Job's boils had started addressing him, saying, "Look here now, Job; this here is your head chief boil speaking to you. You just tell me my name and I'll jump right off your neck and take all the rest of the boils along with me." (*Juneteenth* 304–5)

Every now and then Ellison's allusive impulse even gets the better of his taste: recalling the death of a promising youth, he says the young man contracted lockjaw because "after burning his fingers ... [he] had *cut out the offending flesh* with his pocketknife [emphasis added]." This is a grotesque allusion to Jesus' saying, "If thy hand offendeth thee, cut it off" (*Collected Essays* 657; Matthew 18:8).

Ellison's allusions also amplify the text – as artists have done for centuries – by linking it with a discourse that makes its own radical claims and was still part of the popular imagination when he was writing. Describing his first impressions of New York City, he says he felt his presence was, for some white New Yorkers, like " a dark cloud no larger than a human hand, but somehow threatening" (*Collected Essays* 624). In 1 Kings 18, such a cloud appears to the prophet Elijah and is sent by God to end a drought; it reveals his power to the wicked, especially King Ahab. So Ellison becomes, like the cloud, a small portent of a mighty change that challenges the powerful. Near the end of the Prologue, Invisible Man says, "But I am an orator, a rabble rouser – Am? I was, and perhaps shall be again. *All sickness is not unto death*, neither is invisibility [emphasis added]." (*Invisible* 14) The italics quote Jesus' response at hearing of the death of Lazarus shortly before he restores him to life, and the protagonist is signaling – for those who catch it – the possibility of his own revival, as Ellison acknowledged decades later (John 11: 4; *Letters* 42). Later, when Invisible Man is lamenting his inability to help the people of Harlem after Tod Clifton's funeral, he says "I thought of Jack, the people at the funeral, Rinehart. They'd asked us for bread and the best I could give was a glass eye – not so much as an electric guitar" (*Invisible* 506). This clearly recalls Jesus' poignant comment: "Or what man is there of you, whom if his son ask bread, will he give him a stone?" (Luke 11:11).

There is one more way Ellison uses explicit Christian allusions. He invariably turns to them in his non-fiction when he is honoring someone or something, reverting to the highest terms of praise he encountered as a child. Both tributes to Dawson and Dunjee cited earlier use church-derived images. And when Jimmy Rushing sings at a public dance, he is "preaching"; the result, for all present, is a "feeling of communion" (*Collected Essays* 274–5). In the speech Ellison wrote for the American Institute of Arts and Letters when it honored Bernard Malamud with its Gold Medal for Fiction, he points out Malamud's minority background (Jewish), then praises him with an image found three times in four gospels. Malamud, he says, shows "how, in a nation of minorities, *the last becomes first* and outstanding among equals (*Collected Essays* 467)."²² The same holds true in a poem he wrote after visiting Oklahoma City in 1953, after *Invisible Man* had made him famous. Ellison was deeply moved by being back in his old neighborhood of "Deep Second," especially at a breakfast with old friends where everyone "ate tons of chicken and drank gallons of coffee and just played havoc with the hot biscuits and looked over old photographs." The poem recalls his "second coming into Deep Second"; in the final, climactic lines, he cherishes "how they live in me and I in them" – a close paraphrase of language used by Jesus, and reiterated by Paul (*Trading* 52, 55).²³

Two expositions

Church influence permeates Ellison's work, even his earliest: a 1940 essay in *New Masses* praises a political speaker for being as able a rhetorician as a black preacher, and the 1939 story "Slick Gonna Learn" has echoes of the parable of the Good Samaritan (*Collected Essays* 24).²⁴ But two passages of the second novel offer his gospel full-blown. The first is the *Juneteenth* sermon: it is Ellison's *credo*, his understanding of the African-American role in US history. The second is the narrative of Hickman's conversion; here he embeds his ideas in the scene's action.

Ellison published the sermon in 1964, and the editor John Callahan incorporated it as Chapter 7 of *Juneteenth*. It is set in Alabama during the first two decades of the last century, on the grounds of a tent revival commemorating the Emancipation Proclamation. (Some slaves in Texas got word of their freedom on June 19, 1865, giving rise to the portmanteau word "Juneteenth"). At the revival, several thousand descendants of slaves gather for a few days to mingle and hear a host of preachers enlighten and entertain them. Hickman and Bliss, the white child he has raised from infancy, preach their sermon antiphonally. In a preamble Hickman says its purpose is to "tell ourselves our story" as the "Hebrew children" do at Passover, " so that they can keep their history alive in their memories." Like both the original "chosen people" and Ellison himself, Hickman tells a story to articulate informing truth for incorporation into the character and actions of his listeners. Bliss dons his white tuxedo and takes the role of "the younger generation" (*Juneteenth* 117).

With all the flash and fervor of the best Negro preachers, Hickman tells his story as a series of paradoxes, seeking to draw from them the same rhetorical power that the Gospel writers did. First he stakes his claim that the slaves were fully American, rejecting any notion that they were better off in "heathen Africa" because the "cruel calamity" of slavery "was laced up with a blessing . . . we found the Word of God" (118–19). This is meant to confound white Christians who would exclude them, for if the slaves are Christian, they can claim to be fully human whatever their legal status. (As Paul said in Galatians 3, "There is neither Jew nor Greek, slave nor free, male nor female, for ye all are one in Christ Jesus.") Hickman's emphasis on the power of language – "the Word" instead of, say, the blood of Christ – recurs throughout the sermon. He continues by asserting that the country was "dedicated to the principles of Almighty God," but its beneficiaries "turned traitor to the God who set them free from Europe's tyrant kings" in a "crime . . . like the fall of proud Lucifer from Paradise" (120). Slavery left the Negroes "eyeless, tongueless, drumless, danceless, songless, hornless, soundless, dayless, nightless, wrongless, rightless, motherless, fatherless – scattered" (124). They languished as sacrificial victims, "scattered in the ground for a long dry season." (He is referring to "the Valley of Dry Bones" depicted in Ezekiel 37, a frequent text of black sermons.) Using another paradox, Hickman redefines this diaspora as a broadcast of fertile seed, and the slaves nourish and are nourished by the land over which they have been scattered. "It suited us fine," he says, "It was in us and we were in it" – again echoing Jesus and Paul (125). In fact, he adds, "The land is ours . . . because . . . we fertilized it with our dead." "So" – yet another paradox – "the more of us they destroy, the more it becomes filled with our redemption" (130).

The resurrection occurs thanks to "one solitary vibration of God's true word . . . We were rebirthed dancing, we were rebirthed crying affirmation of the Word, quickening our transcended flesh" (126–7). Finally Hickman redefines, at vivid length, the unmerited suffering of Negro oppression as a sign of God's special favor. He even calls it a discipline:

> He wants a well-tested people to work his will . . . He's going to heat us till we almost melt and then He's going to plunge us into ice-cold water . . . He means for us to be a new kind of human. . . it's all the pressure of God . . . Let those who will despise you . . . [it's a] discipline through which we may see that which the others are too self-blinded to see.   (128–31)

So oppression becomes preparation for leadership, and agency has shifted from the oppressors to God. Or, as another New Testament paradox puts it, the stone which the builder has rejected will become the cornerstone.[25]

Chapter 15 of *Juneteenth* incorporates the narrative nugget depicting Hickman's conversion. Ellison didn't publish it himself, but its power and polish are evident. It is hard to tell when the conversion happens, even for

Hickman: he puzzles over the events surrounding it, trying to determine how "the change" occurred. The sequence begins after the lynching of his brother Robert and murder of his mother, when the pregnant white woman who incited them by falsely naming Robert as her lover shows up at Hickman's door, in labor, begging for help. As always, Ellison presents the animating details: Hickman, the preacher's prodigal musician son, mourning his better-behaved brother with a shotgun, rifle, and two pistols at hand because he expects a mob, and so convinced he will die that he has recorded his death in the family Bible, all but the day; then the woman, also a musician – a church organist – wrapped in a black shawl "coming ... past all those out-houses, yard-dogs and chicken coops, long after dark had come down" (287). Like many white Southerners, she is used to setting the terms of her interactions with black people: she expects to get Hickman's help and does.

The manifest action progresses through the woman's labor and delivery in a "dream-version of the immaculate birth," as Ellison once called it, with Hickman in the thankless role of Joseph (*Conversations* 283). He puts the woman in his mother's bed; dressed in his mother's nightgown, she gives birth, while he watches his "own big black hands going in and out of those forbidden places," using his father's razor to cut the cord. Later he feeds her, "spoon by spoon" (301, 306). In the end, he accedes to her outrageous insistence that he take the child as restitution for his dead brother.

The real action occurs, however, as Ellison plumbs the depths of the mysterious word "forgiveness." Hickman recalls that at the scene's beginning, he was "in the hard cold center of [his] anger ... feasting on revenge and sacrifice" (296). Referring to the Old Testament's *lex talionis* ("an eye for an eye, a tooth for a tooth"), he spares no detail as he looks at the woman and craves:

> Those eyes for Bob's eyes; that skin for Bob's flayed skin ... And remembering what they had done with their knives, I asked myself, But what can I take that can replace his wasted seed and all that's now a barbaric souvenir floating in a fruit jar of alcohol and being shown off in their barbershops.   (296)

But out of the depths of his pain, something emerges. "That's when God shows you his face," he says later, "That's when ... you're about to be nothing and you have a flash of a chance to be something" (298–9). In the midst of his revenge fantasy, Hickman looks at the woman and sees her pain and utter loneliness, though it is far less justified than his, and he extends to her human kindness she in no way deserves. Ellison is moving Hickman out of his Old Testament dispensation based on law and into a New Testament dispensation of grace. He says to himself,

> That's when you got your first peep through the wall of life ... Ha, yes! That's when the alphabet in your poor brain was so shaken up that the letters started

to fall out and spell "hope," "faith," and "charity" – it would take time for them
to fall all the way into place . . . but it was beginning to happen.   (299)

It's no surprise that, in describing the change, Hickman uses language – the
"shaken up" alphabet that regroups into "faith, hope and charity" – as his
metaphor.

The conversion proceeds by fits and starts. After the birth, Hickman
considers poisoning the woman; watching her sleeping, he recalls "just sitting
there and hating . . . and thinking back three generations and more of my
people's tribulations and trying to solve the puzzle of that long-drawn-out
continuation of abuse" (304). He imagines killing both her and himself,
"the way our bodies would look when they found us" (306). At the same
time, he says, "It was like the Lord had said, 'Hickman, I'm starting you out
right here – with the flesh and with Eden and Christmas squeezed together.
Never mind the spirit and justice and right and wrong . . . because this is a
beginning.' He had called me . . . " (305). Yet again, Ellison echoes the Biblical
writers' understanding that human beings don't initiate or control sacred
encounters. Throughout his account, Hickman speaks of being acted upon;
he is "called," and "claimed," and "torn out of his heathen freedom." So he
takes the child hoping that "maybe the baby *could* redeem her and me . . . and
help us all," though he knows it could also "grow into the wickedness his folks
had mapped out for him" (311). The woman acknowledges a special quality in
Hickman and his culture: "Let him share your Negro life and whatever it is
that allowed you to help us . . . Let him learn to share the forgiveness your life
has taught you to squeeze from it" (309). Hickman's conversion is now a fact:
"That was the end of the old life for me, even though I didn't know it at the
time" (311).

Thus Ellison proclaims his gospel in fiction. He depicts a black man
who has undergone profound unmerited suffering yet by some action of
grace can extend sympathy and help to his tormentor, who in no way
deserves it. As a result the man emerges from the furnace of his torment
annealed and qualified to lead others in finding the way to new life based,
as he says in Paul's memorable terms, on faith, hope, and charity (1 Cor.
13). It is unclear, from reading *Juneteeth* and other fragments, just where
Ellison's story was headed. Why, given the love of Hickman and others,
does Bliss (the child) betray his Negro past? Does the cause lie with Bliss,
or Hickman, or both? What does the betrayal say about race in America,
or human nature?

It is impossible to say. But the narrative of Hickman's conversion stands,
not least for the way in which Ellison defines – and redefines – the nature of
dramatic transformation. Like some other fictional heroes, Hickman is

transformed by suffering; unlike them, he in no way causes his own torment. (On the blasted heath, for example, the suffering King Lear sheds his former arrogance and shows pity for "poor naked wretches" [III.iv]. But the king has helped to bring about the downfall that inspires his accession of sympathy.) Instead, what changes Hickman is an action that some would characterize as merely pathetic because it shows – in essence – a bad thing happening to a good person. Ellison dares to ground his scene's drama wholly in the Gospel idea that redemptive transformation can emerge from unmerited suffering. Whether this portrayal will, in Samuel Johnson's phrase, "please many, and please long" is also unknown. But it is clear evidence of the deep penetration into Ellison's consciousness of ideas he first heard as a boy, in church.

Ellison's dissociation

Given the magnitude of his debt to the black Church, Ellison's comments on it are sparse, especially by comparison with his writing on music. He told one interviewer in 1983 – more than twenty years after telling Murray that the preacher Hickman was taking over his second novel – that he was not religious "in any official way" and that "attending church itself I find to be uninteresting." He even sounds something like the sociologists he disparaged, speaking of "religion as a powerful force in Afro-American life, as a stabilizing force, and as a source of tradition" – as though he thought Christianity's historic role in black culture had an accidental rather than substantial cause. Instead of going to church, he said, "I read. I'm aware of the religious content of much of the great literature, and I approach it that way" (West 13–14).

Ellison's diffidence – or dissociation – on the subject of religion makes two glosses especially interesting. In a 1959 letter to Murray, he recalls reading a section of the second novel to students and teachers, and

at the end of two hours they were still in a trance. Old Hickman had them, man; you would have laughed your ass off to see that old downhome Moses rhetoric work. [In Ellison's lexicon Moses refers to any old-style black character, not the Biblical figure.] It's not too difficult to observe when Mahalia cuts loose at such places as Newport, but most of the jazz fans ... have no religion, no sense of literature or art, no way of ... coming to grips with profound feeling – but it's more difficult to reduce Hickman's sermons to mere entertainment; that old bastard knows how to get under even so initiated and tough a skin as mine. He preaches gut, and that comes from depths and admits no absolute control. All I can do is ask him hard questions and write down his acts and his answers.

(*Trading* 204)

In this complex statement, Ellison groups religion with art and literature as ways of "coming to grips with profound feeling," and implies that all three can reach and help order the chaos of the emotions, the element of human nature that is at once most basic and least susceptible to control. But he also says that Hickman's preaching comes "from depths," "gets under [his] skin," and "admits no absolute control," even by himself, so has withstood efforts to use it as "mere entertainment" – gratification – in a way that jazz hasn't.

This raises more questions: given Ellison's love for and debt to music, why does he think Hickman's preaching can resist manipulation better than jazz – is it for extrinsic reasons, such as the temper of the times, or intrinsic ones, such as the nature of language? If Hickman's words have the power of truth, is it because they are true as art or as religion, or both? Perhaps most interesting, how is Ellison's fictional preacher like an artist? Could it be that each must deny chaos the absolute freedom it desires, and instead grant that license to a truth that – in his words – "admits no absolute control?" And that, having granted utter license to truth, both the preacher and the artist must follow it wherever it chooses to go, even if it leads an artist like Ellison to show a black man forgiving a white woman for the most notorious racial crime there is? Again, Ellison doesn't elaborate.

Ellison's other relevant comment on religion surfaces in his acute observations on the debt Stephen Crane owed his own religious past. These illuminate not only Crane but also Ellison, and link both writers with their Protestant heritage, especially the precedence it can give individual conscience when it confronts established authority. Ellison notes that Crane was the product of "two lines of hard-preaching, fundamentalist Methodist ministers," then speculates that the Protestant tradition has affected American literature. In what ways? He suggests that its "emotional intensity and harsh authority" provided Crane with

> an early schooling in the seriousness of spiritual questions – of the individual's ultimate relationship to his fellow men, to the universe, and to God – and was one source of the youthful revolt which taught him to look upon life with his own eyes. Just as important is the discipline which the church provided him [Crane] in keeping great emotion under the control of the intellect, as during the exciting services (which the boy learned to question quite early), along with an awareness of the disparity between the individual's public testimony [in church] and his private deeds – a matter intensified by the fact that the celebrant of this rite was his own father.

Ellison fastens on Crane's Protestant preoccupation with the authority of personal experience; the powerful emotions released in church and the way in which the church sanctioned and structured them; and the often-glaring split between members' public professions and private actions. He infers that such a background made Crane

> concerned very early with private emotions displayed as an act of purification and self-definition, an excellent beginning for a writer interested in *the ordeals of the private individual struggling to define himself against the claims of society.* (emphasis added; *Collected Essays*, 113–15)

This applies to Ellison too; notice how the words in italics exactly describe *Invisible Man*. Writing informally to Murray, he notes the similarities with his own life:

> The little bastard [Crane] was from a long line of preachers on both sides and when we consider this some of the mystery of how he came to think and feel as he did is dispelled. That damned Methodist fire and brimstone along with all that hockey-assed hypocrisy had the boy running like a puppy with the high-life on his balls from a very early age ... The critics have praised Crane for the verbiage he left out, while refusing to see that he wasn't leaving out the religious background of his thought. The other thing which fascinates me is the parallel with his own life: not only the Methodism but the resentment of church folks' shittiness at an early age, the early death of the father, and the strict mother. (*Trading* 223)

Neither did Ellison "leave out the religious background of his thought." What's more, he found its verbiage – i.e. rhetoric – of immense value to his work.

These passages suggest another reason for Ellison's diffidence about the Church. Like many bright, church-immersed youths, he noticed and resented "church folks' shittiness" – the sharp divergence between the ideals as professed and as lived. Churches and church members are notorious for their hypocrisy; like Crane, Ellison surely witnessed his share, especially while living in the rectory on church charity. After an AME clergyman criticized *Invisible Man*, he said that the minister "wishes to out-Bledsoe Dr. Bledsoe ... [but] I know too much about the inner workings of an Afro-Methodist Episcopal Church even to be annoyed with him" (*Letters* 40). Perhaps this is one reason why Ellison, a self-described "loner," resisted churchgoing as an adult and also why he made Hickman a showman evangelist rather than a denominational minister (*Conversations* 332).

In his work, however, Ellison chose not to dwell on the Church's short-comings. In this he diverges from other writers, notably his literary ancestor Melville, who was also immersed in Protestant doctrine as a youth. In his work Melville hardly ever misses a chance to needle the institutional Church, so we witness Ahab's subversive baptism in *Moby Dick*, the hypocritical Mr. Falsgrave's fecklessness in *Pierre*, and the confusing Christian analogues of "Billy Budd." Ellison's non-fiction, however, mentions the besetting sins of

Church and Church people rarely, and then largely indirectly. In *Invisible Man* he rolls them all up into one ball and calls it Rev. Rinehart, who serves more as caricature than full-scale indictment. Like a vice from a medieval morality play, Rinehart is easy to identify and condemn, but he in no way detracts from the towering presence of Hickman. Surely Ellison's restraint also contained an element of good manners, an essential respect for the faith held by the members of "that vanished tribe" he loved and felt loved by, above all his mother.

But there was far more. In the end, Ellison apparently found that what the black Church gave him was of far greater value to his work than its shortcomings were inhibiting, so much so that he set aside his near-constitutional aversion to religion when his art prompted him to draw on the Church's gifts. If, as he noted, his "basic sense of artistic form" derives from music, then it is also true that many of his seminal ideas, as well as his language, images, and techniques, derive from his early immersion in the black Church (*Conversations* 283). And if Ralph's gospel isn't quite the same as the Christian Gospel, there is still a profound overlap that his readers – and anyone interested in the complex relationship between literature and religion, especially in America – cannot afford to ignore. Always happy with a fruitful ambiguity, Ellison reminded one young man who asked about his religion, "Bending the knees isn't the only way to pray" (*Letters* 40).

Notes

1. Ralph Ellison, "'American Culture is of a Whole': From the Letters of Ralph Ellison," ed. John F. Callahan, *New Republic* March 1, 1999:42. Hereafter cited in the text as *Letters*.
2. Ralph Ellison and Albert Murray, *Trading Twelves: The Selected Letters of Ralph Ellison and Albert Murray* (New York: Modern Library, 2000), p. 204. Hereafter cited in the text as *Trading*.
3. Maryemma Graham and Amritjit Singh, eds., *Conversations with Ralph Ellison* (Jackson: University Press of Mississippi, 1995), p. 265. Hereafter cited in the text as *Conversations*.
4. Ralph Ellison, *The Collected Essays of Ralph Ellison.* Ed. John F. Callahan (New York: Random House, 1995), p. 777. Hereafter cited in the text as *Collected Essays*.
5. From an unpublished interview with Hollie West in April 1983, courtesy of Robert O'Meally.
6. Some of the theological ideas discussed in this chapter are so generally accepted that they have no one source. In addition, Ellison himself had no interest in formal theology. I am indebted to Professor Christopher Morse of Union Theological Seminary for reviewing my formulations of these ideas.
7. Albert J. Raboteau, *Fire in the Bones* (Boston: Beacon Press, 1995), pp. 79–87.

8. Lawrence Jackson, *Ralph Ellison: Emergence of Genius* (New York: John Wiley, 2002), p. 27. Hereafter cited in the text as Jackson.

9. Henry M. Mitchell, "African-American Preaching," *Concise Encyclopedia of Preaching*, ed. Willimon and Lischer (Louisville: Westminster John Knox Press), pp. 4–6. Hereafter cited in the text as Mitchell.

10. Ralph Ellison, *Juneteenth* (New York: Random House, 1999), p. 137. Hereafter cited in the text as *Juneteenth*.

11. Albert J. Raboteau, *Slave Religion: The Invisible Institution in the Antebellum South* (New York: Oxford University Press, 1978), pp. 234–5.

12. Dolan Hubbard, *The Sermon and the African-American Literary Imagination* (Columbia: University of Missouri Press, 1994), p. 7. Hereafter cited in the text as Hubbard.

13. Martin Luther, *Luther's Works: Career of the Reformer* II, ed. Forell and Lehmann, vol. 32 (Philadelphia: Muhlenberg Press, 1958), p. 112.

14. It did not originate with Luther of course. In Western rhetorical tradition, the idea of the transforming power of language dates at least to Cicero's "grand style," the purpose of which was to move listeners to action. Augustine and others imported the idea from classical rhetoric into Christian theology; during the Reformation, Luther and other Protestants placed a renewed emphasis on it along with other features of Augustine's thought. This means that both Martin Luther King and Ellison's preacher Hickman are the heirs of Cicero by way of Martin Luther. Ellison may not have known these facts, but his comment on the 'living tradition" of Negro preaching suggests that he correctly sensed that it was both old and rich.

15. Eric W. Gristch, "Martin Luther," *Concise Encyclopedia of Preaching*, p. 314.

16. Louis Menand, *The Metaphysical Club* (New York: Farrar, Straus & Giroux, 2001), p. 318.

17. Herman Melville, *White-Jacket or The World in a Man-of-War* (Northwestern University Press and the Newberry Library, 1970), p. 151.

18. Kenneth Burke, "*A Grammar of Motives*," (Cleveland: World Publishing Co., 1962), p. xxi.

19. Ralph Ellison, *Invisible Man* (New York: Vintage, 1982) p. 574. Hereafter cited in the text as *Invisible*.

20. William H. Ralston, "That Old Serpent," *Sewanee Review* 81 (Winter, 1973): 392.

21. Ralph Ellison, "It Always Breaks Out," *Partisan Review* 30 (Spring 1963): 27.

22. Matthew 19:30, 20:16; Mark 10:31; Luke 13: 30.

23. John 6:56 "He that eateth my flesh and drinketh my blood dwelleth in me, and I in him"; John 15:4 "Abide in me, and I in you ..." Paul famously makes the word "in" do double-directional duty in Romans 8.

24. "Slick Gonna Learn," *Direction* 2 (September 1939): 10–16.

25. This image appears in Psalms 118:22; Matthew 21:42; Mark 12:10; Luke 20:17; Acts 4:11; and Peter 2:7.

3

SARA BLAIR

Ellison, photography, and the origins of invisibility

Among readers of Ellison, it is a truth universally acknowledged that the benchmark for his aesthetics and novelistic style is jazz. His own body of critical writing, as well as received readings of black modernism, insist on a definitive continuity between literature and music, from which visual culture remains at a considerable, historically determined distance. In often-cited essays on such blues and jazz legends as Duke Ellington, Louis Armstrong, Charlie Parker, and Charlie Christian; in remembrances of earlier jazz cultures; in the narrative rhythms of *Invisible Man* (which has been aptly described as "a progression of jazz breaks taking off from and returning to the bass line of invisibility"[1]): everywhere throughout his work, Ellison asks to be read as an "ambidextrous" figure, riffing on jazz and literary histories, thus responding to this American life and forging an authorial identity.[2] Indeed, critic Robert O'Meally has identified jazz in America as "Ellison's metaphor for democracy and love" and "the answer to the complicated question of identity" in one.[3] Ellison's work is thus taken to exemplify the apercu that, throughout their history and in response to the social conditions of their emergence, all black arts aspire to the condition of music – most particularly, the high-flying, mind-bending, magisterial flights, the hot dizzy highs and soulful lows, of improvisatory jazz.

But Ellison's negotiations of racial history and experience in *Invisible Man* owe an as-yet unacknowledged debt to another cultural form with which he purposively experimented: photography. His archive (at least those portions of it currently available to scholars) includes a significant body of materials that document Ellison's life-long, ongoing interests in photographic images, practitioners, and stylistics.[4] As he notes in the preface to *Invisible Man*, Ellison supported himself during the writing of the novel through his work as a photographer, producing a respectable body of commissioned portraits (particularly author portraits, for use by the very same publishers he was trying to interest in his own novel-in-progress), images made on journalistic assignment, and shots of art objects for use in exhibition catalogues. Many of his communications from the late 1940s and early 1950s – the period when he most intensively rewrote the novel and shepherded it into publication – are jotted on his professional letterhead of the time, memoranda sheets that bear the inscription "Ralph Ellison, Photographer." Sorting through various boxes and folders in which have been jumbled Ellison's own photographs, negatives, and prints, his clippings on photography exhibitions and series, his notations on shooting style, his working instructions to himself on the niceties of light-metering, film speeds, and image composition, it becomes clear that photography was far more to Ellison than merely a day job, pastime, or mode for memorializing private events. For Ellison, photography was no less than an interpretive instrument, a resource for critical reflection on American cultural practices and norms.

In this relation to photography, Ellison was to some extent merely one of his generation. He was, in other words, an intellectual who came of critical age in the years spanning the ambitious architecture of recovery from the Depression called the New Deal and a post-war aesthetic, both deeply indebted to photographic canons. Under the aegis of the New Deal's Farm Security Administration, or FSA, a stable of photographers – including such acknowledged masters as Dorothea Lange, Walker Evans, Margaret Bourke-White, Ben Shahn, and Gordon Parks – produced an archive of over two hundred thousand images. During the 1930s and 1940s, this body of work came for good and ill to embody liberalism's project of bureaucratic management of American modernity. FSA images circulated on an unprecedented scale; via their appearance in *Life, Look, Fortune,* and other picture magazines, they not only fed but helped spawn the nation's distinctive post-war image culture. These photographs were, by all accounts, the most lasting and influential body of cultural work produced under the New Deal banner, and they won for photography itself a new-found prestige, glamour, and aesthetic value.

Among black intellectuals in particular, photography seems to have held something of the fascination exerted by the python on the prey it stalks. In the name of documentary reality, ethnography, or liberal consensus, the New Deal camera had (however inadvertently) distorted and reified the realities of black experience in America; in its definitive images of raggedly clothed sharecroppers, shanty-dwellers, and evicted tenant farmers, it created a new iconography of the African-American as atavistic survivor, unfit for the rigors and opportunities of the modernity it celebrated.[5] That very fact made photography irresistible to black writers as a mode of both counter-protest and introspection. Some of Ellison's most soul-searching prose was occasioned in response to *Twelve Million Black Voices* (1941), Richard Wright's photo-text study of black America, an attempt to put his own spin on FSA images of black life in the wake of the Great Migration. As Ellison composed his first critical essays and works of short fiction, a young James Baldwin was collaborating with photographer Richard Avedon on a photo-text study of Harlem, likewise attempting to do justice to the polyphony and mixed cultural resources of its expressive life. A decade later, Langston Hughes would publish his fictive story of a Harlem woman, *Sweet Flypaper of Life* (1955), accompanied by the photographs of photographer Roy DeCarava; Hughes understood it as an antidote to two decades of dehumanizing depictions of black America.[6] In spite – and because – of its instrumentality in "exposing" the racial and class conditions it paradoxically naturalized, photography invited black writers to counter its own dehumanizing trends, to use photographic images to wrest the fullness and mystery of experience out from under the rubrics of poverty, delinquency, and oppression.

Yet if this desire impelled any number of writers and intellectuals of Ellison's generation, it had a particular power, and particular novelistic uses, for him. Such an argument, I should note, runs counter to the received wisdom not only on Ellison's relations with jazz but on vision and invisibility, the core concerns of his landmark novel. Embedded within *Invisible Man* are a myriad of images and symbolic objects that variously challenge longstanding associations between vision, knowledge or self-knowledge, and social progress – and further, implicate photography, the work of the third eye, in the failure of these linked projects. The narrator's achingly durable hope as he is led, blindfolded, to the Battle Royal; the sense of "the veil" being "lowered," rather than lifted, in images of the hallowed Founder of the college [7]; the sightless eyes of the Reverend Homer Barbee; the summons of the veteran at the Golden Day to "look beneath the surface" and "come out of the fog" (*Invisible* 153); Emerson Junior's anxious advice about "what lies behind the face of things" (188); the lobotomizing technician in the Liberty Paints plant hospital, who examines the narrator through the lens of "a bright third eye" (231); the "Cyclopean" glass eye of Brother Jack, bespeaking all he and the Brotherhood choose not to recognize (474): all these and more suggest how apparatuses of vision and insight, real and figurative, work to occlude, to deceive, to produce the expense of hard-fought humanity in the service of false and imprisoning (and racially charged) ideals. No wonder, then, that photography has been in essence written off by Ellison's readers as an instrument of the very logic of invisibility his novel seeks to probe.[8]

But this reductive linkage, by which the camera's eye comes to stand for the institution of photography, occludes a significant tradition within photographic practice dedicated to probing precisely its powers and effects;

further, it occludes Ellison's multiple investments in photographic practice. Close examination of his archival materials, and specifically of Ellison's relationship to the developing history of documentary and street photography defining the cultures of the New Deal and post-war New York, suggests quite the opposite of what his published work allows us to assume. It suggests, that is, that photography serves Ellison powerfully as a resource for the transformation of lived experience into narrative, of social fact into aesthetic possibility – and vice versa. Taking Ellison's photographic work and interests into account, in the context of their emergence and pursuit, allows us a new purchase on the complex cultural politics in which Ellison deftly engaged. In what follows, I begin to reconstruct the meaning of Ellison's self-invention under the sign (and eye) of the camera. I thus aim to provide an alternative, or at least supplementary, account of how invisibility was born.

In an essay titled "Hidden Name and Complex Fate," originally delivered as a lecture at the Library of Congress in 1964, Ellison offers a pointed allegory for his coming-into-being as a son, a writer, and a citizen of these United States (Ralph Waldo Ellison indeed). While "seeking adventure in back alleys" in his hometown of Oklahoma City, the young Ellison serendipitously finds "a large photographic lens":

> I remember nothing of its optical qualities, of its speed or color correction, but it gleamed with crystal mystery and it was beautiful. . . . Mounted handsomely in a tube of shiny brass, it spoke to me of distant worlds of possibility. I played with it, looking through it with squinted eyes, holding it in shafts of sunlight, and tried to use it for a magic lantern. . . . I could burn holes through newspapers with it, or I could pretend that it was a telescope, the barrel of a cannon, or the third eye of a monster – I being the monster – but I could do nothing at all about its proper function of making images; nothing to make it yield its secret. But I could not discard it.[9]

This inability to "find a creative use for my lens" is offered as an analogy for Ellison's frustrated attempts to "master" his over-determined name – at least initially, before the epiphanic readings in T. S. Eliot that are said to impel "the act of will" by which he becomes a writer ("Hidden" 156, 159, 146).[10] In this account, Ellison ultimately comes to terms with the Emersonian challenge of making his name and nationhood his own; he comes to recognize "the sacredness" of his experience as a black American, and its part in shaping "the composite nature of the ideal" national character ("Hidden" 153, 156, 165). His language also implies, however off-handedly, that he comes eventually to master the technical "secret" ("optical qualities," film speeds, "color correction") of image-making. The lens in question may have become "lost and forgotten," "buried" in some lost boyhood "box of treasures" ("Hidden" 153). But the camera as an instrument is a part of Ellison's arsenal, a complex fact of his "own hard-earned sense of reality" ("Hidden" 166).

It is worth taking seriously the nexus this passage proposes: between Ellison's identity as a writer, struggling to articulate a place for himself in an American cultural genealogy, and the instruments of photographic looking. Readers have generally assumed that such moments in which Ellison gestures toward camera work underscore the sociological designs of the camera, its unprecedented power in codifying ethnographic and popular assumptions about "the Negro." Visual historian Nicholas Natanson identifies the repertoire of "positive" photographic images of black Americans under the New Deal as limited to such baneful categories as "the Noble Primitive," "the Colorful Black," and "the Black Victim," relieved only by such differently problematic rubrics as "the glittering Role Model" and "the Transformed Black," with "a dehumanized 'before' giving way to an artifical 'after.'"[11] But Ellison retrospectively imagines himself *behind* the lens, not as its ethnographic or sociological object. In so doing, he simultaneously evades the typology of the New Deal documentary gaze and harnesses the growing power of mid-century camera work to produce allegorical, symbolic, and otherwise richly allusive effects. Like Ellison's given name, the photographic lens represents both an inheritance against which he struggles and a tool of self-creation. Like the invisible man's hibernation, photography as a form and practice serves Ellison as a language for the simultaneous no and yes, the affirmation that is also a form of critical challenge.

The shaping importance of photography to Ellison becomes obvious as one pursues the materials preserved in his archive. In letters, notes and other private writings, he details his ongoing acquisition of cameras and photographic equipment from as early as the mid-1940s. Not only did Ellison purchase an impressive array of cameras, lenses, and other technical apparatuses; his collection reflects – quite self-consciously – the changing styles and imperatives of documentary and street photography. From a classic Leica (the model of choice among key photographic practitioners associated with leftist culture in New York), to a state-of-the-art Pentax (favored by many street shooters for its mobility and ease of loading), to a view camera (a format inextricably linked with the classic work of such practitioners as Edward Weston and Paul Strand), Ellison seems to have experimented with their varying properties of speed, deliberation, monumentality, spontaneity, and anonymity.[12] He thereby produced a notable variety of images, bespeaking wide interests in photographic realism, the conventions of the fashion and glamour shot, experimental art photography, and street work.

I will have more to say below about Ellison's images. Here, I want to emphasize how self-consciously he employed the camera as a tool for self-examination. Each of these different camera models, with its own attendant mythology and history of uses, allowed Ellison to pursue a different relationship to the photographic subject: that of studio professional, producing author portraits; of participant-observer, recording the daily facts of Harlem life; of avant-gardist, testing the possibilities of the medium; of sympathetic outsider, witnessing the lives of the marginalized. Ellison conducted these experiments at the apex of photography's power as a symbol of progress and of its authority as a mode of social critique; he was as interested in the purchases on contemporary urban culture afforded the photographer as in the production of specific images.

Ellison himself left a record of this fascination with the camera as symbolic object. Always a guarded and unrevealing subject, he habitually posed for photographs and self-portraits with camera in hand. An image by his second wife, Fanny Ellison, taken in 1950, around the time of the final revisions of *Invisible Man*, shows a reflective Ellison in Central Park. Turned away from her camera, grasping his own – apparently a 2 × 2 view model – as if in preparation for a shot, Ellison evades the camera's gaze by enacting the role of meditative witness or seer.[13] Other series of portraits show Ellison at work with camera and tripod, apparently preparing to shoot Fanny as she shoots him, or with camera and dog; still others are double portraits of Ellison and other writers – Langston Hughes, Chester Himes – in which Ellison's camera again prominently figures.[14] This penchant for self-presentation as a photographer hardly went unnoticed among Ellison's circle. By way of a Christmas card (undated but probably made in the early 1950s), a journalist acquaintance offers a triple portrait: in it, Fanny Ellison is shot from the rear, holding aloft a camera to take her own shot of Hughes and Ellison, who in turns poses in the act of fingering the camera around his neck, prepared to make a photograph of Fanny.[15]

By turns reflective, authoritative, and absorbed in the delicate intricacies of recording the lived moment, the Ellison who appears in these images wills himself into being as an artist even as he deflects the camera's scrutiny. Of a piece with his life-long self-representations as urbane intellectual and dandy, the image of Ellison as image-maker or auteur affords him a certain cultural authority, and what we might well call invisibility: a mode of open self-concealment. That this strategy was both intentioned and foundational to Ellison's writing life is evidenced in an admission he later made to fellow writer Albert Murray, in a letter requesting the latter's help in purchasing new photographic equipment: "You know me, I have to have something between me and reality when I'm dealing with it most intensely."[16] That "something," often, was the camera, which served at once as a prop for Ellison's self-staging, an instrument for screening contemporary realities, and a mode for negotiating the complex politics of New York's post-war left.

Ellison himself partially acknowledges this state of affairs in the preface to *Invisible Man*, when he describes the genesis of the novel and the conduct of his writing life. There, Ellison figures himself akin to his own character, Mary Rambo, who admonishes the narrator, "Don't let this Harlem git you. I'm in New York but New York ain't in me" (*Invisible* 255).[17] Of "indefinite status" – the writer making his career is "neither a thug, numbers-runner, nor pusher, postal worker, doctor, dentist, lawyer, tailor, undertaker, barber, bartender nor preacher," and thus essentially outside the complex economies of life on the Harlem street – Ellison is accused by the corner "wino lady" of being "some kinda sweetback" – that is, a pimp (*Invisible* x). His unreadability as writer and intellectual is not only linked with, but given form by, his activities as a photographer, as his "woozy" critic suggests: "'…all I ever see *him* do is walk them damn dogs and shoot some damn pictures!'" (ix). It is, Ellison reveals, the presence of the camera and the pursuit of its possibilities that ensures this cherished alterity: "since I was returning home with fifty legally earned dollars from a photographic assignment I could well afford to smile while remaining silently concealed in my mystery" (x). Hiding in plain view behind the lens, Ellison appears to brandish the camera, and photography itself, as a version of Rinehart's hipster shades. Like the invisible man's adoption of the signature symbol of the hipster and jive, this manipulation of the camera as a cultural accoutrement is "flooded with personal significance" (482). Behind the camera, Ellison experiences himself both as "concealed" and self-inventing, occupying a found space – akin to the narrator's "border area" (5) – of both "isolation" (13) and revealing "contact" (3).

Of course, Ellison not only employed his camera as prop, screen, and emblem of post-war cultural "fraternity" (485). He also made photographs by choice and by commission, for "taking notes" and for sale.[18] Widely varied in context and aim, his archived images are remarkable less for their quality as visual objects than for their clear interest in the available range of visual modes defining post-war photographic style. Even the somewhat random, as-yet uncatalogued, photographs housed with Ellison's archived papers suggest a certain rehearsal on his part of the menu of representational possibilities: formalist, socially conscious, reportial, intimate. One dramatic shot shows an unidentified steel structure with a mechanical pinwheel affixed to its apex, surrounded by what appear to be parachutes gracefully wafting toward earth; it rhymes with the celebratory, highly aestheticized images of the George Washington Bridge, Fort Peck Dam, and other emblems of industrial modernity by the most recognized US photographer of the 1940s, Margaret Bourke-White. Featured prominently on the cover of *Life* and in the pages of *Fortune* and *Time*, this work made her the highest-paid photographic professional in the US and a household name. Alternatively, among Ellison's images are various spontaneous portraits made on the streets of Harlem and downtown New York, sites of longstanding interest for documentary and street photography.[19] Substantial numbers of his images take children as subjects – perhaps an outgrowth of Ellison's work collecting their oral narratives, riddles, and jump-rope rhymes in Harlem during 1940–41 as a writer on the New Deal Federal Writers' Project, and a probable response to the emphasis on Harlem and downtown children's cultures of photographers like Lewis Hine and Helen Levitt. In these shots, Ellison tenders subjects who return his gaze confidently or meditatively, as well as those unable to return it at all. He thus recapitulates the essential problem of post-war street work: negotiating documentary photography's own tendency to rob its subjects of the power, the right, or the psychic means to look back.[20]

Other of Ellison's archived images bespeak interests in the longer history of photography – specifically its evolving claims, since the influential work of Alfred Stieglitz in the 1910s and 1920s, to the status of high art. From 1944, when he met the then Fanny McConnell, Ellison made scores of images of her that probe not only her qualities as lover, collaborator, and object of visual attention, but the expressive codes of photography itself. Posed as a figure in the urban landscape, Fanny becomes the focal point of pictorialist, impressionistic photo portraits harking back to Stieglitz's iconic shots of the city streets, bathed in the mists and glow of gaslight, industrial steam, and fog. An unself-conscious model in the nude, striking elegantly rhythmic poses, Fanny enabled Ellison to produce shots reminiscent of the famed work of Edward Weston, whose studies of female nudes in the mid-1930s achieved an extraordinary sculptural quality and an unmatched subtlety of tone. One shot of Fanny posed in front of the leaning tower of Pisa – the stuff of conventional tourist memorabilia – exploits her angular beauty and the famed skew of the structure itself to approximate the visual language of Dada and surrealist photography (as, for example, Man Ray's famed portrait of Lee Miller). Using radical foreshortening and deft cropping, Ellison elides the disparity in scale between his subjects with distinctly graphic and uncanny effects.[21]

As a body of work, these images are scattershot and often experimental in the pejorative sense – that is, tentative or technically unrealized. But they are marked by awareness of the effects they seek to produce, and of the varying, sometimes competing photographic conventions to which they respond. Most realized among them are images that engage with the conventions of street photography, a genre of documentary undergoing radical revision during the 1940s and 1950s, as the tenets of the activist image-making of the previous decade – rooted in direct observation, an affinity for socially marginal subjects, and a commitment to social change through the impact of photographic narrative – were redirected toward a more allusive post-war aesthetic. By the time of the publication of *Invisible Man*, an influential group of photographers, including Weegee, Helen Levitt, Louis Faurer, Ted Croner, Sid Grossman, and Lisette Model, were coalescing into something aptly called the New York School. Highly individualist, often privileging images of marginality and loneliness, they nonetheless cohered in focusing on urban perception and the visual experience of modernity. Their varied histories as photographers of African-American, Yiddish-speaking, working-class, gay and drag, and other marginalized communities in New York contributed to new photographic styles and new ways of apprehending the city.[22] In particular, their work emphasized the tension between the physical proximity, even intimacy, of city dwellers and their psychic distance. Weegee's Bowery alcoholics, Croner's Times Square drifters, Model's solitary women of the urban coffeeshop and bar: such figures collectively limn American modernity as an existential struggle – not with hard luck or poverty, but with alienation from the march of post-war progress, and from the increasingly monolithic cityscape that was its emblem. New York School photographs, in other words, take a certain invisibility as their subject, and they wield the camera not as a tool for "exposure" or "enlightenment" of the conditions that produce it, but as an instrument for heightening our experience of its psychic depths and social meanings.

No wonder, then, that black writers and intellectuals were so fascinated by the evolving history and artifacts of documentary photography. During the period between the end of the war and the emergence of a distinctive civil rights culture in the early 1960s, writers of Ellison's cohort struggled to create transitional forms that would move beyond the logic of the so-called "protest" genre – writing aligned with sociological methods for studying "the Negro" and the conditions of "inferiority," exemplified by Richard Wright's *Native Son*. Documentary photography of the 1930s was utterly implicated in this kind of sociological work, as in Margaret Bourke-White's problematic if powerful images of black sharecroppers in the deep South in *You Have Seen Their Faces*, the FSA's archive of black "rehabilitation" clients in Southside Chicago, and innumerable other photographic studies of black dispossession from modernity.[23] But documentary was nonetheless predicated on a belief in the camera's categorical power to bestow dignity and social value on its subjects. At a moment when the project of black self-affirmation had become both more urgent and newly possible, this facet of documentary tradition continued to suggest itself as a cultural resource.

Black America was hardly ready to abandon the project of rendering visible its obscured, repressed, or forgotten histories, particularly the perdurable facts of white violence and appropriation. Documentary photography offered itself as a way to make claims for that invisible history, to relocate the meaning of social experience within everyday spaces – the tenements and alleys and basements; "the gin mills and the barber shops and the juke joints and the churches" where, as Ellison's narrator argues, a "whole unrecorded history is spoken" (471).

This double understanding of documentary images, as both a source for devastating misrepresentation of black Americans and a resource for combating it, helps explain how the visual genre that Ellison at times so powerfully critiques remains central to his self-imagination as a writer. His own street photographs hardly achieve the taut complexity or technical virtuosity of the most storied images of the New York School. But they nonetheless suggest how Ellison used the evolving canons of street photography as a resource for transforming the essentially didactic logic of documentary into a more richly ambiguous textual mode.

Nowhere is this transformation more graphically attested to than in a binder among Ellison's papers, undated but apparently part of his collection of working materials prior to 1944, and marked "Photographs Miscellaneous Invisible Men."[24] At one point, the binder appears to have included a stack of images; at present, it houses a single print: the photograph of an unidentified woman, shot at relatively close range, lying on a city sidewalk. From the position of the subject's body, it is impossible to determine whether she is dead or merely unconscious; she might be a crime victim or drug user or an unfortunate fallen literally by the wayside. What rescues the image from a kind of documentary banality – and makes such banality, the ease with which the camera affords us a voyeuristic view of failure and pain and want, part of what we confront – is a series of telling details. The woman's hand is placed precisely, in support of her chin, as if she were arrested in deep thought (think Rodin's "Thinker"); the buttons on her dark sweater are enormously oversized, as if, taken beyond the realm of fashion, they had become amulets donned to ward off this very disaster.

Borrowing from the visual appeal of the crime scene images of Weegee, this shot gives us a window onto an otherwise hidden world. But unlike such infamous Weegee photographs as "Their First Murder," "Joy of Life," and "Bodies Taken from Burning Building," this image locates itself in a post-New Deal social space illegible in terms of murderous violence or sensational catastrophe; the logic of the woman's death or misfortune is unavailable to us. Also, the image bears no content or title that would locate (and thus confine) this kind of story within such "underworld" spaces as the Bowery,

Hell's Kitchen, or the Lower East Side – sites metonymic for mid-century Americans with criminality, chronic poverty, ethnic or racial alterity, and low life. Indeed, none of the usual narratives – fallen woman, city-dweller down on her luck, class or ethnic type, victim of crime or the street – helps the viewer make sense of the subject. The camera has refused the project of exposing an underworld for the purposes of shock or rehabilitation. Instead, it limns a more nuanced social condition, an unreadability that troubles the very categories its viewers would invoke to resolve it.

This image may have been shot by Ellison or merely printed for him. In either case he apparently saved it in the "work folder" for his novel-in-progress because it records and enables a crucial transition: from the "Forgotten Man" of New Deal nation-building to the "Invisible Men" of Ellison's writerly imagination. A decade after Franklin Delano Roosevelt's famed address at the Democratic National Convention on April 7, 1932, which inaugurated the New Deal by calling for economic programs "that put their faith once more in the forgotten man at the bottom of the economic pyramid," Ellison's shift in notation suggests a decisive rejection of rhetorics of uplift – New Deal, Communist, black bourgeois alike – and an interest in forms of invisibility, marginality, and social experience resistant to conventional political redress.[25]

At least two points are worth emphasizing here. First, it is the camera, by implication, that provides suggestions for the kind of invisibility in which Ellison is interested; the camera, this shot attests, serves as both an instrument and an emblem of transition from the didacticism of "protest" to the possibilities of expressivity, from uplift to aesthetic critique, from redress for the "forgotten" to imaginative engagement with the worlds of the "invisible." Second, however serendipitous this particular image, its placement within Ellison's personal archive indicates that the body of a woman (and its representation) serve him as some kind of allegory for the conditions of invisibility. I will return to images of the female body and their role in *Invisible Man*. Here, I want to emphasize how fundamentally our picture (as it were) of Ellison is altered when his investments in photography are acknowledged and accounted for. Ongoing debates about his politics and commitments to leftism, about his indebtedness to earlier writers and traditions, about his representations of gender and sexuality: all need to address Ellison's stakes in post-war documentary images, and the role of photography – with its own shifting radicality and modes of critique – in shaping his aesthetics and his narrative strategies. Foregrounding Ellison's interests in image-making may well undermine a received sense of *Invisible Man* as sui generis. But it also heightens our awareness of the suppleness and probity with which Ellison exploits available resources for rethinking the novel as an American cultural form.

The traces of photography, that mode of apprehension defined by its power to retain traces of the real, can be found throughout the pages of *Invisible Man*, and they contribute to some of its most dynamic and controversial effects. From the early incident with Jim Trueblood – staged as a richly ironic riposte to work like Margaret Bourke-White's, in which photographs of black poverty enable the condescension and patronage of white progressive readers – to the narrator's final meditations on "the semi-visible world" of urban modernity, whose hidden truths can only be experienced through willed acts of affirmation, *Invisible Man* offers numerous incidents and narrative moments that riff on photographic history and effect (*Invisible* 574). In particular, Ellison includes a key scene that functions as an allegory for his own interests in documentary. The scene offers an extended meditation on the documentary form: as a vector of opportunity and means of entry (particularly for black intellectuals after the New Deal and the war); as a compromised mode that imposes the imperatives of protest on black writers; as a potential space for immanent critique. It thus clarifies the ways in which Ellison extrapolates from his interests in photography to position himself on the contentious field of 1940s culture, and to rethink the project of the post-war novel.

This scene occurs in Chapter Thirteen of *Invisible Man*, at the text's half-way point. As it begins, Ellison's protagonist – who has just been released from the Liberty Paints factory hospital and ejected from the genteel sanctuary of Men's House – takes to the streets of Harlem. In response to a surge of nostalgia the narrator pauses to buy a "hot, baked Car'lina yam" from a street vendor (*Invisible* 263), savoring the "intense feeling of freedom" afforded by his appetite for such a down-home, folk-tainted, "*Field-Niggeris[h]*" object (264, 265). But the "freedom to eat yams on the street" turns out to be "far less" – far less consequential, that is – "than I had expected" (267). Unlike Proust's madeleine, which opens access to a yearned-for past, the yams leave "[a]n unpleasant taste bloom[ing] in my mouth" (267). They bring the narrator the discomfiting recognition that an identity forged in diametric opposition to "what was expected" is no less conventional, no less forcibly bound by the dehumanizing realities it strains to break (266). Literally central to the novel, then, is a moment of existential and historical crisis: how to generate modes of subjectivity and cultural expression embedded in experiential history, from the geography of slavery to the Great Migration, yet free of the deterministic clutches of the past.

As the episode goes on to suggest, documentary as a stance plays a crucial part in Ellison's response to this question. Having discarded his frost-bitten yam, the narrator continues walking the streets, only to come upon the scene of an eviction – a staple feature of Harlem life throughout the Depression and post-war years. As he attempts to make sense of the event, a new language of visuality becomes insistent: "'Just look what they doing to us. Just look,'" the elderly female evictee urges him; "Just look at what they're doing" (268). Of the "paddies" removing furniture, an outraged bystander yells, "'Look at that'"(268); "'Look, lady,'" one of the dispossessors urges in turn (270). "[F]eeling my eyes burn," resisting his own transformation into a "witness[s] of what [h]e did not wish to see" (270), the narrator "turn[s] aside and look[s]" instead at the household objects thrown pell-mell into the street: the knocking bones of a minstrel; a hair-straightening comb and curling iron; an Ethiopian flag and a cracked plate commemorating the St. Louis World's Fair; a set of tarnished cuff links and a yellowed breast pump. Powerfully auratic in their specificity, these bent and faded objects comprise a material history, a kind of museum, of black life in America, in all its richness and impoverishment of opportunity. But Ellison's catalogue is hardly random. The first thing the narrator "look[s] down to see" is a nineteenth-century portrait of the couple being dispossessed, themselves "looking out of an oval frame" with a gaze that calls to him as both "a reproach and a warning" (271). Their message is clarified only when the narrator completes his witnessing in the present. Last of all, half-buried in the snow, as the narrator searches for "anything missed by my eyes," he finds "a fragile paper, coming apart with age": the free papers of the woman's husband – "*my Negro, Primus Provo*," "*freed by me this sixth day of August, 1859. Signed: John Samuels. Macon*" (272).

Photograph and text; image and testifying narrative: what the narrator encounters, in the form of these framing objects, is the twinned elements of documentary – specifically, the photo-text form so dear to progressive New Deal reformers and black post-war writers alike (among them Wright, Bourke-White, Aaron Siskind, Langston Hughes, James Baldwin, Roy DeCarava, Walker Evans, James Agee, Gordon Parks, and Dorothea Lange). Here, the photo-text form is made central to the mysteries the narrator confronts: who bestows freedom on whom? How is autonomous identity earned, expressed, given shape? The narrator is shocked by the raw intimacy of these objects – so much so that the "unpleasant taste" left by the yams becomes "a bitter spurt of gall" (273); he finds himself in thrall not merely to the objects themselves, but to the very genre of photo-text documentary, the "linked verbal echoes, images," of some lost and collective "home" (273). Hewing to the ideals for camera-work of progressive reformers, this photo-text experience prompts an epiphanic moment of "recognition" that spurs social action (273): a spontaneous oration on behalf of the evictees, a performance that paves the narrator's way to the Brotherhood and a higher education in the realities of power. Invisible Man's public voice, in other words, begins here, in this encounter with documentary – the moment, as Brother Jack suggests, when *"History* has been born in your brain" (291).

In this episode, documentary is transformed from a method of exposure – a technique applied to the hapless, the forgotten, the marginal and unself-conscious – into a powerful exercise, at once aesthetic and political, of self-knowledge. The scene thus serves as an implicit rebuke to the reigning figure of literary naturalism, social realism, and documentary throughout the 1940s, Richard Wright, whose Bigger Thomas (according to Ellison) was fatally denied any trace of the self-understanding of his own creator.[26] Indeed, *Invisible Man's* dispossession episode seems designed to wrest the power of documentary out from under the avowedly sociological uses made of it by Wright, and not only in *Native Son*. Ellison also responds to the essentially evangelic bent of Wright's photo-text project, 12 *Million Black Voices*, and its unrelenting emphasis on black struggle against oppressive conditions:

> The kitchenette is our prison, our death sentence without a trial, the new form of mob violence that assaults not only the lone individual, but all of us, in its ceaseless attacks.
>
> The kitchenette, with its filth and foil air, with its one toilet for thirty or more tenants, kills our black babies so fast that in many cities twice as many of them die as white babies. . . .
>
> The kitchenette scatters death so widely among us that our death rate exceeds our birth rate, and if it were not for the trains and autos bringing us daily into the city from the plantations, we black folks who dwell in northern cities would die out entirely over the course of a few years.[27]

In place of such hortatory rhetoric, Ellison offers the narrator's intensely felt account of his own witnessing, the narrative of an existential nausea born of terrible beauty, of "beautiful absurdity" (*Invisible* 552). Notably, the self-understanding categorically denied Bigger Thomas, by virtue of Wright's documentary commitment to the project of exposing intractable social conditions, is opened as a possibility in Ellison's text through the narrator's encounter with documentary objects as such. But here the logic of photo-text amplifies (rather than "explicates" or "exposes") the mysteries of that encounter. Like the images of the New York School, Ellison's text emphasizes the power of the documentary stance to evoke powerful yet ambiguous responses, states of being that move the subject *"far beyond"* the witnessed artifacts' *"intrinsic meaning as objects"* (*Invisible* 273; italics original).

This outbreak, via documentary, of elusive and allusive significance – or, as the narrator puts it, "more meaning than there should have been" (273) – bespeaks Ellison's interest in the kind of effect produced by post-war street photography. It also suggests how Ellison's interests as photographer and musician shape one another, and his ambitions for his work as a writer. Notably, the confrontation with documentary objects is what precipitates the kind of spontaneous, improvisatory expressive identity usually associated with jazz. Ellison's own riff on documentary makes the images and artifacts of black experience a matter of the urban streetscape, just as it makes the register of witnessing a complex admixture of image and sound, material fact and evanescent memory, black speech rhythms and the cadences of lyric. In Ellison's hands, in other words, documentary becomes both jazz-like and a mode of collage, an experience created out of elements that bear the auratic charge of their own histories of use and survival. The items spilled heedlessly onto the snow – the "useless inhalant" and "tarnished" beads, the "worn baby shoe and dusty lock of infant hair" (272) – evoke such powerful mixed response (the narrator is "both repelled and fascinated" [275]) because they testify not to social fact but to the mysterious alchemy by which lived experience becomes the stuff of history. What Ellison's scene of documentary foregrounds, like the storied images of the New York School, is the perhaps irreparable loss sustained by social beings whose work on the world produces nothing more or less than their own alienation. No wonder, then, that the narrator's spontaneous question to the assembled crowd about the former slave, now dispossessed tenement-dweller, Provo, is so resounding: "Then where did his labor go?" (278).

Photography as a context and a model enables Ellison to stake renewed claims for the American novel, rejecting the instrumentality of protest yet demanding that the conventions of novelistic soul-making answer to the realities of contemporary social experience. Just as the camera serves Ellison as a mode of self-concealment and a strategy for perception and self-representation, the example of its use in the hands of leading post-war practitioners also provides a model for elaborating his own cultural politics – ones that eschewed protest writing, the aesthetics of Communism, and the imperative of authentic blackness alike. The famous conclusion to the novel offers a challenge to the reader cast in the modality of jazz: "Who knows but that, on the lower frequencies, I speak for you?" But the scenes leading up to that conclusion speak eloquently to the context of post-war photography, with its dual emphasis on trenchant critique and social affirmation. These scenes suggest that the author of *Invisible Man* is inseparable from Ralph Ellison, Photographer; they demonstrate how richly the experience of Ellison as an image-maker helps account for the novel's play with invisibility as a historical condition, a mode of urban perception, and a symbolic language.

My final reading, consequently, begins with the extraordinary final chapter of *Invisible Man*. There, the narrator has returned from an ill-fated attempt to seduce Sybil, the wife of a prominent Brotherhood leader, to a Harlem ablaze; in response to the death of Tod Clifton, what one participant calls a "sho 'nough race riot" has begun to break out (552). Steeped in perceptual and moral confusion, the narrator has a devastating epiphany: "Could this be the answer, could this be what the [Brotherhood] had planned...? It was not suicide, but murder. The committee had planned it. And I had helped, had been a tool." (553). Shocked, outraged, he runs aimlessly from one scene of violent encounter to another; the streets on which he flees have become an alien landscape, where shattered glass glitters "like the water of a flooded river" on which "distorted objects," snatched and abandoned by looters, appear "washed away by the flood" (556). In this moment – both a baptism and a drowning – the narrator is stopped short by a ghostly and ghastly vision:

> Ahead of me the body hung, white, naked, and horribly feminine from a lamppost. I felt myself spin around with horror and it was as though I had turned some nightmarish somersault. I whirled, still moving by reflex, back-tracking and stopped and now there was another and another, seven – all hanging before a gutted storefront. I stumbled, hearing the cracking of bones underfoot and saw a physician's skeleton shattered on the street, the skull rolling away from the backbone, as I steadied long enough to notice the unnatural stiffness of those hanging above me. They were mannequins – 'Dummies!' I said aloud. Hairless, bald and sterilely feminine. And I recalled the boys in the blonde wigs, expecting the relief of laughter, but suddenly was more devastated by the humor than by the horror. But are they unreal, I thought; *are* they? What if one, even *one* is real – is ... Sybil? I hugged my brief case, backing away, and ran...   (556; ellipses original)

This climactic moment reiterates the arc traced in Chapter Thirteen, from the fact of documentary eye-witnessing to a more complex form of self-expression. Ellison was himself a journalistic observer of the devastating riots that broke out in Harlem on August 1, 1943, in response to economic stagnation, ongoing institutional segregation, and police harassment of black World War II veterans; he covered the grim mêlée for the *New York Post*, in an article billed as an eye-witness account of Harlem's most devastating civil disturbance of the twentieth century.[28] But Ellison's novelistic account plays serious changes on the work of observation, not least by framing the event of the riot as a decisive moment in the evolution of an artist's self-understanding. In confronting the spectacle of the skeleton and mannequins, Ellison's narrator enters a zone of liminality, a state of being in which the "real" and the "unreal," "humor" and "horror," are continuous if not indistinguishable, and their intersection is the individual's entry into the "devastat[ion]" of "History" (543, 542).

The full force of this liminal moment becomes available only when we read it in the context of a widely disseminated body of photographic images meditating on precisely this intersection. Ranging from early twentieth-century shots by Eugène Atget of the storefronts and small shops on the outskirts of a rapidly industrializing Paris through art world appropriations by Dadaists and Surrealists of the possibilities of the mechanical human form, these images offer up the mannequin as a symbol or allegory of urban modernity and as an object of apprehension – in both senses – that deeply troubles liberal or progressive management of social difference and change. A prop for burgeoning consumer culture; a cause and effect of the cultivation of personal image; a figure for the radical alienation of human labor and consciousness under advanced capitalism: the mannequin as found object becomes a powerful tool for photographers seeking the effect of estrangement from routine habits of perception and self-understanding. Wrenched out of its usual instrumental contexts, the mannequin becomes an over-determined object of fantasy and meditation, richly available for what Ellison calls "dramatic study in comparative humanity" (Introduction, xv).

This is, at least, the logic of certain photographic images of a key practitioner, foundational to the work of the New York School, whose work Ellison studied with care: the Paris-born, briefly New York-based Henri Cartier-Bresson (1908–2004).[29] Ellison's interest in Cartier-Bresson is writ throughout his own archive, and it makes resounding sense. Having begun his career as a painter in the ambit of inter-war surrealism, Cartier-Bresson took up the camera as a more powerful instrument for probing realities hidden beneath the banal, slick, even repellant surfaces of everyday life. Wandering unpremeditatively through the streets – the meaner, the better – of Spain, Italy, Mexico City, Paris, and Eastern Europe, photographing the differently threatened life-worlds of brothels, back alleys, flea markets, and Jewish ghettos, Cartier-Bresson produced images that document intimate local realities. Yet in their fantasmatic quality, their insistence on these venues as sites of drama and adventure, these same images evade the closure of conventional documentary. Within his early body of work, some of Cartier-Bresson's most powerful photographs are shots of storefront mannequins in modernity's outlying districts. One such image ("Untitled," 1929) focuses tightly on a jumbled pile of molds for producing artificial hands and feet, the edges of each appendage roughly severed. Even before the Holocaust, the sense of human labor being obscenely misdirected toward the production of its own false emblem and replacement is palpable. In another shot, the head of a male mannequin presses up against the front of a shuttered shop, its unblinking gaze and the tattered window dressings

Fig. 3.1. Henri Cartier-Bresson, Untitled (Rouen, 1929)

around it belying an adjacent poster, which touts an outmoded vision of the city as source of the bourgeois good life ("Budapest," 1931).[30]

Such images create a far more complex effect than that of obvious irony, which helps explain the power of Cartier-Bresson's work as a significant resource for Ellison's project. In the enigmatic "Rouen, 1929" (Figure 3.1), the camera focuses on a trio of mannequins sporting menswear, placed outside a shop in the downscale market district of that provincial city. Two feature spindles instead of heads; the third has a full complement of appendages – including "African" features and a black face. Carefully calculated to take fullest advantage of its subject, the image makes the experience of commerce, looking, serendipity itself, inseparable from racial feeling, as it raises persistent questions about the presence of the African in this apparently unlikely place. Indeed, the image insists on a rhythmic progression: the two model forms on the left appear almost to give birth to the erect figure on the right, fully clothed down to its three-piece suit and neatly seamed gloves. Yet if this sequence ends in a figure of assimilation, whereby the African is resplendently transformed in the image of a still-coalescing bourgeois modernity, Cartier-Bresson's record of that transformation is far from celebratory. At the still center of the photograph runs the diagonal shutterpole of the shopfront; from the viewer's perspective, it appears to intersect the gleaming metal hoop that holds the mannequin in place – a fettering that uncannily bespeaks the long history of commodification of black bodies in service of Western fantasies.

Like vast numbers of his cultural cohort during the 1920s, Cartier-Bresson would indulge in the liberating effects of veneration of the so-called "primitive." Yet this image, produced in the very moment of the demise of that vogue for the Negro known as the Harlem Renaissance, seems to leave such facile identification behind. Accessorized yet inert, inviting desires it variously troubles, the black mannequin is made the object of social exploration and the viewer's self-understanding alike. Oscillating between literal and symbolic resonances, Cartier-Bresson's photograph limns the centrality of the figure of the African to the business of modernity, probing the entangled facts of visibility, race, longing, and belonging.

If Ellison closely followed Cartier-Bresson's body of work, he was also attentive to the photographs of Lisette Model (1901–83), who (like Ellison) emigrated to New York in 1937. Having (again like Ellison) begun her life in art as a composer and musician, Model inaugurated her photographic career with a series of portraits of bourgeois vacationers on the French Riviera, published in the US January, 1941 in the New York-based Communist weekly *PM Magazine* – a journal Ellison knew intimately.[31] It was, perhaps, not a far step from her unsparing, monumental images of the pampered bourgeoisie, rendered absurd and even surreal in the artificiality of their self-presentation, to her first American body of work. Titled "Reflections, New York," the series comprised images of mannequins, passersby, and their multiple refractions in plate-glass shop windows in the glittering precincts of Fifth Avenue.[32]

Like Cartier-Bresson's, Model's early work can be read as an analogue, if not a direct source, for Ellison's own. Confrontational yet nuanced, linking the spaces of post-war privilege with the realities of life on the other side of the tracks and color line, her "Reflections" images bespeak the perceptual challenge of urban experience, the uncanny fixity of American cultural identity, and the unacknowledged links between the two. In an exemplary shot (Figure 3.2), Model exploits the found realities of the city street to create an image that is both literally illegible and profoundly revealing. With considerable virtuosity, she frames the angled panes of a plate-glass window display so as to locate the mannequins within it, the reflections of facades across the street, and the movements of passersby in what appears to be a unified plane. Deprived of a stable vantage-point or perspectival logic, the viewer confronts the problem of reading the relationship between its subjects; Model's play between transparency and opacity – what we see and what we see through – makes it impossible for us to understand the inert

Fig. 3.2. Lisette Model, Reflection, New York, c. 1939–45

mannequins as a simple metaphor for their human counterparts, drifting yet unmoved. Rather, the photograph asks us to take our affective bearings from its artificial figures. If the stiffly posed torsos framed in Van Raalte's exhibition windows signify commerce and the manufacture of desire, the ghostly reflections dominating the image – the partially visible mannequin and the monumental hand, curved in a receptive gesture that appears to emanate from the distant body – have a very different effect. Imbued with the stillness of religious statuary, the shop-front Madonna or angel emanates a prayerful serenity that is itself a claim on our attention. That its auratic quality is lost on the human passersby below, their faces unfocused, their gazes turned purposelessly elsewhere, is ultimately the point of the image. Playing with the uncanniness of the mannequin, Model uses the camera as an instrument to highlight the complexities and contradictions most fundamental to American social life: what is readily on display offers up a deeper truth, a possibility that remains, by virtue of our habits of perception, utterly invisible.

Fig. 3.3. UPI Untitled (Harlem After Riot) 1943

Model's larger body of mannequin images gestures toward a racialized understanding of this problem of visibility – indeed, she would write of her freelance work for the very journal from which many of Ellison's photographic clippings were made, owned by William Randolph Hearst, that most of it never saw the light of day because Hearst "didn't like black people." Other bodies of photographs link the mannequin as a device securely with Ellison's purchase on black experience. In the photo-journalistic response to the 1943 riots in Harlem, the mannequin was ready to hand as a densely symbolic object. Innumerable photographs focus on the very scene Ellison invokes: broken shop-fronts, the streets littered with debris from looting, particularly the remains of display mannequins decapitated or disassembled in the process. These images circulated in such mainstream journals as the *New York Times*, *New York Post*, and the *Daily News*. Their subjects, composition, and dynamics generally suggest outrage about the destruction of white-owned property and loss of revenues, even as they stoke white readers' anxiety about the implied (or real) threats to (real) white bodies downtown. But some of these shots do more complex work, analogous to Ellison's novelistic aims.

Among them is a widely reproduced UPI wire service photo that appeared most prominently in the *New York Times* (Figure 3.3). In it, the pavement in front of a department store has taken on the look of a battlefield; only human violence could have created such programmatic devastation. The store's display mannequins have been stripped of their clothing, disassembled, and strewn about. Their inert nudity re-enforces the uncanny charge of their likeness to scenes of patriotic gore, the nation's fallen dead. Cropped to produce a tighter focus on the one mannequin with a head that remains upright, the image offers that figure as both a watchful survivor and a haunting testament to the logic that produced this landscape: economic opportunism, unacknowledged labor, a consumer logic predicated on white-owned institutions and Anglo-centric artifacts. With its rouged and hollowed cheekbones, its marcelled hair, its sultry survey of the devastation, the mannequin becomes obscene and foreboding, its knowing glance that of the Sybil – the prophetess whose hypnotic vision foretells the lineaments of disaster. Like the invisible man's Sybil, who drunkenly beseeches him to perform as her own "domesticated rapist" (510), the mannequin seems here to invite a violent response that can only confirm the dehumanizing power of the racial fantasies it embodies.

All the more telling, then, that Ellison invokes the figure of the mannequin, and this body of photographic meditation on it, to articulate the narrator's sense of agency. In witnessing those uncanny objects, bespeaking a humanity they mimic yet lack, the invisible man comes fully to recognize both the lacerating fact of his structural invisibility as a black American, and the liberating possibilities for self-creation in his embrace of that condition. Forced to confront the paradoxes of visibility and identity embodied by the mannequins, the narrator finally ceases to be a mannequin himself: a "zombie," "an automation," "a walking personification of the Negative" (94, 95). Raising the existential question "What if one, even *one*, is real ...?" (556), the invisible man acknowledges the effects of his own attempts to play at invisibility: "By pretending to agree I *had* indeed agreed, had made myself responsible for that huddled form lighted by flame and gunfire in the street ..." (553). This mode of responsibility differs radically from other invocations of the word throughout the text: the narrator's desperate parrot-ing, in his speech after the Battle Royal, of the mantras of "social responsi-bility" and social "equality" (31); Norton's "kindly" denial to Bledsoe of the narrator's responsibility for his injury (103); the narrator's response to the zoot-suiters he observes after Clifton's funeral, who make him feel "respon-sible" for his political failures (444); the Brotherhood's disciplinary response to the invisible man's "personal re-spon-si-bility" (464). For the first time, "responsibility" – the notion that "even an invisible man has a socially responsible role to play" (581) – gestures toward a mode of affirmation that implicates both the narrator's acts in the world of social experience and his narrative about them; both the realities of political struggle and the expressive energies that name and transmit it. Politics and aesthetics, or politics and "love" (to use Ellison's phrase) are at last – however painfully, however tentatively – comprehended in one.

Without the context of post-war photography, such subtle appropriations of its imagery and aspirations remain invisible to us. Yet restoring that context is hardly to diminish the power of Ellison's project as a novelist. Quite the reverse: it allows us to recognize the suppleness with which Ellison exploits documentary history and conventions as a mode of self-creation; as a means of negotiating the fluid political circles in which he moved; as a strategy for evading racialized aesthetic imperatives; as a resource for rethinking the impasses of the novel after the heyday of social realism, documentary, and protest. To foreground Ellison's engagement with photography is to recognize his purposive struggles to respond to, and simultaneously to shape, the conditions of his work's emergence. Even Ellison's controversial commitment to an Afro-Euro-American aesthetic, a kind of cultural miscegenation, looks different in connection with photography, concerned in the post-war years to negotiate the same range of cultural registers and practices: blues and the folk, elite and popular modernisms, black and white rhetorics of uplift and redemption, the stylistics of the hot and the cool. Although that story remains to be fully told, we begin by acknowledging the challenge of Ellison's self-imagination as photographer. Putting the camera back in his hand, we enable him to testify to the powerful achievement of the novel in America at the tumultuous mid-century.

Notes

1. John Callahan, "Preface," *Flying Home* (New York: Random House, 1996), p. xviii.
2. Callahan, "Preface", xv. The argument for African-American writing as inseparable from musical traditions has taken its most influential form in the work of Houston A. Baker, *Modernism and the Harlem Renaissance* (University of Chicago Press, 1987); Paul Gilroy, *The Black Atlantic: Modernity and Double Consciousness* (Cambridge, MA: Harvard University Press, 1993); and Brent Edwards, *The Practice of Diaspora: Literature, Translation, and the Rise of Black Internationalism* (Cambridge, MA: Harvard University Press, 2003). For a vigorous dissent see Kenneth Warren, *So Black and Blue: Ralph Ellison and the Occasion of Criticism* (University of Chicago Press, 2003).
3. Robert O'Mealley, *The Craft of Ralph Ellison* (Cambridge, MA: Harvard University Press, 1980), p. 81, esp. pp. 25–41
4. Ellison's archive is housed at the Library of Congress; the photographic and related materials on which I draw are held in the Prints and Photographs Division. Many thanks to Alice Lotvin Birney, Curator of the Manuscript Division, and to Marcia Battle, Curator in the Prints and Photographs Division, for their aid.
5. See Nathaniel Natanson, *The Black Image in the New Deal: The Politics of FSA Photography* (Knoxville, TN: University of Tennessee Press, 1992).
6. See Arnold Rampersad, *The Life of Langston Hughes, Volume II: 1941–1967, I Dream a World* (New York: Oxford University Press, 1988), p. 244.

7. Ralph Ellison, *Invisible Man* (New York: Vintage, 1995), p. 36. Hereafter cited in the text as *Invisible*.

8. A judicious version of the received view is given by Eric Sundquist: "although Ellison shares with a number of novelists of the 1930s and 1940s an interest in photographic realism, he infused documentary fiction with a heightened sense that the writer's distortion of, and improvisation on, the observed world could bring out more effectively the moral and psychological density of its internal meaning." Sundquist, ed. *Cultural Contexts for Ralph Ellison's "Invisible Man"* (Boston: Bedford, 1995), p. 16.

9. Ralph Ellison, "Hidden Name and Complex Fate: A Writer's Experience in the United States," *Shadow and Act* (New York: Random House, 1964), pp. 152–3. Hereafter cited in the text as "Hidden."

10. Karen Jacobs, "One-Eyed Jacks and Three-Eyed Monsters," *The Eye's Mind: Literary Modernism and Visual Culture* (Ithaca, NY: Cornell University Press, 2001), p. 146, reads this lens as representative of "the aspiring visual mastery and the attendant violence which Ellison associated" with American social science in general. Such a reading, I suggest, moves too quickly from the densely material fact of photographic practice and artifacts to figurative resonances.

11. Nicholas Natanson, "Robert H. McNeill and the Profusion of Virginia Experience," in *Visual Journal: Harlem and DC in the Thirties and Forties*, eds. Deborah Willis and Jane Lusaka (Washington, DC: Center for African-American History and Culture and Smithsonian Institution Press, 1996), p. 99.

12. A useful summation of the technical properties and mythologies attendant on various types of camera available to professionals and advanced amateurs in the context of documentary culture is Eliot Elisofon's "Types of Cameras," *Photo Notes* (August 1938), pp. 3–4. Elisofon was then president of the left-leaning New York Photo League, an important center of photographic activism during the New Deal and wartime years and an institutional player in left cultural politics in New York.

13. One version of this image has been reproduced in *Trading Twelves: The Selected Letters of Ralph Ellison and Albert Murray*, ed. Albert Murray and John F. Callahan (New York: Modern Library, 2000), facing p. 134 (n.p.).

14. Ellison Papers, Prints and Photographs Division, Box 2.

15. Ellison Papers, Prints and Photographs Division, Box 2.

16. Ellison, letter to Albert Murray, March 15, 1956, in *Trading Twelves*, p. 118.

17. The phrase, it is worth noting, was borrowed directly from working notes Ellison made during oral interviews he conducted in Harlem as a writer of local ethnography and documentary pieces under the auspices of his New Deal employer, the New York branch of the Federal Writers' Project. For the full substance of the interview, see Aaron Siskind, *Harlem Document: Photograph, 1932–1940* (Providence, RI: Matrix, 1981), n.p.

18. Albert Murray, letter to Ralph Ellison, February 15, 1956, in *Trading Twelves*, p. 113.

19. See, for example, the street images published in the portfolio included in *Trading Twelves*, n.p.

20. Influential critiques of the documentary tradition with respect to its appropriative and unidirectional gaze have been made by John Tagg, "The Currency of the Photograph: New Deal Reformism and Documentary Rhetoric," *The Burden of Representation: Essays on Photographies and*

Histories (Minneapolis: University of Minnesota Press, 1993), pp. 153–83, and Maren Stange, *Symbols of Ideal Life: Social Documentary Photography in America 1890–1950* (New York: Cambridge University Press, 1989).

21. Ellison Papers, Prints and Photographs Division, Boxes 4 and 5.

22. For definitive discussions of this body of work see Jane Livingston, *The New York School: Photographs, 1936–1963* (New York: Stewart, Tabori & Chang, 1992) and Max Kozloff, *New York: Capital of Photography* (New Haven, CT: Yale University Press and NY: The Jewish Museum, 1992).

23. Erskine Caldwell and Margaret Bourke-White, *You Have Seen Their Faces* (New York: Arno Press, 1975 [orig. 1937]). For reproductions of FSA images of Black Chicago, see Maren Stange, *Bronzeville: Black Chicago in Pictures, 1941–43* (New York: New Press/W.W. Norton, 2003); Natanson, *Black Image*, offers a balanced and insightful reading of the mixed effects of the FSA record with respect to the representation of Black America.

24. Ellison Papers, Prints and Photographs Division, Box 4.

25. Franklin D. Roosevelt, Campaign Address, Albany, NY, April 7, 1932, "The Forgotten Man." Reprinted in *The Public Papers and Addresses of Franklin D. Roosevelt*, Vol. 1, 1928–32, (New York: Random House, 1938), p. 624. Ellison's relationship to the rapidly changing, fraught rhetorics of liberalism, Communism, and socialism has occasioned distinctly varied readings on the part of critics like Barbara Foley, "Reading Redness: Politics and Audience in Ralph Ellison's Early Short Fiction," *JNT: Journal of Narrative Theory* 29:3 (Fall 1999): 323–39; Jerry Gafio Watts, *Heroism and the Black Intellectual: Ralph Ellison, Politics, and Afro-American Intellectual Life* (Chapel Hill, NC: University of North Carolina Press, 1994); Lawrence Jackson, *Ralph Ellison: Emergence of Genius* (New York: John Wiley & Sons, 2002); and Arnold Rampersad, "Baldwin, Ellison and the American Left," paper delivered at the Modern Language Association convention, New York, December 2002.

26. As Ellison famously put it in "The World and The Jug," *Shadow and Act*, (New York: Vintage Books, 1964), p. 114, "Wright could imagine Bigger, but Bigger could not possibly imagine Richard Wright. Wright saw to that."

27. Richard Wright, *12 Million Black Voices* (New York: Thunder's Mouth Press, 1941), pp. 106–7.

28. Ellison, "Eye Witness Story of a Riot: False Rumors Spurred by Mob," *New York Post*, August 2, 1943: 4.

29. Ellison's contact with Cartier-Bresson's work is a matter of cultural conjunction as well as specific contact. In 1934, Cartier-Bresson lived for a time in Mexico City with Langston Hughes, who would launch Ellison's career three years later by hiring him as a secretary, introducing him to Richard Wright and other key cultural players, and discussing photography, culture, politics, and literary matters. In 1935, Cartier-Bresson not only spent significant time on the Harlem club circuit; he became close to Harlem's radical elite and to a number of photographers, later known to Ellison, working in and on black Harlem. By 1947, when Cartier-Bresson had his first retrospective exhibition at the Museum of Modern Art, Ellison appears to have been familiar with the images exhibited there: beginning in the mid-1940s, he maintained clippings files on Cartier-Bresson that span several decades.

30. For reproductions of these images, see Peter Galassi, ed., *Henri Cartier-Bresson, The Early Work* (New York: Museum of Modern Art, 1987).

31. For detailed discussion of Richard Wright's association with *PM*, at the moment of Ellison's most intense engagements with Wright's work, see Michel Fabre, *The Unfinished Quest of Richard Wright*, tr. Isabel Barzun (Urbana: University of Illinois Press, 1993), pp. 258–9, 265.

32. For reproductions of these images, see Ann Thomas, *Lisette Model* (Ottawa: National Gallery of Canada, 1990), pp. 28–9, 38–9, 78–9, 86–9.

4

PAUL ALLEN ANDERSON

Ralph Ellison's music lessons

> Perhaps I like Louis Armstrong because he's made poetry out of being invisible. I think it must be because he's unaware that he *is* invisible. And my own grasp of invisibility aids me to understand his music . . . . Invisibility, let me explain, gives one a slightly different sense of time, you're never quite on the beat. Sometimes you're ahead and sometimes behind. Instead of the swift and imperceptible flowing of time, you are aware of its nodes, those points where time stands still or from which it leaps ahead. And you slip into the breaks and look around. That's what you hear vaguely in Louis's music.
>
> Ralph Ellison, *Invisible Man*[1]

Within the first pages of the 1952 novel *Invisible Man* Ralph Ellison's narrator relates Louis Armstrong's music to his own desires and self-conceptions. "I'd like," the narrator writes, "to hear five recordings of Louis Armstrong playing and singing 'What Did I Do To Be So Black and Blue' – all at the same time" (8). When Armstrong recorded the show tune by Andy Razaf and Fats Waller from the Broadway revue *Hot Chocolates* in 1929 he edited the lyrics to shift a dark-skinned female lover's lament over intra-racial color discrimination (the song's place within the plot of the musical *Chocolate Dandies*) toward a more general lament about racism. Ellison's narrator considers the lyrics but focuses more intently on the specifics of Armstrong's tone and phrasing. Ellison's seemingly central metaphor of invisibility takes on an aural dimension when he attends to Armstrong's "lyrical beam" and rhythmic mastery at creating a "slightly different sense of time." The literary translation and transposition of Armstrong's mastery of swing rhythm opens a window onto the intellectual landscape where the author intertwined his musical and social thought.

Ralph Waldo Ellison was a student at the segregated Frederick Douglass Junior High School in Oklahoma City when Armstrong recorded the landmark Hot Five and Hot Seven sessions. The young Oklahoman witnessed his first Armstrong performance in 1929 but later recalled that he "had been listening to his recordings and admiring the sound of his trumpet for years" while also admiring the local African-American jazz scene.[2] When these players

This essay appears in a different form in *American Literary History*, 17.2 (2005).

"expressed their attitude toward the world," Ellison rhapsodized, "it was with a fluid style that reduced the chaos of living to form." More than a nostalgic idyll from his youth, the scene operated as a regulative norm for the mature Ellison. "The delicate balance struck between strong individual personality and the group during those early jam sessions," he specified about Oklahoma City's burgeoning jazz scene, "was a marvel of social organization."[3]

Ellison's literary portraits of Louis Armstrong and of the legendary post-war figure Charlie Parker (two figures who might be said to exemplify the idiomatic distance between early "swing" and "bop") illuminate the pivotal terms of a "delicate balance" in the author's thought. To pursue the contrasting portraits of Armstrong and Parker is thus also to reconsider the "delicate balance" between Ellison's stated commitments to individuality through masterful self-invention and "a slightly different sense of time," on the one hand, and his idealizations of the "marvel of social organization," on the other hand. A closer look at his skeptical commentaries on Parker's prominent role in the stylistic innovations of the 1940s jazz modernists reveals Ellison's fascinating and rarely discussed inhabitation of the posture of a musical *revanchist* committed to the musical superiority of certain pre-World War II idioms. His tendency toward commemoration in music moves in striking counterpoint to Ellison's prospective tendency toward what he labeled "the futuristic effort of fulfilling the democratic ideal" (*Collected Essays* 466). One might consider these two tendencies as thematic reservoirs from which Ellison drew to fuel his lyrical literary flights. The gaps or points of slippage and irresolution between these seemingly distinct visionary tendencies demanded of Ellison a masterful capacity to "slip into the breaks," a feat all but impossible to maintain.

The frame of ritual action

Ellison attended Tuskegee Institute from 1933 to 1936 on a music scholarship. He later wrote proudly of the oft-misunderstood school and his rigorous studies in music and literature under assorted African-American instructors. "The only form that I studied as a student both in high school and college," he later recalled, "was musical form." "I was kind of stuck with that," he added mischievously. Further reading suggested to Ellison that the form of "the nineteenth-century novel" had itself depended on the prior "form of the symphony." Moreover, Ellison held that symphonic form itself leaned on a prior artistic form: it was "basically a play upon tragic form" (*Conversations* 266). "Tragic form" served Ellison as an umbrella term evoking thematic and functional continuities across artistic media. On this view, structures of artifice generally stood as recognizable frames for ritual activity. Artists employed the occasion of ritual to reveal, contest, solidify,

and transform group values. The challenge Ellison set himself in writing a
first novel was not only the "local" one of translating the symphonic ambitions of African-American musical nationalism into literature. As a "play
upon tragic form," a serious novel also needed to "stage" and work through
the general challenge of balancing the values of individual integrity and
social solidarity.

When Ellison discussed "tragic form" as the novel's dramatic basis he
often noted the influence of André Malraux's writing on him in the 1930s
and later. He held Malraux's post-war treatise *The Psychology of Art*
(1949–50), a book shorn of the author's earlier revolutionary sympathies,
in especially high regard. One can imagine Ellison happily assenting to
Malraux's vaulting judgment that each artistic masterpiece was "a purification of the world." Such purification took place when a masterpiece of world
culture convincingly portrayed the necessarily fleeting "victory of each individual artist over his servitude" to chaotic forces beyond his control. The
individual achievement of formal mastery and promethean creativity served
as a metonym in Malraux's existential vision for a universal human struggle
against destiny, absurdity (an existentialist buzzword he popularized), and
the onward rush of death that defined *la condition humaine*. Each of these
secular victories spread "like ripples on the sea of time" and implemented
"art's eternal victory over the human condition." "All art," Malraux poetic-
ally concluded, "is a revolt against man's fate."[4]

Malraux's heroic vocabulary of servitude, revolt, conquest, and victory,
portrayed art-making and the human condition as decidedly martial affairs.[5]
Such imagery suited Ellison's similarly masculinist vision of the prototypical
African-American artist and culture hero as a male jazz musician. Malraux
presented a framework for interpreting musical compositions and performances in all idioms as reflections on the possibilities of heroic action in a
"victory of each individual artist over his servitude." When music seemed
immune or resistant to translation into a master-code at once existential
and anthropological it remained dull and inert to Ellison. Musical occasions, that is, play no role in Ellison's writing by figuring as sites of untranslatable otherness or estrangement. He regularly displayed a Malrauxian
fervor for ritual interpretation in his explorations of southern and southwestern African-American music and folkways. Especially in Ellison's early
postwar work, a sense of modernization as an abrupt and volcanic process
of cultural upheaval hovered over these explorations. What was happening
to African-Americans' "traditional" cultural tools – what Ellison's friend
Kenneth Burke called "equipment for living" – in the seemingly chaotic
context of northern migration and urban proletarianization?[6] Ellison
adapted the work of Malraux and other theorists to style his own response

to the processes of disruption, survival, and transformation in African-American modernity.

"Rites are there to form and to test character," Ellison once offered, "and I believe speaking abstractly that this is the way I want my fiction to work" (*Conversations* 261). The rhetoric of ritual action within the vortex of African-American modernization would also color his non-fiction commentaries on African-American music and musicians. The New Negro musical doxa taught at Tuskegee officially endorsed vernacular "Negro idioms" – such as work songs, spirituals, blues, and even jazz – as raw or provincial resources for formal cosmopolitan art. But Ellison refused this cultural evolutionist view that folk and popular idioms were or had been merely valuable folkloric resources for formal concert music. After all, the symphonic form held no priority as a social site for the ritualized testing of individual and communal values and the cultivation of tragic consciousness. As Ellison wrote Albert Murray (with whom he developed many of these ideas), "Bessie Smith singing a good blues may deal with experience as profoundly as Eliot, with the eloquence of the Eliotic poetry being expressed in her voice and phrasing." "Human anguish," Ellison added in a universalizing gesture, "is human anguish . . . only expressed in a different medium."[7] An extraordinary philosophical faith in the translatability, if not transparency, of meaning across artistic media shone through Ellison's joint account of racial invisibility and musical technique.

The music of invisibility

Ellison introduces the figure of invisibility on the first page of *Invisible Man* to mark certain characteristics of the US racial regime during the first half of the twentieth century. The maintenance of white supremacy through systematic legal segregation in the South, racially exclusive institutions, and racism nationwide had an inestimable economic and psychological impact upon dominated racial groups as well as the "white" majority. The metaphor of racial invisibility spotlights the power and consequences of what scholars have since come to refer to as the racializing gaze. Simply put, the racializing gaze works to define and objectify another human being not as a fellow subject worthy of equal recognition but rather as a racial other and socially subordinate object. "I am invisible, understand, simply because people refuse to see me" (3). Through the act of non-recognition toward the socially invisible – the refusal "to see me" as a human equal – the white American imagined his own autonomy and superiority. The refusal of recognition crystallized not only the white American's racism, but also his self-deception and irresponsibility to his nation's democratic ideals. It also evidenced the white American's pathological and destructive fear, Ellison insisted. A dominating white majority and a socially submerged black minority – whose "high visibility" as social *objects* overshadowed their invisibility as individualized *subjects* before the white majority's gaze – both suffered and acted irresponsibly. "Irresponsibility is part of my invisibility," the narrator admits. "But to whom can I be responsible, and why should I be, when you refuse to see me?" "Responsibility," in other words, "rests upon recognition, and recognition is a form of agreement" (14).

An ideal of unobstructed visibility and mutuality in a post-racist democracy emerges in *Invisible Man* through images of recognition and care within a reciprocated gaze. While a straightforward corrective progression from invisibility to visibility might seem desirable, the novel's prologue also clarifies invisibility's valuable double-sidedness. "I am not complaining" about being invisible, "nor am I protesting," the narrator offers. He adds that "it is sometimes advantageous to be unseen, although it is most often rather wearing on the nerves" (3). The intelligent and necessary manipulation of invisibility had been and continued to be useful for processing and responding to the experience of racial hierarchy. However, the proper development of self-consciousness does not proceed in a straight line, the narrator concludes, but rather through violent contradiction. The narrator's movement will be "not like an arrow, but a boomerang" (6). At this point, Ellison's reverie on Armstrong's musical achievement becomes paramount for retracing the narrator's progress via turnabout and indirection.

The influential jazz critic Martin Williams once marveled at how often Armstrong's playing seemed to float "majestically over his accompaniment." Moreover, the trumpeter's phrases floated between and ahead of the heard or felt pulse while remaining "in perfect time" or sync with the band.[8] What Williams called Armstrong's "perfect swing" derived from an artful cultivation of sonic discrepancy; Armstrong's playing (whether improvised or not) would carve out and occupy an alternative rhythmic space within a collective performance. His vastly influential approach to swinging a tune included the prying open of unpredictable and even thrilling gaps between his own melodic phrasing, the accompanists' rhythmic support, and the listener's expectation of hearing the familiar melody played "straight." The listener's perception of unity in a group's sense of time is set askew, if not suspended, when a soloist sounds like he or she is floating above or tilting against the accompanists' time. The improvising soloist or vocalist flying "ahead and sometimes behind" the beat has the commanding opportunity to reshape a group's musical journey in the real time of performance. The smooth and flowing ideal of swinging, Armstrong once suggested, was "like a basketball team, everybody passing the ball just right."[9]

Armstrong may have been a representative of an African-American "underworld of sound" but his musical revolution was on intimate terms with the white mainstream of American popular music. The critic Nathaniel Mackey has recently elaborated a theoretical understanding of intimacy and discrepancy through a distinction between "musical othering" and "social othering" that is relevant to this discussion of invisibility's ironic benefits. He introduces the distinction to elucidate "black linguistic and musical practices that accent variance, variability – what reggae musicians call 'versioning.' " Through examples not so far from Ellison's Armstrong, Mackey writes of how practices in minority-based expressive idioms can also stand as critical negotiations with the mainstream. "Such othering practices," Mackey suggests, "implicitly react against and reflect critically upon the different sort of othering to which their practitioners, denied agency in a society by which they are designated other, have been subjected." The machinery of "social othering" is the transformation of groups into "others" or out-groups misrecognized and rendered invisible by majority stereotypes. It operates, for example, through declarations and practices whereby dominant majorities circulate fixed or otherwise restricting notions of minority "authenticity" in the arts. In turn, antiphonal responses found in "musical othering" pursue the critical aesthetic opportunities of being rendered a discrepancy, variation, or point of slippage from the social and aesthetic norm. "The black speaker, writer, or musician whose practice privileges variation subjects the fixed equations that underwrite that denial (including the idea of fixity itself) to an alternative." Thus, musical othering can submit dominant "fixed equations" and aesthetic norms to what Mackey dubs a "dislocating tilt."[10]

For Ellison, the music of invisibility at its best gestured toward an American future of pluralistic integration along the lines of mutual and reciprocal recognition. His championing of the aesthetic and cultural promises of pluralistic integration moved in tandem with his focus on African-American popular music as a singularly prophetic American landmark. After all, something like pluralistic, if unequal, integration characterized a past and present America defined by white domination. His highlighting of African-American music-making as a prophetic site echoed many texts but especially the chapter on the "sorrow songs" in W. E. B. Du Bois's *The Souls of Black Folk* (1903). "Negro Americans have never, as a group, felt alienated from any music sounded within their hearing," Ellison summarized in 1964, "and it is my theory that it would be impossible to pinpoint the time when they were not shaping what [LeRoi] Jones calls the mainstream of American music." Ellison sought to make the erstwhile cultural leadership of an otherwise all but invisible and disenfranchised minority group more visible and more audible to a nation divided over the black freedom struggle. Referring again to the epistemic advantages of a dominated population, Ellison proudly concluded that "the most authoritative rendering of American in music is that of American Negroes." "Whatever the degree of injustice and inequality sustained by the slaves," he added, "American culture was, even before the official founding of the nation, pluralistic" (*Collected Essays* 285). The cultural bases for a social and political revolution in the direction of pluralistic integration – an imagined American future unburdened by "fixed equations" – were already in place.[11] On the level of vernacular culture (if not elsewhere), an invisible but irrepressible "underworld of sound" had already quietly taken over the mainstream. This, too, Ellison heard in Armstrong's popular music. But how was the United States to pass from the sonic and cultural pluralism Ellison discovered to the post-racist social and political revolution of which it offered some kind of foretaste?

Plunging

Armstrong's music imparts lessons in *Invisible Man* about time. Like the boxer who can step "inside of his opponent's sense of time," the expert improviser knows to "slip into the breaks and look around" – with similarly stunning effects (8). Ellison's notion of *slipping* "into the breaks" refers, most simply, to those places within a performance where the rhythmic accompaniment goes silent, as if halting the crafted flow of time, or merely punctuates in stop-time a soloist's break. At these points, the improvising soloist (usually singular) fills the otherwise empty sonic space with dramatic solo obligatti, usually without abandoning the overall performance's established feel or its tempo of rhythmic propulsion. Armstrong moved to master playing the breaks during his apprenticeship in King Oliver's Creole Jazz Band in the early 1920s. Ellison suggested elsewhere that solo breaks are nothing less than moments when "the jazzman must lose his identity" in separating himself from the ensemble "even as he finds it" as a solo voice and individual (*Collected Essays* 267).

The prologue's image of slipping "into the breaks" foreshadows the narrator's resistance to the Brotherhood's rigid vision of time and historical change. Immediately following a violent street encounter with Ras the Exhorter, Tod Clifton confides to the narrator, "I suppose sometimes a man has to plunge outside history ... turn his back." "Otherwise," he adds, "he might kill somebody, go nuts" (377). Clifton's remark on the "plunge outside history" shows his understanding of Ras's alienation from American life. Clifton himself straddles two worlds: he has one foot in the white-dominated, downtown-based Brotherhood and another in the street life of black Harlem. Once he leaves the Brotherhood, Clifton loses his balance and fatally plunges "outside history" without finding or crafting a strong new identity. The narrator will need to calculate his alternatives more carefully if he is to plunge out of the Brotherhood and its deterministic vision of history. Instead of moving up in New York City, the protagonist only finds himself slipping downward again and again. A series of slips and plunges – including the final "plunge down, down ... upon a load of coal" (565) – demand that he learn how to make more productive use of such unplanned slips. The "movement vertically downward" in the novel, Ellison later explained, is ultimately "a process of *rising.*" Plunging, slipping, and falling give the protagonist opportunities to rise "to an understanding of his human condition" (*Collected Essays* 111). Ultimately, the narrator will summon Armstrong's "beam of lyrical sound" as a heroic model for transforming slips, breaks, and plunges into opportunities to master "the swift and imperceptible flowing of time." A dawning transvaluation of slips and plunges derived from the African-American blues, one of Armstrong's chief idiomatic sources, will also enrich the narrator.

What the French began calling "existentialist consciousness," Ellison once noted, had long been a central "property of the blues" (*Conversations* 138). Blues was not a folk music per se but rather a symptom and response to the "seething vortex" of modernity, on Ellison's account. It preceded and carried more practical value, Ellison decided, than the comparatively arid abstractions of French existentialism. "While the Frenchmen must plunge from the springboard of thought into reality," he noted to Richard Wright, "that is hardly a problem of us who live too often beneath the surface and in the texture of that reality."[12] The force of the blues, Ellison wrote in an admiring 1945 review essay on Wright's *Black Boy*, is captured in how "they at once express both the agony of life and the possibility of conquering it through sheer toughness of spirit" (*Collected Essays* 143). The agony and potential for spiritual conquest dramatized in the blues illustrated how contemporary "Negro life does not exist in a vacuum, but in the seething vortex of those tensions generated by the most highly industrialized of Western nations" (*Conversations* 138). *Invisible Man* elaborates a kind of blues modernism in several episodes, one being the narrator's street encounter with Peter Wheatstraw, a blues singing street character. The episode suggests Ellison's sense of the human condition's absurdity and indeterminism by addressing the unreliability of prefabricated abstractions or overconfident blueprints. Wheatstraw's name refers to both a mythic African-American folk figure and a historic blues artist, Peetie Wheatstraw. Born William Bunch, the St. Louis pianist and singer recorded widely in the 1930s and died in 1941 at the age of thirty-nine. The novel's Wheatstraw pushes a cart full of blueprints through Harlem's streets. "Here I got 'bout a hundred pounds of blueprints and

I couldn't build nothing! ... Folks is always making plans and changin' em."
"Yes, that's right," the narrator answers, "but that's a mistake. You have to
stick to the plan." "You kinda young, daddy-o," Wheatstraw retorts, "suddenly grave" (175).

In "Richard Wright's Blues" Ellison foreshadowed Wheatstraw's existential lesson: "It is only when the individual, whether white or black, *rejects* the
pattern that he awakens to the nightmare of his life" (*Collected Essays* 142).
Facing modern life as an unpredictable "seething vortex" compels the awakened individual to find a new "toughness of spirit." In sticking "to the plan,"
Ellison's protagonist naively evidences his social blindness and somnolence
before a chaotic reality. Wheatstraw's blues wisdom offers entry into a world
where plunging is inevitable, but mastery is possible too. Ellison's
Wheatstraw wants the narrator to turn away from a mechanical dutifulness
to an old blueprint of racial uplift and peer into Wheatstraw's cart of leftover
and unused blueprints. The protagonist needs to re-value himself not as the
object of someone else's blueprint but as a self-authored and open-ended
blueprint. A dawning "toughness of spirit" helps the narrator hold cynicism
and despair at bay after his disillusioning experiences with the Brotherhood.

Invisible Man concludes as the narrator considers the discrepancy between
a racist society and a prospective post-racist ideal. The latter ideal can be
understood in terms of what Ralph Waldo Emerson once dubbed "this new
yet unapproachable America."[13] A striking double-movement takes place
when the narrator shifts registers from blues individualism to idealistic nationalism. On the one hand, the existentialist blues voice of Wheatstraw convincingly derided the naïve determinism of a "hundred pounds of blueprints." On
the other hand, the narrator follows the well-worn path of the American
jeremiad to resuscitate another grandiose and unfinished blueprint in the
epilogue. "A novel," Ellison wrote in a revised 1981 introduction to
Invisible Man, "could be fashioned as a raft of hope, perception and entertainment that might help keep us afloat as we tried to negotiate the snags and
whirlpools that mark our nation's vacillating course toward and away from
the democratic ideal"(xx–xxi). Less than a blueprint and more than a cipher of
despair, the democratic "raft of hope" figures as a saving remnant and a make-
shift instantiation of the national community. In such a case Ellison redes-
cribed the African-American blues as a raft, if not a generating motor, for
moving closer to the "democratic ideal." At least on some occasions the blues
came to the aid of his anti-racist dialectic of democratic national becoming.

Alongside the notion of plunging outside history, Ellison evokes another
kind of dramatic plunge below everyday waking consciousness. He once
noted that as an eleven-year-old he had dipped into Freud's *Interpretation
of Dreams* (1905). Ellison's quest for models of behavioral complexity

appropriate to the richness of "human personality" led him to stock his novel with dream sequences and hallucinatory or surreal evocations of the unconscious and its libidinal pulsions. Not surprisingly, music triggers many of these sequences in *Invisible Man*. Readers encounter the novel's first dream or hallucinatory sequence with the narrator's reflections on Armstrong's "slightly different sense of time" (8). Armstrong's music acts as a trigger or key to open an "underworld of sound" otherwise unknown to the narrator. The opening portion of the scene includes the following passage:

> I not only entered the music but descended, like Dante, into its depths. And *beneath the swiftness of the hot tempo there was a slower tempo and a cave and I entered it and looked around and heard an old woman singing a spiritual as full of Weltschmerz as flamenco, and beneath that lay a still lower level on which I saw a beautiful girl the color of ivory pleading in a voice like my mother's as she stood before a group of slaveowners who bid for her naked body, and below that I found a lower level and a more rapid tempo and I heard someone shout.* (9)

The passage's excavation of what, for the narrator, lies beneath Armstrong's "Black and Blue" amounts to a vertical tour through the psychic underworld. Italics mark the psychological descent, as is the case with numerous dream sequences or eruptions from or within the unconscious throughout *Invisible Man*. Beneath and behind Armstrong's bluesy rendition of a romantic lament lies the condensed matter of African-American memory. The narrator could consciously summon and process the italicized journey, of course, only after the worldly journey packed between the novel's prologue and epilogue. According to this psychic topography the "movement vertically downward" through a series of vignettes returns as another "process of rising to an understanding of the human condition."

The Dantean journey into the unconscious in the prologue of *Invisible Man* builds on familiar tropes within African-American literary modernism. Numerous novels and short stories associated with the interwar Harlem Renaissance or Negro Renaissance, for example, included scenes where black protagonists experience acute psychic distress and destabilization during episodes of musical listening. Some critics have described a psychological or social "movement vertically downward" as nothing less than elemental to the African-American literary tradition. Facing an imagined "primitive" Other buried within their psyches, black protagonists in works like Jean Toomer's *Cane* (1923) and Nella Larsen's *Quicksand* (1928) lose their sense of psychic stability at the site of certain "unrefined" African-American musical performance. The dislocation of racial identity can coil around a disturbing experience of class differentiation when protagonists plunge in the company of musical performers or ritual participants cast as either rural folk or their newly urbanized kin. Such limit-case experiences of racial identification cause a kind of psychological and epistemological vertigo. The models of black identity these New Negro characters had previously assumed, comfortably or otherwise, now seem altogether unworkable: a tide of irrational *jouissance* erupts within them, bringing repressed libidinal energies closer to the ego's now destabilized surface. The extent of the characters' disquiet during these plunges from the psychic stability of everyday experience into (what Ellison would ironically term) "the blackness of blackness" roughly equals their measure of repressed and unreleased libidinal energy.

The representation of moments of plunging, however, had a double edge, for such depictions flirted with primitivism. In remarks about some Harlem Renaissance authors, Ellison asserted: "As Americans trying to win a place as writers, they were drawn to the going style of literary decadence represented by [white author] Carl Van Vechten's work." In addressing the taste for decadence among a predominantly white reading audience, Ellison concluded, these predecessors "insured, even more effectively than the approaching Depression, the failure of the 'New Negro' movement." (*Conversations* 114). Van Vechten's "literary decadence" and his exoticizing appreciation of the blues and jazz (as in his 1926 bestseller *Nigger Heaven*), Ellison was convinced, had been anything but productive for African-American literature.[14] The supposedly unrepressed psychic abandon energizing black popular music offered some whites a *frisson* of bohemian decadence while transvaluating and reinscribing an exoticizing logic of racial difference. In response to the strain of racial romanticism in literary modernism, Ellison's commentaries on African-American music and art-making typically stressed the centrality of discipline and artifice. While "the Negro" functioned as a guilt-inducing and thus repressed or demonized presence within white American culture, a psychoanalytically informed post-war modernism might point to more sober possibilities for working through the nation's racial pathologies. Here was another reason for Ellison's blues aesthetic to eschew the romanticization of unmediated expression or naturalness in favor of a nearly classicist stress on restraint and self-control. The latter provided the firmest stabilizing equipment for the existential plunge into the "seething vortex" of modernity.

Coursing through *Invisible Man* were Ellison's critical concerns with the African-American's aesthetic management of social masks and performances, on the one hand, and (as we have stressed here) existential plunges into the psychological world beneath any naively accepted blueprint for uplift or social progress. Near the novel's end, the Reverend B. P. Rinehart offers the startling image of a character purely made of surfaces. What we might call the Rinehart scenario speaks to the plunge into the "underworld of sound" in a philosophical valence related to the legacy of epistemological skepticism within modern Western philosophy. Such philosophical skepticism (a core component of most transatlantic literary modernist discourses) contests the belief that the world presented to us by our senses is also the one that may exist independent of our necessarily limited human perceptions. Rinehart serves *Invisible Man* as a limit-case mystery: like the "transitional" zoot-suiters of Harlem who appear to the narrator as "men out of time," Rinehart too has plunged "outside of historical time" (441). Fleeing from Ras's violent henchmen late in the novel, the narrator can only escape them by disguising himself – perhaps dissembling for the first time. He buys a pair of dark sunglasses and finds himself immediately "plunging into darkness and moving outside" (482). People in the street mistake him for Rinehart at which point he reconsiders the confidence man's multiple identities and constituencies:

> I had heard of it before but I'd never come so close. Still, could he be all of them: Rine the runner and Rine the gambler and Rine the briber and Rine the lover and Rinehart the Reverend? Could he himself be both rind and heart? What is real anyway? But how could I doubt it? He was a broad man, a man of parts who got around. Rinehart the rounder. It was true as I was true. His world was possibility and he knew it. He was years ahead of me and I was a fool. I must have been crazy and blind. The world in which we lived was without boundaries. A vast seething, hot world of fluidity, and Rine the rascal was at home. Perhaps only Rine the rascal was at home in it: It was unbelievable, but perhaps only the unbelievable could be believed. Perhaps the truth was always a lie. (498)

Where a person's identity is "both rind and heart" there can be no fully differentiated "inside" to regulate the truthfulness or sincerity of the shifting surfaces made available to the public. Thus the narrator wonders "What is real anyway?" Without a capacity to unambiguously "*plunge* from the springboard of thought into reality," access to truth or a foundational reality is threatened by endless vertiginous plunging.

Ellison later glossed Rinehart's doubleness as both a negative "personification of chaos" and a positive cipher of American fluidity. The dissembling confidence man embodies the "constant threat of chaos" beneath and beside the fragile patterns upon which people impose the meaningfulness of their experiences. As Ellison put it, chaos signaled the "irrational, incalculable forces that hover about the edges of human life like cosmic destruction lurking within an atomic stockpile" (*Collected Essays* 324). The multifarious threats of chaos, he insisted, had wreaked a special havoc on the psychology of African-Americans transplanted from the South. "Negro life," Ellison wrote in preparatory notes for *Invisible Man*, has moved at an extraordinary "tempo of development from the feudal-folk forms of the South to the industrial urban forms of the North." The tempo was "so rapid that it throws up personalities as fluid and changeable as molten metal rendered iridescent from the effect of cooling air" (*Collected Essays* 343). Here was an ominous image of the "the swift and imperceptible flowing of time" against which Ellison would pose the idealized jazz soloist and his heroic work of conquering and recrafting time.

Ellison countered the negative and anomic aspects of Rinehart with more positive visions of an aesthetic master armed with African-American folk wisdom. As a mysterious and cynical character on intimate terms with a chaotic "country with no solid past or stable class lines," Rinehart "knows how to manipulate" these conditions artfully (*Conversations* 18). To master chaos by creating a web of masks, mediating structures, and virtuoso performances: here was the charge of the Ellisonian hero. But Ellison's essays often set to the side the ambiguities of Rinehart and the anonymous changeling he would later celebrate as "the little man at Chehaw Station." Instead he would sometimes spotlight figures from the past like Oklahoma City's African-American jazzmen of his youth or musicians who played in continuity with earlier big band idioms. They had been true masters of reducing "the chaos of living to form" while unambiguously fulfilling some of the black community's most important ritual needs (*Collected Essays* 229).[15] Only in holding themselves close to their native community and its rituals of socialization were these men able to cultivate the deepest level of individuality and artistry. Mastering musical form in the swinging guises of jazz and the blues committed these musicians to what we might call a centripetal ethos of lyrical transition even as they enacted "from performance to performance" a more centrifugal and decentering process of what Kimberley Benston calls "multiplication and substitution."[16]

Lyricism and the semblance of wholeness

After publishing *Invisible Man* Ellison moved slowly to confront the immediate postwar era's most influential and celebrated virtuoso improviser, Charlie Parker. Ellison described the alto saxophonist, also known by the names "Bird" and "Yardbird," as "a confidence man and a practical joker." Like a mockingbird, he would "take off on the songs of other birds, inflating, inverting and turning them wrong side out" (*Collected Essays* 258). The final collapse of bebop's central figure in 1955 at age thirty-four, Ellison concluded, stemmed from Parker's flawed understanding of his opportunities as an artistic mockingbird and confidence man. The mythic mockingbird of bebop was a peerless improviser at peak tempos who took flight in musical "moments of sustained and meaningful integration through the reeds and keys of the alto saxophone." As a man deviled by outsized appetites and lethal addictions, however, Parker's incapacity for "sustained and meaningful integration" elsewhere in his life grounded and destroyed him. Bird was "many things to many people," Ellison asserted, but in the end he remained a confidence man "essentially devoid of a human center" (*Collected Essays* 264). Unlike those survivors the centerless Rinehart or the protean narrator who recounts his own education in *Invisible Man*, Ellison's Parker lost all balance and plunged heedlessly into the "seething vortex" of a vertiginous world. The mockingbird's wings turned "wrong side out" and a period-defining musical genius lost everything. The essay, "On Bird, Bird-Watching, and Jazz," shows the full force of Ellison's musical boomerang, striking themes reaching far beyond the particularities of Parker's musical genius.

Parker, as Ellison describes him, enjoyed too few moments of stability to safely secure his daring plunges into a fevered chaos captured in the break-neck tempos and brilliance of his daring music. Parker stood for Ellison as an alternative kind of modernist. As we have seen, Ellison wrote regularly with Malrauxian brio about the "constant threat of chaos" in all corners of modern life. Yet, he took more and more care to distance himself from the heat of political battle or social risk. Perhaps one explanation for this distance is Ellison's uneasy response to the givens of modernist discourse. Ellison recognized, to borrow the words of William James, the metaphysical homelessness of "finite experience" where "nothing outside of the flux" that is our "tramp and vagrant world" can secure or vouchsafe the truths issuing from our inevitably partial and finite experience.[17] But this recognition impelled Ellison, as it did James, to hold fast to ideals and elements of his cultural heritage that he perceived as relatively secure centripetal anchors in an centrifugal environment of increasing disorientation and protean trans-formation. While the "out of stride and seemingly arbitrary" sounds of bebop music accurately captured the harried jolts and chaos of African-American urban life in the 1940s, Ellison later clung harder still to pre-war idioms of African-American popular music as exemplified by ensembles led by Count Basie, Duke Ellington, and Louis Armstrong (*Collected Essays* 240).

The Ellison scholar Robert O'Meally once noted that Ellison was obviously "deaf to virtually all jazz beyond Basie and Ellington."[18] One might add that the older jazz of the southwestern territory bands (in which many of the "beboppers," including Parker, had apprenticed) seemed to offer Ellison what James called "a go-between" or "smoother-over of transitions." As such, the music exerted if not "a minimum of jolt," then certainly "a maximum of continuity."[19] "Lyricism" was a key term Ellison used to convey his sonic and social sense of preferred centripetal anchors or Jamesian "go-betweens." The big band blues singing of his friend Jimmy Rushing, for example, imposed a "romantic lyricism upon the blues tradition . . . a romanticism native to the frontier" (*Collected Essays* 276). Ellison's preferred mode of lyricism in African-American music belonged to what struck him as a comparatively optimistic pre-bebop music of social romance. The tempered longing of its "romantic lyricism" deliberately sounded the Orphic impulse in music – the impulse through which music "gives resonance to memory" (*Collected Essays* 240). Ellison's appeal to centripetal lyricism in music, it must be said, did not commit him to commemorate a Golden Age amidst the restrictive climate of Jim Crow segregation. Instead, his lyricism – or what Jerry Watts has pointedly framed as "folk pastoralism" – functioned as an aestheticizing "smoother-over" between a chaotic present and a childhood past that could be remembered in terms of an idealistic temper of individual assertion and mobility (rather than static satisfaction) within a context of African-American social cohesion.[20] But as Watts rightly notes, the barnyard whiff of "folk pastoralism" in Ellison's thought sometimes threatened to coagulate into the implication "that if a subjugated people feel good about themselves, their situation is not desperate."[21]

Ellison's myth-making account of what he elsewhere dubbed "the curse of Charlie Parker" provides an apt bookend to his metaphoric uses of Armstrong and the blues in *Invisible Man* (*Trading* 205). In the "Bird-Watching" essay Ellison admits to the virtuosity and occasional brilliance of Parker and the "beboppers," but nonetheless finds in him a new symbol of decadent tendencies. Of Parker's acolytes – "screwedup" purveyors of "miserable hard-bopping noise (defiance with both hands protecting their heads)" – Ellison wrote to Albert Murray that "they believe in the witchdoctor's warning: If Bird shits on you, wear it" (*Trading* 193). Although his "moldy fig" criticisms suggested otherwise, Ellison (born in 1914) was Parker's elder by only six and a half years. Ellison certainly recognized the serious "thrust toward respectability" that unified Parker's peer group of African-American modernists. A campaign of cosmopolitan vindication, after all, marked Ellison's aggressive efforts to solidify his own reputation as a cutting-edge social commentator and American novelist. At the center of the bebop movement, Ellison noted, was an "understandable rejection of the traditional entertainer's role," a role that a Parker acolyte like Miles Davis saw exemplified by Louis Armstrong (Davis's elder by twenty-five years) (*Collected Essays* 259). We recall the comments from *Invisible Man* about Armstrong's genius for making "poetry out of being invisible." "I think it must be," the narrator concluded, because Armstrong is "unaware that he *is* invisible." Parker, Davis, and the other inventors of the "bebop" idiom during World War II, by contrast, were all too aware of their racial invisibility and the racism that sustained it. In response to their relative invisibility as virtuoso professionals the African-American jazz modernists crafted a forbiddingly complex idiom to help them pry open a market niche in the wartime world of white-dominated "swing music." Having interpreted Armstrong's stage persona – a smiling southern black virtuoso eager to draw laughter and delight from all audiences – as an embarrassing reminder of minstrelsy, the new generation "demanded, in the name of their racial identity, a purity of status which by definition is impossible for the performing artist" (*Collected Essays* 259).

In making the demand for a "purity of status," Ellison argued, the bebop musicians lost the firm cultural footing enjoyed by earlier jazz practitioners. Behind the specifics of the case lay Ellison's conviction that performers should not seek to transcend the impurities of mediation in performance for the sake of immediate expression. The so-called impurities of most public performances of jazz – announcements, jokes, and other forms of explicit interaction with the audience – struck Ellison as essential to bringing to life the ritual action that bound together performers and their audience. These interactions served almost literally as Jamesian "go-betweens" or accessible points of transition between centrifugal displays of metamorphic improvisational prowess. To operate otherwise, Ellison's foreboding note on the "curse of Charlie Parker" implied, was to court personal disaster and cultural irrelevance. In other words, disaster shadowed the antinomian and alienated response to the predicament of racial invisibility. Parker's example also demonstrated how the quest for "purity" was especially dangerous for African-Americans who entered the music business already facing a gauntlet of constricting stereotypical expectations. The hub of professional bebop performance moved during the war years from the legendary Harlem clubs that incubated the idiom (most notably Monroe's Uptown House and Minton's Playhouse) to the higher-paying downtown clubs of 52nd Street. The new scene catered to a mixed, but primarily white audience. Ellison argued that many of these listeners held up a constricting and ultimately racist stereotype of black musical purity. According to the stereotype, such purity resided in the black musician's distinctive surplus of emotional expressivity that could be summoned free of the impurities of mediation or artistic sublimation.

Ellison's Parker (who should be distinguished from the historical Parker) sought a purity of artistic expression free of the mediation of stagecraft. In so doing, he inadvertently fell or plunged into the stereotype of the instinctive black musical genius from whose saxophone poured a formless ocean of expressivity for a club's predominantly white customers to play in. In

Ellison's hands, Parker ended up "a sacrificial figure." His "struggles against personal chaos, onstage and off, served as entertainment for a ravenous, sensation-starved, culturally disoriented public which had only the slightest notion of its real significance" (*Collected Essays* 261). Ellison's cultural critique of Parker and his "ravenous" and "cultural-disoriented public" paralleled his running Du Bois-styled denunciation of Carl Van Vechten's influence (especially through his racial exoticism and "literary decadence") over the Negro Renaissance authors whose work preceded that of Wright and Ellison. Moreover, the lurid tableau of Parker's plunge into self-degrading performance before a "ravenous, sensation-starved" white audience closely follows a fictional precedent from *Invisible Man*: Tod Clifton's final appearance as a vacant-eyed street performer indistinguishable from the paper Sambo doll he manipulates for small change. "Who wants Sambo, the dancing, prancing? . . . There's no license for little Sambo, the joy spreader. You can't tax joy, so speak up, ladies and gentlemen" (433). Here was the full price of vertiginous plunging.

Ellison's Armstrong (who should also be distinguished from the historical Armstrong) may have been unaware or not fully conscious of his racial invisibility; nevertheless, Ellison presumed that the musician had distinguished his private life from his public performances. He had, in other words, mastered the artist's ritual function in the deft manipulation of mediating frames. According to Ellison, "certain older jazzmen possessed a clearer idea of the division between their identities as performers and as private individuals" (*Collected Essays* 260). An essay from 1948, for example, went so far as to identify "folk jazz" as the "embodiment of a superior democracy." Earlier jazzmen, it implied, enacted richer relations with each other as ensemble performers and between themselves and the audience. Ellison contrasted the embodiment of democratic interaction in "folk jazz" against more recent alternatives (bebop serving as the obvious target for opprobrium) that failed to intertwine the musicians' pursuit of aesthetic mastery with the fulfillment of communal ritual needs. "The lyrical ritual elements of folk jazz" were the "artistic projection of the only real individuality possible for [the Negro] in the South." That projection of individuality and minority-group cohesion also embodied "a superior democracy in which each individual cultivated his uniqueness and yet did not clash with his neighbors." The pre-war "lyrical ritual" idyll had "given way to the near-themeless technical virtuosity of bebop, a further triumph of technology over humanism" (*Collected Essays* 325). The merely "technical virtuosity" of bebop musicianship offered only a mechanistic and impersonal response to the "seething vortex." Ellison's criticisms moved half-way toward Theodor Adorno's stinging denunciations of jazz in toto: the new idiom, according to

Ellison, presented a dehumanizing mimetic defense against the alienating industrialized conditions that inhibited the "lyrical ritual elements of folk jazz." The "artistic projection" of an individuality fulfilled within a democratic and affirmative ritual practice, Ellison suggested, was falling out of style. In his 1958 essay on Jimmy Rushing, the long-time featured vocalist of the Count Basie Orchestra, Ellison wrote warmly of the "feeling of communion which was the true meaning of the public jazz dance." "The thinness of much of so-called 'modern jazz,'" he asserted again, "is especially reflective of this loss of wholeness" in the decline of the public jazz dance. While Ellison wrote elsewhere in a pluralistic vein on the theme that "American culture is of a whole," he also lamented the "loss of wholeness" within the particularities of the African-American life he knew as represented by "the small Negro public dance." Rushing symbolized a fading communal life where rituals played out to the danceable lyric music of big band jazz and blues "helped to give our lives some semblance of wholeness" (*Collected Essays* 275–6).

Ellison's criticisms of bebop as the post-war lingua franca of "modern jazz" were so sweeping because they were primarily cultural rather than musical. Some bebop leaders, most notably the composer and trumpeter John Birks "Dizzy" Gillespie, did not forgo the on-stage role of announcer and raconteur inherited from Armstrong, Ellington, and others. Ellison's lament centered on his view that a "total culture" crystallized in pre-war public performances by the great black big bands was disintegrating. For him, decline and fragmentation was following an earlier moment of crystallization – what hindsight revealed as a classical moment offering "some semblance of wholeness." Ellison's musical nostalgia, however, was not that of a Spenglerian pessimist stuck on an image of decline. There were, for example, complex motivations behind his avid interest in high-fidelity stereo and his admitted obsession "with the idea of reproducing sound with such fidelity that . . . it would reach the unconscious levels of the mind with the least distortion" (*Collected Essays* 234). In order to move with fidelity toward the distant new world of an idealized pluralistic and post-racist America, an older segregated African-American world, with its joys and its restrictions, had to give way. Ellison could at least maintain fidelity to that past world through his home-made stereo and private archive that sonically reproduced the beautiful world of his youth as he imagined it.

When playing his Emersonian song of the future, Ellison would celebrate his nation's ideal identity as an ever-expanding fabric of overlapping pluralistic influences and brilliant "motley mixtures." "Here, theoretically, social categories are open, and the individual is not only considered capable of transforming himself, but is encouraged to do so" (*Collected Essays* 503). As a kind of Rinehart-like confidence man, Ellison issued conflicting prose rhapsodies, by turns retrospective and prospective, centripetal and centrifugal. Thus, the epilogue of *Invisible Man* boomerangs back against the disillusioning thrust of the novel's preceding chapters with a dramatic shift toward affirmation as the narrator considers emerging from hibernation to speak for an anti-racist and integrationist strain of liberal American nationalism. Echoing the preacherly cadences heard throughout his youth and summoned during his career as a Brotherhood spokesman, the narrator's secular sermon takes the form of an American jeremiad. While Emerson pledged himself to "this new yet unapproachable America which I have found in the West," the narrator of *Invisible Man* plays on the ideal nation's unapproachability – whether its impossibility or its necessity – by presenting the views in the form of questions about his cryptic grandfather. Inquiring as to his grandfather's deathbed advice, the narrator asks:

> Could he have meant – hell, he *must* have meant the principle, that we were to affirm the principle on which the country was built and not the men, or at least not the men who did the violence. . . . . Was it that we of all, we, most of all, had to affirm the principle, the plan in whose name we had been brutalized and sacrificed – not because we would always be weak nor because we were afraid or opportunistic, but because we were older than they, in the sense of what it took to live in the world with others and because they had exhausted in us, some – not much, but some – of the human greed and smallness, yes, and the fear and superstition that had kept them running (574).

The dialectical form of the Brotherhood's theory about how the predicament of racial invisibility might be transcended through class consciousness and revolution, shifts register in this passage into the protagonist's new liberal nationalist dialectic of American self-becoming. Precisely because they were still victimized by America's distance from its non-racist democratic principles, African-Americans "most of all" remained the truest keepers of the nation's ideals. Only they could teach other Americans how to become truly American and "what it took to live in the world with others." The narrator allies himself first with the Brotherhood's vision of history but rejects their class-based, anti-racial interpretation. In rejecting the Brotherhood's rationalist theory of history as class warfare, the narrator of *Invisible Man* moved toward identifying with the passed over (or dialectical residue) represented not only by Peter Wheatstraw's cart of discarded blueprints, but by Brother Tarp's chain link, the blues records of the evicted Harlem tenants, the street vendor's hot sweet yams, and other reminders of his southern heritage. Putting his blues modernism to work on a nationalist project, Ellison transforms the embrace of the remainder into a new dialectic and an American jeremiad in an African-American idiom. Here he sides with the ideal of an unbuilt and prospective America. Rejecting one dialectical model of history but identifying with all that is left out of that model, the narrator brilliantly uses these very residues to fuel another dialectic of history.

Ellison followed the existentialist "*plunge* from the springboard of thought into reality" with an ascent or perhaps a retreat from the "irrational, incalculable forces" of chaos and fragmentation into a more orderly world of "romantic lyricism" offering "some semblance of wholeness." His rejection of the rationalist's world of philosophical abstraction, in other words, was only partial. He laced his Americanist project, however impure and variegated, with a tincture of idealism as ineradicable as the drop of black dope that makes possible the purity of "Optic White" paint in *Invisible Man*. A first plunge landed Ellison in an invisible African-American underworld "beneath the surface" of a dominant reality. It was an underworld where an ultra-modern existential individualism possessing a finely honed tragic sense and bias toward improvisation mingled freely with centripetal anchoring-points offering affirmation and release in communal musical rituals. A public intellectual who described himself as "a true outsider," Ellison preferred not to plunge further still beneath an established repertoire of lyrical forms of musical sociality (*Collected Essays* 663). Hence his chastening references to "the curse of Charlie Parker."

Rather than plunge further into the metamorphic possibilities of alternative models of African-American musical and literary modernism, Ellison fastened himself more firmly to idealized images of social integration – whether of a segregated black community brought together by the assertive lyricism of Jimmy Rushing and other legends of southwestern jazz or a prospective post-racist America buoyed by a pluralistic and democratic ideal. He wrote of Armstrong's "different sense of time" in terms of being sometimes "ahead and sometimes behind" the beat; Ellison's genius, and perhaps his limitation, resided in being both at once. If the tragicomic blues spirit of collective affirmation he identified with a music born in his youth was less frequently heard with the passing of time, Ellison worked all the more to commemorate the "romantic lyricism" of a receding world. Thus he offered the following dedication to his never-published second novel: "To That Vanished Tribe Into Which I Was Born: The American Negroes."

Notes

1. Ralph Ellison, *Invisible Man* (New York: Vintage Books, 1995), p. 8. Hereafter citations will appear in the text.
2. Ron Welburn, "Ralph Ellison's Territorial Vantage" (1976), in *Conversations with Ralph Ellison*, eds. Maryemma Graham and Amritjit Singh (Jackson:

University Press of Mississippi, 1995), p. 311. Hereafter citations will appear in the text.

3. Ralph Ellison, "Living with Music" (1955), in *The Collected Essays of Ralph Ellison* (New York: Random House, 1995), p. 229. Hereafter citations will appear in the text as *Collected Essays*.

4. André Malraux, *The Voices of Silence*, trans. Stuart Gilbert (Princeton University Press, 1978), p. 638.

5. For a useful overview of the martial theme in Malraux, see Roger Shattuck, "Malraux, the Conqueror," in *Andre Malraux*, ed. Harold Bloom (New York: Chelsea House, 1988), pp. 57–72. For a detailed examination of Malraux's existential aesthetic over the course of his career, see Geoffrey T. Harris, *Andre Malraux: A Reassessment* (New York: St. Martin's Press, 1996), esp. pp. 169–95.

6. Burke wrote of works of art as "strategies for selecting enemies and allies, for socializing losses, for warding off evil eye, for purification, propitiation, and desanctification, consolation and vengeance, admonition and exhortation, implicit commands or instructions of one sort or another. Art forms like 'tragedy' . . . would be treated as equipment for living, that size up situations in various ways and in keeping with correspondingly various attitudes." Kenneth Burke, "Literature as Equipment for Living" (1937), in *Perspectives by Incongruity*, ed. Stanley Edgar Hyman (Bloomington: Indiana University Press, 1964), p. 109.

7. Ralph Ellison to Albert Murray (June 2, 1957), in *Trading Twelves*, eds. Albert Murray and John F. Callahan (New York: Vintage, 2001), p. 166. Hereafter citations will appear in the text.

8. Martin Williams, *The Jazz Tradition: Second Revised Edition* (New York: Oxford University Press, 1993), p. 56. Williams is referring specifically to an Armstrong recording of "I Gotta Right to Sing the Blues," and adds that "one has to wait almost until the jazz of the 'sixties for such freedom of musical phrase"(56).

9. Louis Armstrong, *In His Own Words: Selected Writings*, ed. Thomas Brothers (New York: Oxford University Press, 1999), p. 166.

10. Nathaniel Mackey, "Other: From Noun to Verb," in *Discrepant Engagement: Dissonance, Cross-Culturality, and Experimental Writing* (Cambridge University Press, 1993), pp. 266–7, 284.

11. Ellison later credited Alain Locke as an early advocate of an open-ended vision of cultural influence and American pluralism capable of seeing "members of a minority group" who "affirmed and defined not only the black experience, but what was basically an American experience, and, when it was most transcended, the experience of human beings living in a world of turbulent transitions" (*Collected Essays* 444). For connections between Locke's pluralism and his music writings, see Paul Allen Anderson, *Deep River: Music and Memory in Harlem Renaissance Thought* (Durham: Duke University Press, 2001), esp. pp. 113–66.

12. Ralph Ellison to Richard Wright (June 24, 1946), Richard Wright Papers: Personal Correspondence, James Weldon Johnson Collection, Yale University, Series ii, Box 97, Folder 1314, p. 3.

13. Ralph Waldo Emerson, "Experience," from *Ralph Waldo Emerson: Essays and Lectures,* ed. Joel Porte (New York: Library of America 1983), p. 485.

14. Langston Hughes kindly protected his friend Van Vechten from this knowledge when Van Vechten praised Ellison's novel.
15. For an alternative discussion that stresses "The Little Man at Chehaw Station" as Ellison's pragmatist critique of identity logic in the tradition of William James and Alain Locke, see Ross Posnock, *Color and Culture: Black Writers and the Making of the Modern Intellectual* (Cambridge: Harvard University Press, 1998), pp. 184–91, 200–7.
16. Kimberly W. Benston, *Performing Blackness: Enactments of African-American Modernism* (London: Routledge, 2000), p. 13. For a recent analysis stressing the non-identitarian, centrifugal, and "avant-gardist" elements of Ellison's aesthetic, see, for example, Kevin Bell, "The Embrace of Entropy: Ralph Ellison and the Freedom Principle of Jazz Invisible," *Boundary 2* 30.2 (Summer, 2003): 21–45. For a recent analysis that sketches the distance between the novel's framing sections and its more disorientating contents, see Fred Moten, *In the Break: The Aesthetics of the Black Radical Tradition* (Minneapolis: University of Minnesota Press, 2003), pp. 63–73. By focusing on Ellison's comments on swing and bop my discussion instead stresses Ellison's coherent and consistent interest in what might be called centripetal lyricism as a dream of stability and mastery amid chaos and flux.
17. William James, *Pragmatism* (Indianapolis: Hackett Publishing Company, 1988), p. 117.
18. Robert G. O'Meally, *The Craft of Ralph Ellison* (Cambridge: Harvard University Press, 1980), p. 169.
19. William James, *Pragmatism*, p. 31.
20. I mean to highlight here the centripetal or commemorative element of Ellison's temperament without neglecting his centrifugal assertion elsewhere that "our cultural wholeness ... offers no easily recognizable points of rest, no facile certainties as to who, what or where (culturally or historically) we are. Instead, the whole is always in cacophonic motion. Constantly changing its mode, it appears as a vortex of discordant ways of living and tastes, values and traditions, a whirlpool of odds and ends ... Deep down, the American condition is a state of unease." Ralph Ellison, "The Little Man at Chehaw Station," (*Collected Essays*, p. 504). As for music as a resting-point or centripetal and Orphic force-field, consider Ellison's assertion that "one of the chief values of living with music lies in its power to give us an orientation in time. In doing so, it gives significance to all those indefinable aspects of experience which nevertheless help to make us what we are. In the swift whirl of time music is a constant, reminding us of what we were and of that toward which we aspire" (*Collected Essays* p. 236).
21. Jerry Gafio Watts, *Heroism and the Black Intellectual: Ralph Ellison, Politics, and Afro-American Intellectual Life* (Chapel Hill: The University of North Carolina Press, 1994), p. 109. Watts' harsh denunciation of Ellison's "folk pastoralism" (and its presumed antidemocratic and elitist political implications) and his (Emersonian) idealism in general offers a stunning riposte to Ellison's romanticization of a tough-minded blues existentialism and tragic view of life. "Pastoralism," however, does not strike me as an appropriate description of Ellison's modernist and conflict-bound urban vision.

5

GREGG CRANE

Ralph Ellison's constitutional faith

Over the years, critics have disagreed about the relation between aesthetics and politics in Ralph Ellison's work. Early evaluations of *Invisible Man* often praise the richness of Ellison's literary invention without comment on its political significance. Others have disapproved of what they see as Ralph Ellison's preference for the aesthetic over the political. In "Black Boys and Native Sons," Irving Howe famously criticized Ellison and James Baldwin for lacking the confrontational zeal appropriate to a minority writer in a racist society. More recently, Jerry Watts faults Ellison for his "elitism" and "extreme ... political disengagement."[1] Much of this criticism, whether sympathetic or unsympathetic, appears to wish Ellison would choose between art and politics, high culture and folklore, universal themes and the particularities of black experience; otherwise, either his aesthetics or his politics become tangled and suspect.[2] Ellison, however, steadfastly refuses this choice. Instead, his fiction and essays suggest an artistic and democratic vision of justice combining aesthetics and politics, ethics and law, high and vernacular culture, a vision that "plays havoc with conventional ideas of order," such as the categorical division of art and law.[3]

Simultaneously committed to a continuity of ethical principle and the fluid processes of democratic consensus and believing that art plays an important role in shaping that consensus, Ellison is part of a hybrid transcendental and pragmatist tradition in American aesthetic and jurisprudential thought which includes Ralph Waldo Emerson, Frederick Douglass, Charles Sumner, James Weldon Johnson, Alain Locke, W. E. B. Du Bois, William James, Oliver Wendell Holmes, Benjamin Cardozo, and Kenneth Burke.[4] By depicting the intersections and dialogue between Ellison and this line of intellectuals, I hope to furnish a fuller sense of the aesthetic and political engagements of his work and to add an ethical dimension to the current recovery of Ellison's pragmatist emphasis on change and experiment.

Ellison's brief but telling characterization of the Civil Rights movement and *Brown* v. *Board of Education* in a letter to his friend Albert Murray provides a revealing glimpse of his vision of justice as a mix of art and law, universal and particular, continuity and change:

> I feel a lot better about our struggle though, mose is still boycotting the hell out of Montgomery and still knocking on the door of Alabama U ... and he's still got his briarpatch cunning; he's just been waiting for a law, man, something solid under his feet; a little scent of possibility. In fact, he's turned the Supreme Court into the forum of liberty it was intended to be, and the Constitution of the United States into a briar patch in which the nimble people, the willing people, have a chance. And that's what *it* was intended to be.[5]

A composite of Moses and Brer Rabbit, "mose" seeks the promised land of an American democracy living up to its republican and egalitarian ideals, and he brings to that quest the folk tale trickster's "briar patch cunning." In the well-known folk tale, Rabbit, having been caught in the tar baby made by Wolf, tells his adversary that the death he most fears is being thrown into the briar patch. Wolf takes the bait and throws Rabbit into the briar patch where he escapes.[6] Merging the Exodus story as universal symbol of liberation (though it is also, of course, the creation of a particular people) with the African-American folk tale as the symbol of a particular people's historic struggle against oppression, "mose" embodies what Kenneth Burke describes as a dual vision in which the "Negro ... recognizes that his particular act must be adapted to the nature of his historical situation, ... yet at the same time, he can view this situation universally (thereby attaining the kind of transcendence at which all men aim)."[7] A lawgiver and escape artist, Ellison's "mose" is a folk hero and a new incarnation of the universal values of freedom and fair play.

In a similarly paradoxical fashion, the law, as "briar patch" *and* something solid under [mose's] feet," is both fluid and stable. Through his wits, agility, and fortitude, "mose" is able to transform the law, so often a trap for the powerless, into a means of escaping the rule of force and the supposedly fixed or natural hierarchies of Rabbit and Wolf, slavery, and Jim Crow. In *Invisible Man*, the novel's unnamed narrator finds a similar freedom in the realization that certainty is an illusion. If he rejects a vision of "the world [as] nailed down" and the false certainties of "rank" or "limit," Ellison's protagonist discovers, his world can "become one of infinite possibilities," a surprising and ironic outcome for a black man living in a racist society.[8] Such fluidity, however, is not by itself sufficient. "Mose" needs something "solid under his feet," some bit of ethical and legal certainty, to provide the point of leverage necessary for creating movement or change.

Ellison expressly addresses the simultaneous continuity and fluidity of legal and aesthetic values in "Perspective of Literature," an essay considering whether and how literature contributes to law and jurisprudence. Ellison quotes Paul Freund, an influential constitutional scholar:

> Does not law, like art ... seek change within the framework of continuity, to bring heresy and heritage into fruitful tension? They are not dissimilar, and in their resolution, the resolution of passion and pattern, of frenzy and form, of convention and revolt, of order and spontaneity lies the clue to the creativity that will endure.

The prolonged existence of legal discrimination compels Ellison to qualify Freund's words as describing an "ideal" rather than a daily reality. With a keen awareness of how commonly the rule of law devolves into an expression of majority power and bias, Ellison claims the authority of aesthetic and ethical principles in order to affirm *and* transform those principles. Unlike the policeman or even the jurist, the artist has greater flexibility in addressing the law. The function of writers in "the tradition of Mark Twain, Emerson, and Thoreau" includes disruption, "yell[ing] 'Fire' in crowded theaters," and, by pushing American democracy, such artists become "an irreplaceable part of the social order" (*Collected Essays* 773).

Ellison's conception of aesthetic and ethical judgment

"Little Man at Chehaw Station" represents Ellison's most complete articulation of the relation between change and continuity in aesthetic and ethical judgment. The essay begins with a reminiscence of Ellison's days as a music student at the Tuskegee Institute. After a technically proficient but uninspired trumpet recital, Ellison "sought solace" from one of his teachers, Hazel Harrison, a highly respected concert pianist, student of Ferruccio Busoni, and friend of Sergei Prokofiev. Instead of comforting him, Miss Harrison challenged Ellison to "play [his] best, even if it's only the waiting room at Chehaw Station [a 'lonely whistle-stop'] because in this country there'll always be a little man behind the stove ... and he'll know the music, and the tradition, and the standards of musicianship." The little man, Miss Harrison herself, and the janitors Ellison describes encountering in the basement of a Manhattan apartment building arguing about grand opera embody the hopeful improbabilities of American society and the way in which the interaction between artist and audience has the potential to confound hierarchy, materializing even "at the depth of the American social hierarchy" (*Collected Essays* 490, 515–19).

Appealing to the audience "on the basis of what it assumes to be truth as a means of inducing it into new dimensions of artistic truth," Ellison writes, "the artist seeks to shape its emotions and perceptions to his vision, while it, in turn, simultaneously cooperates and resists, says yes and says no in an it-takes-two-to-tango binary response to his effort" (*Collected Essays* 492). Aesthetic values and norms are not static in this dialogue. The artist's articulation and the audience's understanding of these values is a medium of communication, and each side plays an important role in the exchange. The artist uses established themes and figures as the basis for innovation and experiment, which modifications the audience resists and accepts. Ultimately, new applications or formulations of the old, "assumed" truths emerge from the interaction. For Ellison as for Kant, Emerson, Douglass, and other more immediate precursors, the ethical relevance of a process in which aesthetic values are invoked and transformed is plain – just as one's sense of artistic form and experience can be transformed so can one's sense of basic ethical principles, such as fair play.

In sections 40 and 41 of the *Critique of Judgment*, Kant describes how the faculty of judgment assimilates new or discrepant events and facts to the categories we use to structure and organize our aesthetic experiences.[9] One result of the interplay between particular experience and category is that our categories change, as, for instance, when a different kind of fiction recalibrates our definition of the novel. While sections 40 and 41 of the *Critique* focus on aesthetic discernment, as section 60 states, this form of judgment "is at bottom a faculty for judging of the sensible illustration of moral ideas."[10] The Kantian version of judgment is, as Samuel Fleishacker notes, "at home most familiarly in law and literary and other aesthetic criticism." Aesthetic judgment "provides the foundation of the kind of conversation relevant to morality: conversation about particulars that must be placed in some valuative category but are, often, too distinctive to fit easily into any single such category." Aesthetic and ethical judgment share an "unnerving endlessness of moving between universals and particulars" and an "uncertainty that permeates moral thinking at its best."[11] Borrowing Ronald Dworkin's terms, we can describe this movement as a dialogue between concepts and conceptions. Concepts are large principles or values never fully or finally defined, and conceptions are our specific attempts to achieve and illustrate those abstractions. In this creative and dialogic process, new examples and unforeseen instances stretch and modify our sense of the concept. As a result the concept has continuing vitality – it is dynamic, and alive as a consequence of its capacity for expansion and modification by new particulars. Under pressure from new and heterodox experiences, our ideas of beauty or justice shift, creating an uncertainty not in the concept itself but in the finality of any attempt to define or articulate the concept.[12]

The creative and open-ended nature of this mode of judgment and its emphasis on human agency appealed tremendously to Ellison as it did to

Frederick Douglass and "that earlier Ralph Waldo" (*Collected Essays* 423). As "transcendent forms of symbolic expression," aesthetic and ethical norms are, as Ellison puts it, "agencies of human freedom" (*Collected Essays* 514). All three resist any attempt to curb the frequently unsettling process of agency and transformation in the name of a specious certainty. Ellison's protagonist in *Invisible Man* rejects the desire to have "the world nailed down" in order to secure a false "feeling of security" (*Invisible* 573). And Emerson excoriates attempts of proslavery apologists to fix the meaning of the Constitution once and for all: "They would nail the stars to the sky. With their eyes over their shoulders, they adore their ancestors, the framers of the Constitution ... They wish their age should be absolutely like the last." To acquiesce in this "desperate grasp of the past" is, in Emerson's view, to reject ethical and aesthetic principles, which call us to the difficult but liberating project of revision.[13]

For Ellison, Emerson, and Douglass, literary or aesthetic experience exemplifies the ceaseless process of revision involved in value judgments. "It is the very *spirit* of art to be defiant of categories and obstacles," Ellison writes, thereby opening up our "forms of symbolic expression" to new meanings (*Collected Essays* 514). By intruding on our habitual ways of thinking about and experiencing the world, literature opens new perspectives on fundamental concepts, such as beauty and justice. "Literature," Emerson says in "Circles," furnishes "a point outside of our hodiernal circle through which a new one may be described":

> In my daily work I incline to repeat my old steps, and do not believe in remedial force, in the power of change and reform. But some Petrarch or Ariosto, filled with the new wine of his imagination, writes me an ode or a brisk romance, full of daring thought and action. He smites and arouses me with his shrill tones, breaks up my whole chain of habits, and I open my eye to my own possibilities.

Douglass describes aesthetic experience as an appreciation of nature's or art's ceaseless "Creating, unfolding, expanding, renewing, changing, perpetually, putting on new forms, new colours, issuing new sounds, filling the world with new perfumes, and spreading out to the eye and heart, unending scenes of freshness and beauty [and] all pervading and never resting life." The flux of aesthetic experience, in Douglass's view, exemplifies and illuminates the fact that our lives are and should be a continuing process of transformation:

> Men talk much of a new birth. The fact is fundamental. But the mistake is in treating it as an incident which can only happen to a man once in a life time; whereas, the whole journey of life is a succession of them. A new life springs up in the soul, with the discovery of every new agency by which the soul is raised to

a higher level of wisdom, goodness and joy. The poor savage, accustomed only to the stunning war whoop of his tribe, and to the wild and startling sounds in nature, of winds, waterfalls, and thunder, meets with a change of heart the first time he hears the Divine harmonies, of scientific music: and the child experiences one with every new object, by means of which it is brought into a nearer and fuller acquaintance with its own subjective nature. With every step he attains a larger, fuller and freer range of vision.

Whether aesthetic or ethical, judgment produces, in Emerson's words, "new views & broader principles ... to fit the natural expansion of the times."[14]

In creating new perspectives, the faculty of judgment thrives on diversity. Consequently, Douglass contends, we should "welcome to our ample continent all nations, kindreds, tongues and peoples, and as fast as they learn our language and comprehend the duties of citizenship, we should incorporate them into the American body politic."[15] Ellison describes this ongoing process of incorporation as a "ceaseless contention" between various parochial conceptions of American identity "whose uneasily accepted but unrejectable purpose is the projection of an ever more encompassing and acceptable definition of our corporate identity as Americans" (*Collected Essays* 500).[16] Because the "American cultural identity" is "tentative, controversial, constantly changing," Ellison finds that "the ideal level of sensibility to which the American artist would address himself tends to transcend the lines of class, religion, region, and race – floating, as it were, free in the crowd" (*Collected Essays* 495). Accepting such diversity and fluidity, however, is not painless. As Ellison notes, "we shy from confronting our cultural wholeness because it offers no easily recognizable points of rest, no facile certainties as to who, what or where (culturally or historically) we are. Instead, the whole is always in cacophonic motion" (*Collected Essays* 504). In response, some retreat to the counterfeit and regressive certainties of "blood magic and blood thinking" – the notion that an inherited and innate racial or ethnic identity determines one's behavior, associations, and judgment (*Collected Essays* 505).[17]

By moving in a distinctly cosmopolitan direction from "specifically imagined individuals to the group, to the nation and, it is hoped, to the universal," art exceeds and defies the determinism of such "blood theory" (*Collected Essays* 533, 750). As Ross Posnock has shown, the cosmopolitanism Ellison shared with W. E. B. Du Bois and Alain Locke "means that 'culture has no color.' Nor do individuals, groups, or nations possess 'special proprietary rights' to culture."[18] Ellison credits Locke with the insight that culture is not pure but hybrid and cannot be imprisoned in blood (*Collected Essays* 443). As Locke put it, "out of the depths of his group and personal experience," the "Negro artist" speaks to "a vital common background."

Even African-American spirituals, an artform ostensibly bound to racial identity, "transcend," Locke states, "the very experience of sorrow out of which they were born."[19] Frederick Douglass similarly observed that, while the slaves' sorrow songs express a particular and private experience unknown to those "outside the circle of slavery," the sympathetic outsider's perspective is required to appreciate the songs' public and political import: "I did not, when a slave, understand the deep meanings of those rude, and apparently incoherent songs. I was myself within the circle, so that I neither saw nor heard as those without might see and hear." Though the songs give Douglass his "first glimmering conceptions of the dehumanizing character of slavery," it is only after he has access to different perspectives furnished by literacy and travel (for example, his hearing "the same *wailing notes*" in Ireland during the famine of 1845–46) that Douglass can fully comprehend and articulate the universal political significance of their beauty: "A sense of human wrong and oppression has ONE language the world over."[20] Ethical and aesthetic insight in Douglass's and, later, Ellison's formulations benefits from movement, shifting perspectives, and changing points of view, and defies any containment by the parameters of a given identity.

From Douglass to Ellison, African-American intellectuals and artists have been keenly aware of the political significance of a cosmopolitan perspective on culture. James Weldon Johnson, executive secretary of the NAACP, lawyer, writer, and musician, contended that a "cosmopolitanism of spirit and intellect" was essential to the possibility of interracial justice in the United States.[21] Conceiving of art generally and music in particular as "the touchstone, the magic thing, by which the Negro can bridge all chasms," Johnson's novel, *Autobiography of an Ex-Coloured Man* (1912), one of many precedents for *Invisible Man*, tells the story of an unnamed African-American narrator whose light skin and native gift for languages and music enables him not only to move across cultural and social boundaries but also to translate between different cultures. Ultimately choosing to pass as a white man, Johnson's narrator feels he has forsaken his "birthright," which is not some metaphysical blackness carried in his blood but is rather his native and cosmopolitan gift as a musician to bridge the chasm between white and black Americans. Abandoning his vocation costs the narrator his chance to participate in the noble effort to improve the lot of black Americans and transform the nation's conception of justice and citizenship.[22]

Conscience and consciousness: Ellison's constitutional faith

In its embrace of change, improvisation, and revision, Ellison's conception of aesthetic and ethical judgment closely parallels a pragmatist strain of

American jurisprudence. In *Pragmatism*, William James describes changes in our idiom of justice as part of the general mutability of language and meaning: "Truth grafts itself on previous truth, modifying it in the process, just as idiom grafts itself on previous idiom, and law on previous law. Given previous law and a novel case, and the judge will twist them into fresh law."[23] Behind the judicial decision's "language of logic" and "certainty," Justice Oliver Wendell Holmes writes in his famous essay "The Path of the Law," "lies a judgment as to the relative worth and importance of competing legislative grounds, often an inarticulate and unconscious judgment" which is "the very root and nerve of the whole proceeding."[24] Inspired by James and Holmes, Justice Benjamin Cardozo describes judicial interpretation as a "perpetual flux" driven by "forces which [judges] do not recognize and cannot name ... inherited instincts, traditional beliefs, acquired convictions; and the resultant is an outlook on life, a conception of social needs, a sense in James's phrase of 'the total push and pressure of the cosmos,' which, when reasons are nicely balanced, must determine where choice shall fall." And Judge Learned Hand, who studied with James at Harvard, argues that judges define the law's orienting values, such as freedom and equality, in an ongoing process of trial and error: "knowledge is hard to get, that man must break through again and again the thin crust on which he walks, [and] the certainties of today may become the superstitions of tomorrow, that we have no warrant of assurance save by everlasting readiness to test and test again. William James was its great American apostle in modern times; we shall do well to remember him."[25]

The archenemy of this kind of judicial experimentalism is strict construction, which attempts to fix the law's meaning, once and for all, at its moment of origin. When it comes to the Constitution, Kenneth Burke argues, strict construction is not viable. As something broader, more durable, and more flexible than any mere code section (e.g., a highway weight limit or age restriction for the purchase of alcoholic beverages), the nation's charter requires a pragmatist approach to its interpretation. Constitutional principles, such as the idea of freedom in the First Amendment and the idea of equality in the Fourteenth Amendment, are ideals we aspire to but which we do not pretend to achieve in any final sense. These values call for something more than mere compliance; they compel a never-ending project of revision and improvement. A "*strict* interpretation of [such] 'principles,'" Burke writes, "is simply a contradiction in terms." Echoing Emerson, who advocates replacing "literal construction" with a "visionary" and "inventive" approach to the nation's charter, Burke contends that, as "highly generalized wishes," constitutional principles must be interpreted "according to the 'spirit' rather than the 'letter' of the Constitution."[26] To adopt strict construction would be to disregard, as Ellison puts it, the nation's origin in "revolution" and its "dedicat[ion] to change through basic concepts stated in the Bill of Rights and the Constitution" (*Collected Essays* 757). For Emerson, Burke, and Ellison, to confine the Constitution to the framers' worldview is to destroy its creative potential as part of the lexicon of justice, which has to be more capacious and more fluid than the particular outlook of any given generation.

The Constitution's embrace of change and experiment, however, cannot be total. As Emerson points out, the "incessant movement and progression which all things partake could never become sensible to us but by contrast to some principle of fixture or stability in the soul."[27] In "Little Man at Chehaw Station," Ellison characterizes this "principle of fixture" as a "rock" or:

> terrain of ideas that, although man-made, exerts the compelling force of the ideal, of the sublime: ideas that draw their power from the Declaration of Independence, the Constitution, and the Bill of Rights. We stand, as we say, united in the name of these sacred principles. But indeed it is in the name of these same principles that we ceaselessly contend, affirming our ideals even as we do them violence.   (*Collected Essays* 501)

Though our particular illustrations and applications of freedom, equality, and fair play are contingent, tenuous, and fluid, we register and believe in these values as constant. As John Dewey explains in "Freedom and Culture" (1939), while we experiment with "the forms and mechanisms" of law and society, "the ideal aims and values to be realized" by our political and legal scheme "remain unchanged in substance."[28] "[A]bstract, ideal, spiritual," these principles, Ellison maintains, "prod us ceaselessly toward the refinement and perfection of those formulations of policy and configurations of social forms of which they are the signs and symbols" (*Collected Essays* 501).

"Conscience and consciousness" is Ellison's shorthand for the process by which we continue to affirm and revise the nation's governing ethos and fundamental law – a binary conception which Ellison expressly links to Emerson, "I can only fall back upon the teaching of that earlier Ralph Waldo and suggest conscience and consciousness, more consciousness and more conscientiousness" (*Collected Essays* 423). Ellison's phrase combines moral inspiration and individual agency, the ability to put ethical insight into democratic practice through the processes of dialogue, consent, and action. "[A]s the still-vital covenant by which Americans of diverse backgrounds, religions, races, and interests are bound," the Constitution is perpetually refashioned by the interplay of individual conscience and collective consent (*Collected Essays* 773). As "covenant," the nation's charter is a kind of contract – a diverse assembly's binding exchange of promises and reciprocal obligations, but it is also something more than any mere quid pro quo. It represents, however imperfectly, a sacred agreement about the ethical basis of American law and society, deriving its ultimate authority from a plausibly universal moral consensus about the terms of justice and citizenship. This consensus becomes *plausibly* universal when it becomes hard to imagine any sentient being not agreeing to such basic values of coexistence.

Of course, the oppression we observe in our own and previous historical moments may well cause us to wonder whether the appearance of genuine consent does not await a still distant transition, as Antonio Gramsci puts it, from the "reign of necessity" to the "reign of freedom." Following Gramsci, we may suspect that what seems to be consent is an illusion produced by hegemony to hide or justify various forms of oppression. We might recall how the Supreme Court used the idea of consent to strike down progressive legislation aimed at protecting workers. In *Lochner v. New York* (1905), for instance, the Court characterized legislation protecting workers from being made to work in excess of sixty hours a week and ten hours a day as an unconstitutional interference with the contractual freedom of the employees as well as the employer, entirely disregarding the radically unequal bargaining power of the parties, the absence of any negotiation of contractual terms, and how the workers' "consent" was made inevitable by their economic circumstances. Recalling Louis Althusser's warning that "people are always coming across themselves in the act of consenting to their own coercion," we might suspect with considerable historical justification that reformers advocating a consensual model of justice are deluded. Sacvan Bercovitch has charted in considerable detail how nineteenth-century invocations of the "rhetoric of consensus" hid the substitution of a form of intellectual and material domination for actual consent. However, though such observations often prove apt, they do not utterly negate the distinction between consent and coercion. In fact, these comments depend on that distinction for their comprehension. Without a sense of the difference between consent and coercion, we cannot recognize the coercion Althusser says we "consent" to, and we cannot distinguish between the "*rhetoric* of consensus" and actual consensus.[29] For those not willing to capitulate in a fatalistic vision of power as the sum and substance of social and political forms of association, the desire to root out and expose oppression masquerading as consent betokens a desire for the possibility of genuinely consensual human association. For the Constitution to be something better or more than a mere expression of political power, it has to be, in Ellison's view, a "still-vital" ethical agreement unifying "Americans of diverse backgrounds and interests," and the continuing process of constitutional interpretation and revision has to recognize and include all morally competent citizens as co-authors or parties to the bargain.

Ellison illustrates the central importance of mutual recognition and agreement to the ethical authority of American law in the Prologue to *Invisible Man*, which famously begins with the narrator's murderous assault on a tall blond man who insults him after they accidentally bump into each other. Attempting to force some form of recognition, the narrator repeatedly screams, "Apologize! Apologize!" (*Invisible* 4). The blond man's complete failure to acknowledge the narrator amounts to a denial of his humanity and a rejection of the changing yet permanent covenant of American democracy. Consequently, the narrator feels free to deny culpability for the attack, arguing that "Responsibility rests upon recognition and recognition is a form of agreement" (*Invisible* 14). Because legal and ethical duties are reciprocal, matters of shared perception and consent, the blond stranger's failure to acknowledge the narrator transforms an illegal act, a crime, into an extralegal act. The narrator's formula of responsibility, recognition, and agreement encapsulates American jurisprudence's thorough grounding in a logic correlating power and liability, rights and duties, agency and responsibility, and it recalls earlier observations by Douglass, Martin Delany, and Mark Twain that the notion of slaves committing crimes is a contradiction in terms.[30]

In the ethical and political significance of its violence, Ellison's scene recalls Frederick Douglass's fight with Covey the slave breaker. Early in his career, Douglass discovered that "what any people will quietly submit to" furnishes "the exact measure of injustice and wrong which will be imposed upon them, and these will continue till they are resisted with words or blows, or with both."[31] If oppression is underwritten by passivity and self-effacement in words and actions, as Douglass suggests, it follows that resistance may be expressed through violence as well as speech. As exemplified in Douglass's fight with Covey, violence can be an elemental statement of human agency, a way of forcing recognition of one's humanity.[32] In *My Bondage and My Freedom*, Douglass sums up the meaning of his fight as the discovery that "A man without force, is without the essential dignity of humanity. Human nature is so constituted, that it cannot *honor* a helpless man, although it can *pity* him; and even this it cannot do long, if the signs of power do not arise."[33]

"As If": how art shapes the constitution

As Ellison puts it in his essay "Perspective of Literature," by permitting slavery, the founding fathers created the "nation's drama of conscience" and made the African-American "keeper of the nation's sense of democratic achievement, and the human scale by which would be measured its painfully slow advance toward true equality" (*Collected Essays* 778). Ellison's phrase "drama of conscience" suggests the literary or imaginative nature of the

Constitution's ethical grounding. The stories we invent to portray American society both shape and are shaped by our imaginings of the Constitution as a moral document. When the constitutional system stagnates, becoming merely an expression of the majority's biases and will, writers perform an "irreplaceable" function by pushing the nation's fundamental law in the direction of justice (*Collected Essays* 773). Notwithstanding the relative dearth of lawyers and judges he finds in American fiction, Ellison contends that "the prevalence of black figures in our literature" registers the constitutional crisis at the heart of American history (*Collected Essays* 770, 778). Ellison's belief in the importance of both literature and minority experience to the nation's constitutional jurisprudence was shared by two prominent legal actors in the nation's "drama of conscience" – Senator Charles Sumner, a leading antislavery politician and architect of Reconstruction, and Chief Justice Earl Warren, the author of the Supreme Court's unanimous opinion in *Brown v. Board of Education*. In his first major address as a Senator, Sumner characterizes fugitive slaves as "the heroes of our age" whose stories "claim kindred with all that is noble" and argues that popular resistance aroused by literature "more potent than laws" would effectively nullify the infamous Fugitive Slave Law of 1850. In his address "All Men Are Created Equal," Warren quotes Emma Lazarus's famous poem, "The New Colossus," ("Give me your tired, your poor/ Your huddled masses yearning to breathe free") as illustrating the ethical core of American law, and he attributes Justice Cardozo's ability to separate the egalitarian aspirations of the Constitution from its racist implementations to his first-hand experience of discrimination as a Jewish-American.[34] All three suggest that the pursuit of justice in a democratic society requires the heterodox perspective of political minorities and that literature, in certain circumstances, offers greater insight into the ethical basis of American law than any legal precedent.

As an important part of the context for its interpretation, what Kenneth Burke calls "the Constitution behind the Constitution," literature plays a role in constitutional jurisprudence whether that role is acknowledged or not.[35] For Burke and Ellison, literature shapes the Constitution by pretending that, despite all present and past facts to the contrary, it is more than an expression of political power and bias, that its ethical values are real, and that, as Burke says in describing *Invisible Man*, it "holds out the same promise to us all." Burke and Ellison called this form of pretense the game of "as if." Burke uses this term to identify the constitutional alchemy performed by *Invisible Man*:

> In his *Critique of Practical Reason*, Kant says that, although we cannot scientifically prove the grounds of a belief in God, freedom, and immortality, we should harbor such beliefs and frame our conduct on such a basis. You did a

Kantian "as if" by acting as if the constitutional promise [of the Civil War amendments had] the markings of reality – and within feasible limits, it worked![36]

Here Burke is thinking of, among other things, the ending of Ellison's novel where the narrator wonders whether his grandfather's enigmatic advice "to keep up the good fight" and "to overcome 'em with yeses" meant "that we were to affirm the principle on which the country was built ... because he knew that the principle was greater than the men, greater than ... all the methods used to corrupt its name?" In the narrator's circumstances, affirmation is no simple task; it has to include speculation, contradiction, and acting as if certain ideals are real though they seem dreamlike, ephemeral, and unconnected to the narrator's daily existence, hoping somehow that the contrast between the real and the ideal can push society in the direction of the ideal. In his introduction to the thirtieth-anniversary edition of *Invisible Man*, Ellison echoes Burke's assessment,

> fiction is ... a mere game of 'as if,' therein lies its true function and its potential for effecting change. For at its most serious, just as is true of politics at its best, it is a thrust toward a human ideal. And it approaches that ideal by a subtle process of negating the world of things as given in favor of a complex of man-made positives. (*Collected Essays* 482)

In its conclusion, Ellison's novel affirms through pretense and speculation that the principles of democracy can and should be severed from the nation's racist history and that democracy need not boil down to oppression: "Did he mean to affirm the principle, which they themselves had dreamed into being out of the chaos and darkness of the feudal past, which they had compromised to the point of absurdity even in their own corrupt minds?" (*Invisible* 574). Dreamed into existence, these ideals, like Ellison's novel itself, offer a way of imagining a reality which remains only a possibility. Though "corrupt," this imaginative vision can, by saying "as if," bring something new into the world.

While it is difficult, if not impossible, to gauge the legal or jurisprudential impact of even an extraordinary literary work, telling signs exist that *Invisible Man* has entered the lexicon of justice, such as a lawyer's reading from it as his closing statement in a voting rights case, and a family court judge quoting it as illuminating the court's role as "intervenor between the individual struggling to be recognized as human and the vast bureaucracy which tends to dehumanize him." Perhaps most striking is Richard Kluger's use of the central trope of Ellison's novel to assess the ultimate achievement of *Brown* v. *Board of Education* in *Simple Justice*, a sweeping study of the decision and its history: "At a stroke, the Justices had severed the remaining conditions of *de facto* slavery. The Negro could no longer be fastened with the status of official pariah. No longer could the white man look right through him as if he were, in the title words of Ralph Ellison's stunning 1952 novel, *Invisible Man*."[37]

Notes

1. See, e.g., Richard Chase, "A Novel is a Novel," *The Kenyon Review*, 14 (Autumn 1952): 678–84; Irving Howe, "Black Boys and Native Sons," *Dissent* 10 (Autumn 1963): 353–68; Jerry Gafio Watts, *Heroism and the Black Intellectual: Ralph Ellison, Politics, and Afro-American Intellectual Life* (Chapel Hill: University of North Carolina Press, 1994), pp. 115, 119.
2. Valerie Smith, "The Meaning of Narration in *Invisible Man*," in *New Essays on Invisible Man*, ed. Robert O'Meally (Cambridge University Press, 1988), p. 26.
3. Ralph Ellison, "The Little Man at Chehaw Station: the American Artist and His Audience," in *The Collected Essays of Ralph Ellison*, ed. John F. Callahan (New York: Modern Library, 1995), p. 513. Subsequent references to this text are made parenthetically in the body of the essay. My approach here is synchronic, focusing on a relatively consistent perspective found in *Invisible Man* and Ellison's critical writings; a more diachronic or developmental approach might focus on Ellison's changing views of communism.
4. For an extended discussion of this jurisprudential tradition, see Gregg D. Crane, *Race, Citizenship, and Law in American Literature* (Cambridge University Press, 2002).
5. Letter, dated March 16, 1956, from Ralph Ellison to Albert Murray, in *Trading Twelves: The Selected Letters of Ralph Ellison and Albert Murray*, ed. Albert Murray and John F. Callahan (New York: Vintage, 2000), pp. 116–17.
6. Lawrence Levine, *Black Culture and Black Consciousness: Afro-American Folk Thought From Slavery to Freedom* (New York: Oxford University Press, 1977), pp. 106, 114.
7. Kenneth Burke, *A Rhetoric of Motives* (Berkeley, CA: University of California Press, 1969), p. 195; For a thorough examination of the "marginal" Emersonianism of Burke and Ellison, see Beth Eddy, *The Rites of Identity: The Religious Naturalism and Cultural Criticism of Kenneth Burke and Ralph Ellison* (Princeton University Press, 2003), and, for an astute assessment of the intersection of Burke's and Ellison's views of democracy, see Timothy L. Parrish, "Ralph Ellison, Kenneth Burke, and the Form of Democracy," *Arizona Quarterly* 52 (Autumn 1995): 117–48.
8. Ralph Ellison, *Invisible Man* (New York: Vintage, 1980), pp. 573, 576. Subsequent references to this text will be made parenthetically in the body of the essay.
9. Immanuel Kant, *Critique of Judgment* (New York: Hafner Press, 1951), pp. 135–40.
10. Kant, *Critique of Judgment*, p. 202.
11. Samuel Fleishacker, *A Third Concept of Liberty: Judgment and Freedom in Kant and Adam Smith* (Princeton University Press, 1999), pp. 7, 31, 40.

12. Ronald Dworkin, *Taking Rights Seriously* (Cambridge, MA: Harvard University Press, 1977), p. 134.

13. Ralph Waldo Emerson, "Lecture on Slavery," in *Emerson's Antislavery Writings*, ed. Len Gougeon and Joel Myerson (New Haven: Yale University Press, 1995), pp. 95, 96.

14. Ralph Waldo Emerson, *The Selected Writings of Ralph Waldo Emerson* (New York: Modern Library, 1950), pp. 288, 285; Frederick Douglass, "Our Composite Nationality," in *The Frederick Douglass Papers*, ed. John Blassingame, 5 vols. (New Haven: Yale University Press, 1982) 4:244; Douglass, "Pictures and Progress," in *The Frederick Douglass Papers*, 3:460; Emerson, "WO Liberty," in *The Journals and Miscellaneous Notebooks of Ralph Waldo Emerson*, ed. William H. Gilman et al., 16 vols. (Cambridge, MA: Harvard University Press, 1960–82) 14:421.

15. Douglass, "Our Composite Nationality," p. 256.

16. Diversity has a practical political benefit in democratic society. "[L]et man keep his many parts and you'll have no tyrant states," Ellison writes, recalling the spirit of James Madison's proposal of diversity as a bulwark against tyranny of the majority (*Invisible* 577). "Extend the sphere" of society and "take in a greater variety of parties and interests," Madison argues, and "you make it less probable that a majority of the whole will have a common motive to invade the rights of other citizens." James Madison, Alexander Hamilton, and John Jay, *The Federalist Papers* (New York: Penguin, 1987), p. 127.

17. Ivan Hannaford helpfully elucidates the difference between identity (*ethnos*) and politics (*politikos*), a distinction he traces back to Aristotle. Politics, for Aristotle, is a distinct human activity expressed in citizenship as a form of civic participation and emerging when a social order no longer depends "on the observation of hierarchical rules pertaining to the household, family, clan, and tribe." The political disposition sees "people not in terms of where they come from and what they [look]ed like but in terms of membership." Politics, in this formulation, means the consensual creation of basic standards of coexistence by and for a diverse citizenry: "The *politikos* refers to men of various origins and social standing who leave the household realms of necessity to engage in rational debate and judgment." Those outside the political sphere and excluded from the language of politics, says Hannaford, were called *ethnos*, the root of ethnic, or termed as *barbaros*, embedded in nature, confined to blood relations, and reliant on the habits and folkways of forebears. In Hannaford's account, race and other forms of identitarianism represent the antithesis of politics. Ivan Hannaford, *Race: The History of an Idea in the West* (Baltimore: The Johns Hopkins Press, 1996), pp. 8–9, 12, 21, 51.

18. Ross Posnock, *Color and Culture: Black Writers and the Making of the Modern Intellectual* (Cambridge, MA: Harvard University Press, 1998), p. 10.

19. Alain Locke, ed., *The New Negro* (New York: Atheneum, 1992), pp. 47, 200–1. For a striking account of the cosmopolitan and modernist implications of Du Bois's quotation of African-American spirituals in *The Souls of Black Folk*, see Posnock, *Color and Culture*, pp. 263–5.

20. Frederick Douglass, *My Bondage and My Freedom* (New York: Dover Publications, 1969), pp. 98, 99; Douglass, "Persecution on Account of Faith, Persecution on Account of Color," in *The Frederick Douglass Papers*, 2:291.

21. James Weldon Johnson, *Negro Americans What Now?* (New York: Viking, 1938), p. 81. While an undergraduate at Fisk University, Ellison's wife Fanny worked for Johnson as his secretary. Lawrence Jackson, *Ralph Ellison: Emergence of Genius* (New York: John Wiley, 2002), p. 298.
22. James Weldon Johnson, *The Autobiography of an Ex-Coloured Man* (New York: Hill and Wang, 1960), p. 211. Lawrence Jackson notes the importance of Johnson's novel as a precedent for *Invisible Man*. *Emergence of Genius*, p. 411. Ellison shares with James Weldon Johnson and other African-American artists and intellectuals a belief in what Johnson called "the Art approach" to improving the civil status of black Americans. "[N]othing will go farther to raise the status of the Negro in America," Johnson writes, "than work done by great Aframerican creative artists." "American Negro Poets and Poetry, Address Delivered at Howard University, April 10, 1924," Beinecke Library, Yale University, p. 2. The art approach works, in Johnson's view, because he, like Ellison, connects recognition with agreement or exchange. Artistic and cultural achievement forces recognition at the same time that it indebts others. It forces others to recognize the "Negro as a creator as well as a creature . . . a giver as well as a receiver." Letter, dated March 6, 1927, from James Weldon Johnson to Carl Van Vechten, Beinecke Library, Yale University. The artistic and cultural "gifts of the Negro to America," in Johnson's view, "entitle him to opportunity for full development." James Weldon Johnson, "Address at Fisk University Dinner, Chicago, April 5, 1938," Beinecke Library, Yale University, p. 21.
23. William James, *Pragmatism* (New York: World Publishing, 1969), p. 158.
24. Oliver Wendell Holmes, Jr., "The Path of the Law," *Harvard Law Review* 10 (1897): 465–6. John Dewey interpreted this passage of Holmes's essay as arguing for a more "experimental and flexible logic" of "search and discovery" that would address the "flux of events" more helpfully than the "logic of rigid demonstration," which seeks a "specious" certainty in the artificial "fixity of concepts" (Dewey, "Logical Method and Law," *Cornell Law Quarterly* 10 (1924): 20, 22.
25. Benjamin Cardozo, *The Nature of the Judicial Process* (New Haven: Yale University Press, 1921), pp. 13, 28; Learned Hand, "Sources of Tolerance," *University of Pennsylvania Law Review* 79 (1930): 13.
26. Kenneth Burke, *A Grammar of Motives* (Berkeley, CA: University of California Press, 1969), pp. 366, 386; Emerson, "WO Liberty," pp. 420–1.
27. Emerson, "Circles," *The Selected Writings*, pp. 288–9.
28. John Dewey, "Freedom and Culture" (1939), in *The Later Works, 1923–53*, ed. JoAnn Boydston (Carbondale: Southern Illinois University Press, 1986) 13: 174.
29. Antonio Gramsci, *Selections from the Prison Notebooks of Antonio Gramsci* (New York: International Publishers, 1971), pp. 404, 268; *Lochner* v. *New York*, 198 US 45 (1905); Louis Althusser, "Ideology and Ideological State Apparatuses (Notes Towards an Investigation)," in *Lenin and Philosophy and Other Essays* (New York: Monthly Review Press, 1971), pp. 156–7, 167–8; Sacvan Bercovitch, *The Rites of Assent: Transformations in the Symbolic Construction of America* (New York: Routledge, 1993), pp. 45–50.
30. The best known formulation of the law's emphasis on agency and rights as the necessary correlative for the imposition of legal duties and obligations is Wesley Hohfeld's essay, "Some Fundamental Legal Conceptions as Applied in Judicial Reasoning," *Yale Law Journal* 23 (1917): 16. In *Puddn'head Wilson*, Mark

Twain characterizes the petty theft of slaves as the just rejoinder to the larger theft of slavery. *Pudd'nhead Wilson* (New York: Penguin, 1969), pp. 67–8. And Martin Delany similarly contends that the usual terms of criminal responsibility do not apply within the inverted moral world of slavery where the greater theft of total domination frames all slave behavior. *Blake: or The Huts of America* (Boston: Beacon Press, 1970), p. 31. In *My Bondage and My Freedom*, Douglass recalls that being "deprived of the necessaries of life" by the slaveholder, "necessaries supplied by my own labor – it was easy to deduce the right to supply myself with what was my own." Employing the logic of exchange and contract, Douglass turns the vocabulary of crime on its head: "the morality of *free* society can have no application to *slave* society. Slave holders have made it almost impossible for the slave to commit any crime, known under the laws of God or to the laws of man. If he steals, he takes his own; if he kills his master, he imitates only the heroes of the revolution ... Freedom of choice is the essence of all accountability." *My Bondage and My Freedom*, pp. 189, 190–1.

31. Frederick Douglass, "The Do-Nothing Policy," in *Life and Writings of Frederick Douglass*, ed. Philip S. Foner, 5 vols. (New York: International Publishers, 1950–75) 2:403.

32. Henry Louis Gates, Jr. shows how Douglass's strategy of reversal tends to break down the binary oppositions of master/slave, spiritual/material, aristocratic/base, human/beast. *Figures in Black: Words, Signs, and the "Racial" Self* (New York: Oxford University Press, 1987), pp. 92–3. I would add words/blows to this list.

33. Douglass, *My Bondage and My Freedom*, pp. 241, 242, 246–7.

34. Charles Sumner, "Freedom National, Slavery Sectional," in *The Works of Charles Sumner*, 15 vols. (Boston: Lee and Shepard, 1872) 3:184. Earl Warren, *"All Men Are Created Equal"* (Association of the Bar of the City of New York, 1970), pp. 13, 11.

35. Burke, *Grammar of Motives*, p. 341.

36. Burke, "Ralph Ellison's Trueblooded Bildungsroman" in *Speaking for You: The Vision of Ralph Ellison*, ed. Kimberly Benston (Washington, DC: Howard University Press, 1987), pp. 353, 355.

37. *Griffin* v. *Burns*, 431 F.Supp. 1361, 1363 (DRI 1977); *In The Matter of Carlos P.*, 78 Misc. 2d 851, 851, 358 NYS 2d 608, 609 (1974); Richard Kluger, *Simple Justice* (New York: Vintage, 1977), p. 749.

6

ANNE ANLIN CHENG

Ralph Ellison and the politics of melancholia

In the Prologue to Ralph Ellison's *Invisible Man*, the narrator explicates the novel's central metaphor by telling us that he is invisible because "[white] people refuse to see [him]."[1] The narrator proceeds to illustrate this assertion with a story about a violent confrontation that took place between himself and a white man:

> One night I accidentally bumped into a man . . . he looked insolently out of his blue eyes and cursed me . . . I yelled, "Apologize! Apologize!" But he continued to curse and struggle, and I butted him again and again until he went down heavily . . . I kicked him profusely . . . when it occurred to me that the man had not *seen* me, actually; that he, as far as he knew, was walking in midst of a walking nightmare . . . a man almost killed by a phantom. (4)

This passage offers a striking yet enigmatic vision of the nature of racial blindness. Seemingly explicit, the description nonetheless opens up layers of complicated questions about the differences between perception and projection, between action and reaction, in a racial encounter. From the narrator's perspective, we see the white man's "insolence" as anger from having to confront what he presumably did not want to see. The white man's curse, upon being bumped, expresses a wish to deny the black man who is no longer "invisible" and who is now actively demanding his right of way. The white man's resistance to this presence reminds us that "black invisibility" grows out of dominant culture's privilege to see or to not see, a privilege substantiated by a history of longstanding material, legal, and social discrimination. The metaphor of invisibility thus alerts us to the repercussions of this long process of social and legal exclusion.

At the same time, when we attend to Ellison's description more fully, we have to ask: is the white man the only one suffering from blindness in this scene? The writing is ambiguous. Who is the invisible one? If the narrator bumps into the white man, is not the white man the one who is invisible to the black man? The narrator bumps into what *he* did not see and then accuses the other of blindness. If we do not take the narrator's account at its surface value, it is conceivable that the white man cursed the black man for his clumsiness rather than for racist reasons, that masculine rather than racial privilege may be at stake, and that the narrator's detection of the white man's insolence may itself be a projection growing out of the former's own self-denigration and wounded pride in the face of "blue eyes," a historically incendiary sign for whiteness.

This ambiguous scenario highlights the fraught consequences of the history of racism for both dominant and minority cultures. The point here is not to discount the invisible man's interpretation of the event, nor to dismiss the possibility of racism at work. The issue is, more crucially, the realization that because of the historic relation between whites and blacks in this country the possibility of a rac*ist* response haunts every potentially rac*ial* encounter. A pre-written script compels, if not dictates, this confrontation. In this loaded exchange, mutual invisibility as the result of mutual projection seems unavoidable. Indeed, the incident becomes a racial one, not because a black man and a white man are involved per se, but because of the over-determined history between them.

The insight that invisibility rarely presents a one-sided projection poses a challenging notion for a liberal politics dedicated to social progress and the amelioration of racism and racist effects. For Ellison's careful composition of the encounter above suggests that one of the most insidious effects of discrimination may be that it perpetuates itself, even on the part of the discriminated. "Racial injury" thus alludes to a fraught nexus of implications that revolve around psychical as well as material effects. More than fifty years after the publication of *Invisible Man*, the issue of racial injury and its effects continue to present a central problem for civil progress. On the one hand, progressive politics criticize the perspective that racism has wreaked psychical damage on racial minorities for its potential to re-victimize these individuals. (That is, it can be damaging to say how damaging racism has been.) On the one hand, there is wide agreement that the discourse of racial injury has played a key role in promoting civil rights reform during the past half century. The task of acknowledging the grief of racial injury without denying or sentimentalizing its legacy presents a central challenge for contemporary politics. Recent debates over the polemics of reparation, for instance, highlight the complexities haunting the issue of racial damage and compensation. While institutional recognition of historic wrongs (in the forms of monetary and/or symbolic acknowledgments) are important, it also raises a host of ethical and pragmatic questions: does material compensation absolve ethical responsibility? How much compensation is enough? How, indeed, does one *quantify* injury? With its bold explorations of the double binds that structure the effects of racism on the discriminated, *Invisible Man* remains remarkably germane at the beginning of the twenty-first century as we continue to scrutinize the meanings of multiculturalism and pluralism.

Underneath the narrator's angry grievance (that he has been made invisible) runs a narrative about grief: how does one mourn or get over profound social and personal losses (in the narrator's case, to the point of becoming invisible, nameless, and homeless) in the face of discrimination? What are the psychological as well as material impacts of discrimination, and what constitutes a "proper" response in the face of such damage? *Invisible Man* asks, what can political agency or action mean for someone operating in a symbolic, cultural economy that has already preassigned them as non-presence?

The rhetoric of progress or cure can unwittingly overlook the repercussions, both historical and personal, of this ongoing history. An over eager attachment to progress, anticipating a color-blind society, tends to disregard how racialization continues to operate in contemporary life: how is a racial identity socially secured, and how does it generate its seductions and limitations for both the dominant and the marginalized? When it comes to the future of the race question, to borrow Faulkner's words, the past is not dead; it is not even past. Rather than prescribing how we as a nation might go about "getting over" that history of profound discrimination, it is useful to ask what it means, for social, political, and subjective beings *to grieve*.

To help us think through these questions, let us take a detour through the writings of Sigmund Freud, who in his essay "Mourning and Melancholia" (1917) offers one of the most evocative treatises on the nature of grief. In this study Freud suggests that there are two different kinds of responses to grief: mourning and melancholia. According to him, the former is healthy because it is finite in character and accepts substitution (that is, in the healthy work of mourning, the lost object can be relinquished and is eventually replaced). In mourning, Freud tells us, "we rest assured that after a lapse of time, [the grief/loss] will be overcome."[2] Melancholia, on the other hand, is pathological; it is interminable in nature and refuses substitution (that is, the melancholic cannot "get over" loss.) The melancholic is, one might say, psychically stuck.

Several aspects of Freud's work on melancholia are intriguing in light of our exploration of the phenomenon of racial injury. First, stepping outside of his usual preoccupation with sexuality, Freud in this study is interested in losses that an individual suffers that are not necessarily erotic in nature. When Freud speaks about the "lost object" in this essay, he refers to more than a loved person to include abstract ideas such as "fatherland, liberty, ideal, and so forth" (164). (Coincidentally, it is precisely the loss of a social "ideal" and its effect on one's "liberty" that we will soon be examining in what follows, but for now I wish to note simply that the kinds of profound losses that Freud alludes to may be ideological in nature.) Second, he suggests that the melancholic individual, in failing to mourn and give up the lost object, ends up incorporating (almost like psychically eating) the ghost of the lost object, creating a crypt within the self and identifying with it – what Freud describes as a psychological form of cannibalism. This means that the lost person or thing is now both dead and yet kept alive in a suspended way, making this lost person/idea a spectral presence. And since the melancholic holds all kinds of ambivalent feelings toward the lost object – including both desire and resentment – by taking in and identifying with the object, Freud tells us, the melancholic has taken in also all the ambivalent feelings he/she has for that object. If we were to follow the logic of incorporation (that the thing taken in is now the ego), then we would also have to see that all those ambivalent feelings for the object must now be directed against the self. The melancholic is thus never truly an individual per se, but the effect of an interaction, even if purely psychically, with an Other. In this sense, the melancholic is not melancholic because he/she has lost something but because he/she has psychically incorporated that which he/she all at once denigrates, longs for, and is now part of. So in the paradoxical dynamics of melancholia, loss gets denied and yet maintained, resulting in an internal identification that is both self-sustaining and self-deploring. Melancholia in Freud's account therefore refers not to a mood in the vernacular sense of being "moody" but to an intricate, ambivalent psychological structure developed in the face of loss. As a mode of identity formation, melancholia highlights the *inter*subjective basis of *intra*subjectivity.

We might say that Ellison's scene of confrontation between the black and white men dramatizes what might be called *racial melancholia* on the part of both characters. For the white man, the encounter means that he ran into a ghost of his own making – a ghost, furthermore, whose ghostliness has historically guaranteed his social privilege and integrity. Part of the central dilemma of white power in this country is that its authority is constituted, sustained, and made productive by the very other that it excludes. Racist discrimination is rarely about completely "losing" the racial other; it is often about keeping the other in some controlled, excluded space. The economics of racism that sustained American slavery and colonialism, for example, have often meant that racism is not so much about annihilating the other as about keeping the other in its proper place. This means that there are a host of lost citizens (phantoms) in the heart of American nationalism. White racial melancholia thus refers to the institutional process of producing a dominant, standard, white national ideal, which is sustained by the exclusion-yet-retention of racialized others. The white man in the Ellison account, consequently, can be said to have "bumped" into his own racial melancholia.

If one of the ideals that sustained the American nation since its beginning has been its unique proposition that "all men are created equal," then one of America's ongoing national mortifications must be its history of acting otherwise. As Michael Rogin reminds us, "racial exclusions, be it chattel slavery, the expropriation of Indian and Mexicans, or the repressive use and exclusion of Chinese and Mexican American labor, were the conditions of American freedom rather than exceptions to it."[3] It is at those moments when America is most shamefaced and traumatized by its betrayal of its own democratic ideology (the genocide of Native Americans, slavery, segregation, immigration discrimination) that it most virulently – and *melancholically* – espouses human value and brotherhood. As Eric Lott demonstrates in his studies of blackface minstrelsy, dominant white culture's relation to the raced other displays an entangled, and I would call melancholic, network of repulsion and sympathy, fear and desire, repudiation and identification.[4] White American identity and its authority are secured through the melancholic introjection of racial others that it can neither fully relinquish nor accommodate and whose ghostly presence nonetheless guarantees its centrality. It is precisely the slippery space between loss (what does not seem to be there) and exclusion (what *must not* be there) that racist myopia effects.

But if the white man in Ellison's Prologue represents white racial melancholia, what about the invisible man? Let us return to the latter's intense reaction to being bumped on the street. In a response at once macho and hysterical, the narrator reveals that he is trapped not only by having been seen as invisible but also by *suspecting himself to be so*. His perception is subject to a script that he is unable – and indeed cannot afford – to ignore. To overlook the racist potential in the scene is to be blind to history, but to assume that potential is to be enslaved by that history. If the white man is caught in a melancholic bind of denying that which fortifies his authority and integrity, then the black man is caught in a *double* melancholic bind: he is *both* a melancholic object and a melancholic subject, the one lost and the one losing, the one excluded and the one performing the exclusion. This internalization of the dominant ideal and its accompanying denigration dramatize racial melancholia for the raced subject: the taking in of a rejecting other, creating a negative self-perception that one must continually negotiate in some form or the other, whether it is to be complied with or resisted. Only in the light of this double melancholia can we understand how the narrator's racial radar may be simultaneously paranoid and perspicacious.

One of the insights afforded by the concept of racial melancholia is that the notion of the "individual" is really illusory, especially when it comes to racial identification. That is, as Ellison demonstrated in the anecdote above, when it comes to racial negotiation, every *intra*subjective process is potentially an intersubjective exchange. The "personal" or the "individual" is always potentially colored by historical relations and contingencies. The dynamics of racial melancholia thus highlights the inherent theatricality and plurality of racial claims. Ellison has written eloquently elsewhere on the fraught relationship between the American democratic ideal of individualism and liberty and its contradictory racial history. In *Shadow and Act*, he suggests: "When American life is most American it is apt to be most theatrical."[5] Alluding to the Boston Tea Party (1773) and how the colonials donned "Indian" masks in their act of insurrection as an originary moment in American founding, Ellison points out that the tradition of masking – here the adopting of racial masks to veil and authenticate a new national project – has played a persistent role in the process of Americanization. Quoting Yeats, Ellison proposes a connection between theatricality and discipline:

> 'There is a relation between discipline and the theatrical sense. If we cannot imagine ourselves as different from what we are and assume the second self, we cannot impose a discipline upon ourselves ... Active virtue, as distinct from the passive acceptance of a current code, is the wearing of a mask. It is the condition of an arduous full life.' (53–4)

According to Ellison, Yeats' insight into the intimacy between self-discipline and theatricality has much to say about the *making* of Americans. In light of the subsequent treatment of Native Americans, this spectacle of identification is more than ironic, of course, but it is also highly significant that the origin of American authenticity turns on a theatrical gesture. In addition to availing themselves of a nativist claim, the colonials were also enabled to "act out," so to speak, by borrowing the supposedly "savage" faces of the other. This speaking-through-the-other in the making of self-discipline through theatricality is deeply resonant with the melancholic dynamic that we have been discussing. If, according to Freud, melancholia is the dramatic (and, at times, manic) acting out of the-other-within whom we both desire and decry, then Ellison directs us to see the Boston Tea Party as an enactment of the racial melancholia in the heart of Americanization. The performances of blackface and yellowface more than a century after the Boston Tea Party tells us that the "arduous" task of making "real" Americans continues to rely on acts of taking on the face of the denigrated yet desired racial other: a (melancholic) drama of identification and dis-identification.

Invisible Man reminds us that, well after the phenomenon of minstrelsy, versions of such masking continue. Even more disturbingly, such masking may be assumed by the racial others themselves. Dr. Bledsoe, who thinks he has to "act the nigger" (142) in order to realize his career and self-potential, offers one such example. (This problem has not disappeared from contemporary life. Spike Lee's recent film *Bamboozled* highlights the persistence of this disturbing phenomenon). The question of what it means when objects of discrimination assume stereotypical images of themselves remains a complicated one, one that continually haunts Ellison's writings. White dominant ideology (dependent on the denigrated racial other in order to fortify its own integrity) and the racial minority (bound by the very ideals he/she resents) form an affectively powerful and politically vexing reflexive dynamic. Throughout *Invisible Man*, we are given a series of these painful reflexive dramas. There is Mr. Norton, the supposedly progressive white supporter of black education, who cloaks his blindness to black particularity in a rhetoric of progress and philanthropy. Norton claims that he sees his destiny in the future of the black students, but he hardly sees the young black man driving him. "Racial progress" serves as a guise for what Norton calls his "first-hand organization of human life" (42). His generosity towards the young black men in the college eerily echoes the ideology of paternalistic mastery in slave discourse. Norton's focus on black education also turns out to involve a perverse desire. Informing the invisible man that the "state college for Negroes" is really a memorial to his dead daughter, Norton describes her in obsessive terms: "'[My daughter] was a being more rare . . . , purer, . . . than the wildest dream of a poet. I could never believe her to be my own flesh and blood. Her beauty was a well-spring of purest water-of-life . . . a work of purest art . . . I found it difficult to believe her my own . . . She was too pure for life, too pure'" (42–3). The repetition of the word "pure" is highly charged, revealing Norton's preoccupation with his daughter. It also recalls the historic discourse of white racial purity tied in to the fear of miscegenation, its concomitant idealization of white womanhood, and the fear of black sexuality as a threat against that sanctity.

Mr. Norton's vision of black progress turns out to be a monument to regressive, sepulchral whiteness. That Mr. Norton's daughter and her promise of "white purity" represents not only an incestuous but also a racialized desire on his part exposes the extremity that the ideal of racial purity can become. After all, is not incest the perversely logical conclusion of the pursuit of racial purity? It is therefore hardly a coincidence that Mr. Norton's story runs into Trueblood's story, the two fathers being foils for one another. But where the white man's incestuous desires remain on an unspoken, fantastic, and hence supposedly civilized level, the black man commits the sin "for real," so to speak, making him a primitive enactment of what Norton can only fantasize. This view is what drives Norton to exclaim with "envy and indignation": "'You did and are unharmed!'"(51).

Trueblood's seemingly barbaric story, however, turns out to be itself a painful reflection of the historic conditions produced by white civil society. For Norton's fantasy of black animality as a veil for entertaining his own dark desires is encapsulated within Trueblood's dream, which is all about the fantasies and projected fears of/indictment against black male sexuality. We remember that on the night of the transgression when Trueblood violated his own daughter, he was having a dream. In fact, it was during the dream that the incest happens, irrevocably entwining the dream and the act. Trueblood tells Mr. Norton about his dream:

> Everything in the room was white and I'm standin' there knowin' I got no business in there . . . It's a woman's room too . . . I tried to git out, but I don't find the door . . . Then I . . . sees one of them tall grandfather clocks and I hears it strikin' and . . . a white lady is steppin' out of it . . . .Then she starts to screamin' . . . she runs up and grabs me . . . tryin' to keep me out of the clock. (58)

In the dream, Trueblood finds himself in one of the worst situations that a black man can get into historically: to be caught with a white woman. His presence alone is enough to compromise, even condemn, him. The dream offers a barely veiled parable about the prohibition against black male sexuality, evoking the history of white anxiety over miscegenation that has informed much of the affective core of white racism, as well as the very real history of lynching and violence that accompanied that anxiety.

We should remember that Trueblood has told (we may even say performed) this story many times for the white audience, including now Mr. Norton. Even as the dream satisfies the white audience's prurience, it exposes the devastation of African-American family life effected by slavery and its legacies. The sexual images in Trueblood's dream are clear enough, but Ellison's writing reminds us that we cannot separate the sexual content from its historic, racial context. The claustrophobic atmosphere in the dream echoes the claustrophobic conditions of Trueblood's impoverished family where a family of three adults had to sleep in one bed. If we understand the grandfather clock in the dream as symbolizing patriarchal, civilized time/history and the white woman as the supposed guardian of that history (and as such, a threat to, even as she threatens, the black man), then we would see this dream as acting out Trueblood's traumatic encounter with time and history. His forced entry into that time and history (the moment that he breaks through the door of the grandfather clock in dream time and the moment that he violates his daughter in real time) propels him into yet another nightmare. "Black masculine savagery" stands on both sides of the clock, an inescapable trap – the trap, once again, of racial projection. Trueblood's transgression reflects the savagery embedded in white racial history itself and critiques by mirroring – by literally naming (true blood) – the horrific consequences of racial purity.

Just as Trueblood and his family are literally kept at the margins of the white community for the latter's gratification and denigration, so are other minority subjects in this novel, literally, often served up for consumption. This lack of privacy and individuation is symptomatic of a society embroiled in racial melancholia, where there is no gaze that is not already a mirror of another's gaze. Consequently, in this novel, individualism shows itself to be at best an untenable ideal and at worst a deceptive form of coercion. The narrator, too, finds himself served up for entertainment at the very moment when he believes he has won hard-earned social recognition. Consider, for another example, his high school graduation. Instead of addressing an audience in his carefully prepared speech, the narrator finds himself the object of humiliation arranged for the enjoyment of the white audience. The blonde dancer placed amid the Battle Royal allows the white audience to witness the "bestial" nature of the black boys. The description of the woman offers a curious mixture of inanimation and bestiality:

> The hair was yellow like that of a circus kewpie doll, the face heavily powdered and rouged, as though to form an abstract mask, the eyes hollow and smeared a cool blue, the color of a baboon's butt. (19)

The dancer's face and body mirror the animalistic qualities that the white patrons have attributed to the black young men. At the same time, her presence mediates the white patrons' visual attention to the half-naked black bodies. The blonde dancer and the black young men thus occupy similarly debased positions in the scopic regime of white male visual desire. Misogyny, repressed homoeroticism, and racism converge.

This conscription of the black male body for white visual pleasure-and-denigration exercises an even more insidious psychical violation, for it is not just black bodies that are put on display but also what is imagined to be black psychology. More than the young men's stripped-down bodies, the battle royal exposes their sexual appetites. When the narrator, along with the other young men, reacts to the dancer with desire and hatred, wanting "to caress and destroy her, to love and murder her" (19), he is but performing the inseparability of desire, shame, and rage that he, according to white fantasy, is *supposed to* feel as a black man gazing at a white woman. The blonde's display highlights the spectacle of the boys' arousal and shame, which in turn reflect and veil the arousal of the white audience. The *mise en scène* is designed to exhibit black murderous desire. The invisible man is thus caught in a setup where his personal response is always already a historical response.

Is there any escaping this trap of history? In other words, what might be a basis for political change if individualism is always inevitably compromised? Given the possibility repeatedly demonstrated by this novel that every individual speech or act may be but an act of ventriloquy or disguise, Ellison's novel proceeds to explore how this problem might be transformed. More than delineating the symptoms, Ellison's writing offers a sustained meditation on the question of *strategy* in the face of this challenge. That is, the novel repeatedly investigates the challenge of "how to master the master's tongue": How can one speak effectively even as one has but the words of the other? In short, we might say that Ellison works toward developing a melancholic strategy for the melancholic condition. Throughout the novel, there is a persistent exploration of different versions of assimilation, accommodation, and internalization. Metaphors of mirroring, swallowing, and even gagging abound in *Invisible Man*. These images of "taking in" appear in many guises: the yes'em-to-death of the grandfather, the mad internalized cynicism of the vet, the inbred narcissism of Trueblood, and later the incorporating politics of the Brotherhood. Each incident bespeaks a mutual counter-incorporation, whereby the white man and the black man mime each other, both trying to approximate their identity through the projected image of the other. The Brotherhood, for example, offers an inverse version of the white progressive politics represented by Mr. Norton: both exercise the rhetoric of progress that hides the opposite.

Ellison is not an accommodationist, as is evidenced by his satirization of Booker T. Washington throughout the novel, but neither is he a separatist. This, after all, is a writer whose protagonist notices that it takes a drop of black paint to produce true whiteness, yet another symbol for the melancholic imbrication between blackness and whiteness. Rather than denying racial melancholia and its binds, Ellison works to transform the symptom into a strategy by experimenting with a range of figures who negotiate the binds of incorporation/invisibility in different ways, with both successes and limitations. One such figure is Todd Clifton. The one character who manages to "fall outside history," Clifton does so by acting out, rather than denying, that history. After recognizing that he has been duped by the Brotherhood, Clifton takes to the streets of New York performing with the Sambo doll. Rather than reading his action as a concession to stereotype, I suggest that he is dramatizing and exposing the role that had been assigned to him. In taking up the Sambo doll, by becoming all too visible, he is melancholically acting out what the Brotherhood has made him. The idea of a healthy progressive history, in which events can be successfully mourned and left behind, echoes far too closely the kind of blind, corrective, historical logic that undersigns projects like the Founder's dream ("the history of the race a saga of mounting triumphs"[134]) or the Brotherhood's idea of progressive history. Clifton's parodic strategy, however, has its limitations. He critiques history but at the price of being outside of it altogether.

Another character who offers an alternative strategy in the face of invisibility is the spectral figure of Rinehart. Perhaps the real invisible man in the text, Rinehart never appears – except as pure appearance: Rinehart the runner, Rine the gambler, Rine the briber, Rine the lover, pimp, and reverend. He stands as the figure of a figure. He represents form without substance, yet his substancelessness provides him with pure potential. The narrator muses:

> Could [Rinehart] himself be both rind and heart? What is real anyway? ... His world was possibility and he knew it. He was years ahead of me and I was a fool ... It was unbelievable, but perhaps only the unbelievable could be believed. Perhaps the truth was always a lie.   (498)

To try to locate Rinehart's "true" identity would be to miss the lesson of Rinehart: who you are depends on whom you are talking to, which community you are in, and who is watching your performance – what we may call the politics of representation and performance. Embodying dissimulative potentials, glaringly visible in his invisibility, Rinehart operates and structures a network of connections in Harlem from religion to prostitution to the law. He is at once the ultimate outsider and insider, making visible the contingency of division and perverting the lines of power – or at least, exposing power as *positionality*. As a parable for plurality, as a continually re-signifiable sign, Rinehart undermines the ideal of implacable individuality.

Indeed, this figure of re-signable *tabula rasa* subverts the integrity of racial categories. Rinehart is all too easily recognizable as "Rinehart" in his glasses, his hat, and even shoes. As a type ("poppa-stopper," "daddy-o," the "stylin'" one), Rinehart seems more stylized than racialized. He personifies the idea that racial*ization* is always a matter of style, rather than essence – a performance of type that can either be stereotyping or employed by the Other as self-identification. As the narrator says, "I was recognized [as Rinehart] not by features, but by clothes, by uniform, by gait"(485). It is no coincidence that the narrator does not run into Rinehart but *becomes* Rinehart, dramatizing the (con)fusion of identities that racial melancholia delineates – except here, the narrator is turning the condition of melancholia into a kind of strategy. The narrator's disguise (the dark glasses which throws him into a sequence of "dreamy, distorted" events) literally calls forth Rinehart. Rinehart as an event of visual performance demonstrates: first, that to identify with or as someone is not far from gestures of representation, suggesting that the performance of authenticity may be precisely that, a performance; second, that any act of identification tends to involve simultaneously an act of dis-identification. This means that the faith we tend to place in "identity" as an inviolable essence has to be questioned.

At the same time, this is not a postmodern scenario where we are allowed to imagine that there is sheer freedom in the lack of essence, that "we can be anything we want to be." By assuming Rinehart's subject position, the narra-tor wins some freedom, but he also has to ask himself repeatedly, "who actually was who?" There is a *cost* in every identificatory staging. "It" is not just a costume. To impersonate Rinehart is to personify Rinehart. The narrator finds himself not only acting like Rinehart, but *acting* Rinehart. The narrator tells us, "Something was working on me, and profoundly" (486). This lesson that what seems like a mere masquerade may have penetrating effects on the one doing the masking can have productive as well as inhibiting implications. By dissimulating the dissimulator, the narrator perceives for the first time the originating potentials of *enacting identification* rather than a stable identity: " ... being mistaken for him ... my entire body started to itch, as though I had just been removed from a plaster cast and was unused to the new freedom of movement ... you could actually make yourself anew" (498–9). It is crucial, however, to note the limitations of this self-revision. The liberation that the narrator experiences through his impersonation of Rinehart, although seem-ingly brimming with possibilities, can also be provisional, if not downright destructive.

By impersonating Rinehart, the narrator arrives not at an identity, but at the fantasm that is the mode of identification, suggesting the mechanisms of racial identifications are equally fantasmatic by nature. To follow Rinehartism is to plunge into the very heart of racial melancholia:

> So I'd accept it, I'd explore it, rine and heart. I'd plunge into it with both feet and they'd gag. Oh, but wouldn't they gag .... Yes, and I'd let them swoller me until they vomited or burst wide open. Let them gag on what they refuse to see. (508)

The metaphor of gagging instantiates the melancholic condition of race in America: *we gag on what we refuse to see.* American culture is continually confronted by a ghost (the ghost of race) that it can neither emit nor swallow. Rinehart, the "Spiritual Technologist" who preaches "Behold the Invisible" (495), recommends a remedy for that social malady by insisting on the awareness that invisibility serves as the precondition for visibility. His play with in/visibility reminds us that the racialization and phantomization of African-Americans exist *to condition* "American" presence. His very characterization emblematizes the insight that the act of delineating absence *preconditions* presence.

Rinehartism as a strategy of omnipresent-nondescription provides the foundation for the narrator in developing a strategic response to the (pre)-condition of racial melancholia. The narrator comes to recognize that description itself – the delineation of presence and absence – may prove to be the symptom and the critique of invisibility. Beyond the standard reading of invisibility as a metaphor for exclusion (that the black man is invisible because white society refuses to see him), the narrator offers us invisibility as a strategy of critique: a metaphysical, intellectual meditation about invisibility as it comes to be associated with abstraction, the power of disembodiment and illusion. The narrator's invisibility is not only an effect of, but also affects social reality. He gives us the vocabulary with which to conceptualize reflexivity in a critical way:

> I am invisible .... Like the bodiless heads you see sometimes in circus side-shows, it is as though I have been surrounded by mirrors of hard, distorting glass. When they approach me they see only my surroundings, themselves, or figments of their imagination ... (3)

Within that mirroring structure, who distorts whom? As much as racial blindness renders the narrator invisible, surely his invisibility reflects emptiness back on those gazers as well. If he has been assimilated only through his invisibility, then he also dissimulates – renders dis-similar – the status of *their* visibility. Here we have the potential for a kind of subversive assimilation. The fantasm of the narrator's invisibility imitates the fantasm that *is* mainstream society. While blackness has traditionally been seen as all too visible, whiteness also in a way operates through invisibility. Critic Richard Dyer explains:

> Trying to think about the representation of whiteness as an ethnic category ... is difficult, partly because white power secures its dominance by seeming not to be anything in particular .... This property of whiteness, to be everything and nothing, is the source of its representational power.[6]

The narrator in the Epilogue assumes this representational power for himself through camouflage. He hides under the city, so *in* its innards, that he becomes undetectable: the city's "Monopolated Light & Power" company observes a source draining their energy but whose origin they cannot determine. The narrator as that source is at once everywhere and nowhere.

Invisible Man finally hints that the first solution to racial melancholia is not to recover a presence that never was, but to recognize the disembodiment that *is* both the master and the slave. Disembodiment, metaphorized by Rinehart, becomes literalized in the narrator's own epiphanic hallucination, the scene of castration. In that state of neither dreaming nor waking, he confronts the groups that he has encountered and their particular brands of incorporative histories and ideologies:

> I lay the prisoner of a group consisting of Jack and Emerson and Bledsoe and Norton and Ras and the school superintendent . . . . they were demanding that I return to them and were annoyed with my refusal.
>
> "No," I said. "I am through with all your illusions and lies . . . "
>
> But now they came forward with a knife . . . and I felt the bright red pain and they took the two bloody blobs and cast them over the bridge, and out of my anguish I saw them curve up and catch beneath the apex of the curving arch of the bridge, to hang there, dripping down through the sunlight into the dark red water.
>
> "Now you're free of illusions," Jack said, pointing to my seed wasting upon the air. "How does it feel to be free of one's illusions?"
>
> And now I answered, "Painful and empty . . . But look . . . there's your universe, and that drip-drop upon the water you hear is all the history you've made, all you're going to make" (569–70)

This agonizing hallucination returns us to a question we asked above: How do we imagine agency in a situation where agency has been denied? Here the narrator envisions liberty in a world where liberty has been severed. Not surprisingly, this vision of liberty is fraught, difficult, and costly: "painful and empty." This scene speculates that freedom comes not from historical or social liberation, but specifically from identificatory renouncement ("to be free of illusions"). Because the vocabulary of freedom itself can be deployed by the rhetoric of enslavement (as illustrated by the rhetorics of the Brotherhood), freedom in the light of this wisdom must paradoxically and crucially mean the freedom from ideologies of authenticity and selfhood.

Like the white man in the Prologue whose reality can only be shaped by his nightmare, the narrator's own perceptions have for most of the duration of the novel (that is, the narrative between the Prologue and the Epilogue) been shaped by the ideologies that have consumed and defined him. Throughout the body of the narrative, he had been searching for visibility, individualism, as well as communal identification – all of which turn out to be illusory, producing what he calls "soul-sickness"(575). The closet approximation to "individualism" comes from the state of disappearance, of pain and emptiness – a shattered rather than integral individual. In that scene of castration and relinquishment, invisibility has been theorized as a condition of disembodiment and abstraction, as an escape from "illusions."

Ellison thus locates identity, not in uncompromising individualism, but in painful interpersonal negotiations. Consequently, the narrator's dismemberment – his scattered, castrated ego – becomes the resistance against group consolidations. This vision is quite radical. It relocates political agency, not in an individualism that is inevitably compromised, but in the consciousness of the mutual complicity of racial identities, black and white. By trying to recruit the narrator as a mirror image of themselves, by castrating him to do so, the various social organizations incorporate the very loss that they instigate. If history enacts denigration, then history will be structured by that brutalization. This scene demonstrates that "to be free of illusions and lies" is viscerally brutalizing and produces loss, but the scene also theorizes the possibility that *that* place of violent intra-subjectivity might also be the very place where freedom lies.

In light of Ellison's critique of uncomplicated individualism, it is not surprising that the resolution of *Invisible Man* remains far from certain. What is the "socially responsible role" that the protagonist will play by the end of the novel? He informs us: "So it is now I denounce and defend ... I condemn and affirm, say no and say yes, say yes and say no .... So I approach it through division" (580). The politics of this novel lie, not in prescription, but in the critique of description: how society describes and inscribes personhood. Since inclusion and community are ideas that invariably embody their inverse – exclusion and isolation – *Invisible Man* remains wary of the very group ideologies which create and isolate African-American communities in the first place. As the enclave that protects but also marginalizes, Harlem is not free from that "soul-sickness." The narrator tells us that he had been "as invisible to Mary" (the nurturing 'mother' in the heart of Harlem) "as [he] had been to the Brotherhood" (571). The discourse of identity can paradoxically foster division and dis-identification (I am this; therefore I am not that). The Brotherhood provides a quintessential example of such group ideology: its membership requires the forsaking of other identities, even as its recruitment works through the borrowed rhetoric of communal ideals: black brotherhood. When the narrator asks of Clifton's death, "Why did he choose to plunge into nothingness, into the void of faceless faces, of soundless voices, laying outside history" (441), he anticipates his own falling underground, significantly on the edge *between* the margin of Harlem and the mainstay of the city. *Invisible Man* collapses the literal question of "where you stand" into the metaphoric and political question of "where you stand" and exposes the contingencies behind having "a position."

Many critics in Ellison's time as well as in our own have been troubled by what appears to be the lack of political resolution in *Invisible Man*. Yet Ellison's political thesis has always seemed to me more courageous and radical than traditional identity politics would find comfortable. It is radical in its willingness to confront the illusions of identity, group ideology, and communal possibilities. The political platform of *Invisible Man*, contrary to the appeal of the representative ethnic novel, relies not on identity – because the protagonist never arrives at one – but on the non-existence of identity, on invisibility with its assimilative and dissimulative possibilities. Ellison offers meditations on the problems of prescription and description, meditations that political protocols have often foreclosed. The place of political discomfort in which Ellison's novel places us may finally provide the most intense vantage point from which to examine what it means to adopt a political stance.

As the invisible man reminds us in the Epilogue, "you carry part of your sickness with you" (575). *You carry the burden of the other inside.* This malady of doubleness is the melancholy of race: a dis-ease of location, a persistent fantasy of identification that *cleaves* and *cleaves to* the marginalized and the master.

Notes

1. Ralph Ellison, *Invisible Man* (New York: Vintage Books, 1990), p. 3. All further citations in this chapter are from this edition.
2. Sigmund Freud, "Mourning and Melancholia (1917)." *Collected Papers: Vol. IV* (London: Hogarth Press, 1953), p. 152. All further citations in this chapter are from this edition.
3. Michael Rogin, *Black Face, White Noise: Jewish Immigrants in the Hollywood Melting Pot* (Berkeley: University of California Press, 1996), p. 24.
4. See Eric Lott, *Love and Theft: Blackface Minstrelsy and the American Working Class* (New York: Oxford University Press, 1993).
5. Ralph Ellison, *Shadow and Act* (New York: Vintage, 1972), p. 53. All further citations in this chapter are from this edition.
6. Richard Dyer, "Whiteness," *Screen* 29 (August 1988): 44–5.

7

TIM PARRISH

Invisible Ellison: the fight to be a Negro leader

In his moving story, "Boy on a Train," written approximately fifteen years before the publication of *Invisible Man* (1952), Ellison portrays through the eyes of an eleven-year-old child the conflict that was to consume him both as an artist and as a cultural critic until his death in 1994: How to represent the distinctiveness of Negro American culture without being consumed by the soul-killing racism endemic to American life.[1] James, the protagonist of the story, is riding with his mother and brother in a Jim Crow train car away from their home in Oklahoma City to begin a new life after the death of James's father. The reader sees the boy first as his mother directs his attention to the fall colors of the passing trees and tells him that Jack Frost "made the leaves pretty" and that he "paints the leaves all the pretty colors."[2] This moment of innocence between mother and child contrasts sharply with the anger James witnesses from his mother when "a butcher had tried to touch her breasts" (*Flying*, 13). Her response is defiant: "she had spat in his face and told him to keep his dirty hands where they belonged" (13–14). Traveling in the Jim Crow car, seeing that the hostile treatment his family receives is in part a consequence of others' perception of their skin color, the boy begins to understand his place in a racially divisive society. From this point forward, the history the mother carries as a Negro will structure her child's understanding of the world. She tells the child of his dead father how she and the father moved to Oklahoma from the South "because we had heard that colored people had a chance out here" (17). The mother impresses the symbolic importance of the train ride on to the boy: "Son, I want you to remember this trip," she says. "You understand, son. I *want* you to remember. You *must*, you've *got* to understand" (17–18). Not only must the boy understand that their trip has a symbolic meaning, but she wants him to be responsible for that meaning. The boy's initial response, though, mirrors his mother's response to the groping butcher. He senses only a nameless enemy that he promises himself (and thus his mother) to avenge: " 'I'll kill it when I get big,' he thought. 'I'll make it cry just like it's making Mama cry!' " His love for his mother is so great and his will to protect her so strong that he extends his defense to a pledge that, if need be, "'I'll kill God and not be sorry!'" (20). The comic nature of his rebellion against God is overwhelmed by the pathos of the recognition of his situation: the love he and his mother share is bounded by the hatred that the white world (and their God) aim at them. A question the story raises but cannot resolve is whether the love the boy feels for this mother can overcome the anger that the world's ignorant hatred instills in him.

What is remarkable about the story is the brilliance with which Ellison conveys the unusual closeness between mother and son. It captures the moment, gestating in the child, when the mother's impressions and even her history, become an ineradicable part of the child's perspective. Like much of Ellison's work, "Boy on a Train" is autobiographical and reveals very powerfully not only the lasting influence his mother's life had on him, but also that even as an adult he never outgrew the moment of self-recognition the boy experiences on the train. Ellison would always be striving to live up to his mother's ambition for him. Later in life Ellison would frequently acknowledge that his mother raised him to be not only a leader, but a Negro leader true to the heritage that had brought his parents from the Deep South in search of freedom in Oklahoma. For his fifth birthday she gave him a toy typewriter, roll-top desk, and a chair to match. She often told him that "the hope of our group depended not on older Negroes but upon the young, upon me."[3] Moreover, as he also recounted many times, his father had given him the name Ralph Waldo Ellison after Ralph Waldo Emerson. Many critics, including Ellison, have made much out of Ellison's complicated attempt to come to terms with his Emersonian heritage bequeathed him by his father (and by being an American, Ellison would add). The protagonist of *Invisible Man* is advised to "Be your own father, young man. And remember, the world is possibility if only you'll discover it."[4] Claiming authority – or authorship – of one's self in order to claim the world as one's own is certainly a theme that comes from Emerson to Ellison. Yet "Boy on a Train," Ellison's tribute to his mother and the ambition she had for him, suggests a reading of Ellison's career that differs from the generally optimistic Emersonian one Ellison associated with his father. The view inflected through the mother requires us to be more skeptical about whether "the world is possibility." More important, out of this skepticism comes the mother's demand that her son be a witness to and spokesman for the pain their family experienced as a consequence of their identity within a particular ethnic group – what Ellison would later refer to in the epigraph to his unfinished second novel, "That Vanished Tribe Into Which I Was Born: The American Negroes."[5]

My contention in this chapter is that Ralph Ellison did grow up to become a Negro leader – someone who was in his way a peer to Martin Luther King, Jr.

and to Malcom X. Ellison dedicated his life and his art to drawing critical attention to and improving the status of African-Americans in American society. Ellison, of course, is ordinarily thought of as a demanding artist who completed one novel, failed to complete another, and in the meantime wrote some highly influential cultural and literary criticism. If discussed as a political figure, he is usually regarded as one who eschewed politics in favor of the "higher" realm of art.[6] However, in light of the recent publication of *Trading Twelves* (2000), a collection of letters between Ellison and Albert Murray, *Juneteenth* (1999), a highly edited fragment of Ellison's never finished second novel, and Lawrence Jackson's impressive biography of Ellison that follows his life up through the publication of *Invisible Man*, we can now recover an Ellison radically at odds with previously established views of him. If *Invisible Man* culminated Ellison's career as a public novelist, its publication also initiated his career as a Negro leader. Indeed, reading Ellison's eloquent letters to Murray and Jackson's account of Ellison's writing of his novel, one sees how even *Invisible Man* was in fact Ellison's answer to his mother's charge to become a Negro leader. Such a claim may seem to many ironic given that, except for Mary Rambo and perhaps the slave woman in the Prologue, the novel contains no significant maternal figures. Yet, if Ellison does not seem to give his narrator a mother, Ellison's own mother nonetheless still hovers over every page. What is arguably the novel's central theme is in fact a version of the duty Ida Ellison had assigned to her son: the task of becoming an effective Negro leader. Bledsoe at one point tells invisible man that "the race needs good, smart, disillusioned fighters" and the novel's action is driven by the protagonist's quest to become a meaningful voice for social change (*Invisible* 143). While Ellison's hero never surrenders his will to fight, just as his mother was unafraid to confront white racism when it appeared before her, he nonetheless learns that his process of disillusionment requires that he distance himself from the roles available to Negro leaders like Bledsoe or, later, Ras the Exhorter. Ellison's narrator changes from "ranter" to "writer" largely out of his recognition that society offers no structure for expressing himself in which he can be true to his vision of himself and his people whose story he represents. As Ellison explained in a lecture he gave at West Point in 1969 about creating such a leader, "it was very important for this young man, this would-be leader, to understand that all political parties are basically concerned with power and with maintaining power, not with humanitarian issues in the raw and abstract state" (*Collected Essays* 538).

The narrator's progress from speaker to writer has suggested for many readers, including sometimes Ellison himself, a kind of modernist triumph of the individual artist. As a speaker, Ellison's narrator could inspire but not control crowds. The narrator writes his fictional memoir, as perhaps Ellison wrote his novel, in despair over the possibility of being a part of any political movement that would not be cynical or self-defeating. Over and over his words would move audiences to action but the action his words provoke repeatedly threatens either the speaker's or the audience's immediate interests. No possibility of productive change seems to exist. In the Battle Royal chapter he raises the ire – and interest – of his hostile Jim Crow audience by substituting the word "equality" for "responsibility" (*Invisible* 31). He retreats from his accidental "slip" but not because his words have failed to get his audience's attention or, perhaps, reminded them of their own hypocrisy toward the high ideals they would profess. His last speech (before the one that becomes the novel) unleashes a riot that threatens to send Harlem up in flames. He escapes the riot, falling through a manhole in the street before being killed by the rioters, and eventually achieves the insight required to identify and assess the meaning of his "invisibility." The conclusion to the rioters' actions is not depicted, though, except insofar as the energy of the riot has been appropriated and transformed by invisible man's narrative. His words, and the riot it produced, lead only to the narrator's own epiphany and this, it seems, is what can only matter. The concluding line of the novel, "who knows but that, on the lower frequencies, I speak for you?," invites the audience to share his recognition but it does not compel group assent (*Invisible* 572). Moreover, he speaks to whoever might read this book, not, as he did in his last speech for the Brotherhood, to a specifically Negro audience. One certainly can argue that this is a formula for great literature in the sense that it demands, in Ellison's words, "a human protest against that which *is*, against the raw and uninformed way we come into the world," but not effective Negro leadership (*Collected Essays* 541).

In his 1955 interview with *The Paris Review* Ellison says that *Invisible Man* began as he was "speculating on the nature of Negro leadership in the United States" (*Collected Essays* 218). He repeated this claim often through the years without to my knowledge ever specifying what conclusion the novel reaches regarding leadership. To most readers, *Invisible Man* is at best an extremely ambivalent text about the prospects of Negro leadership. No question is more vexed in Ellison criticism than how to read the book's ambiguous ending. The narrator himself seems to criticize his book's ending when he says that "even hibernations can be overdone . . . Perhaps that's my greatest social crime, I've overstayed my hibernation, since there's a possibility that even an invisible man has a socially responsible role to play" (572). Historically, from Irving Howe on down, readers who have wanted to agree with the narrator's self-accusation have suggested that the ending provides conclusive evidence of Ellison's habitual "social and political disengagement."[7] It is an extreme irony of social and literary history that this argument makes more sense if we think of Ellison only as a Negro leader rather than as an American leader, since as his novel's narrator progresses he switches from speaking to the black audiences of Harlem to the literate, largely white audience of Ellison's novel. This perspective is especially ironic when one remembers that the goal of the Negro leaders born during Ellison's generation was *integration* with broader American society. As a representative of democracy that happens to be embodied in the history of African-Americans, the narrator's larger point is that no existing social structure allows him to speak and be heard as a leader. Ellison, through his narrator, must create the context which will enable him to become a leader. He resembles Emerson in "Self-Reliance" writing "whim" on his doorpost and hoping that his gesture is not whimsical but will become an incentive for others to follow and build on his example.

The publication of *Invisible Man* made Ellison a world-famous novelist: a stunning debut with no obvious sequel. One cannot help but wonder why he apparently never completed the novel he would work on for the rest of his life. "If I'm going to be remembered as a novelist," he said as late as 1982, "I'd better produce it soon" (*Conversations* 382).[8] Why did Ellison surrender the idea of publishing another novel and instead decide to become an orator? Yet, given the theme Ellison identified as central to his novel and what became of Ellison, the question needs to be addressed. Whereas Ellison's protagonist moved from being a speaker to being a writer, Ellison's career moved from being a writer to being primarily a speaker. Ellison knew very well what an ironic situation this was. Explaining his novel to Arlene Crewdson and Rita Thomson in 1974 for Chicago television, he paused to reflect on the irony of having switched roles with his own creation: "because you notice that the [invisible] man moves from someone who talks all the time (the exact reversal of what has happened to me, I now talk all the time) but he started out as an orator in school, and he really ends up, though he doesn't say so, by writing a book?" (*Conversations* 264). In the long period between the publication of *Invisible Man* and Ellison's death in 1994, Ellison fashioned for himself a career as a Negro leader. In his essays and lectures, Ellison argued for the Negro's crucial place in American society. Unlike his narrator, Ellison kept on speaking and never retreated in the face of often hostile audiences. He was, I think, forever doing what he demanded his protagonist do: "run[ning] the risk of his own humanity" (*Collected Essays* 221). If readers have failed to recognize what a challenging social and political novel *Invisible Man* is, then they have also failed to see how Ellison's post-*Invisible Man* career was both an extension and a refinement of his novel's politics.

Readers have misunderstood Ellison's career as a retreat into the ambiguities of his novel rather than the daring confrontation of those ambiguities that his career actually was. *Trading Twelves*, for instance, shows both how defiant and fundamentally unimpressed Ellison was by his remarkable and seemingly sudden rise into the American literary pantheon. That ascent was as unpredictable as James Baldwin's and Richard Wright's, and rivaled the transformation of Mark Twain – a hero of Ellison's and clearly a model for him not just as an author but as an author-celebrity – from frontier comedian to living American classic author. Ellison's letters, however, register less his surprise at his rise in the world and more a sense of having had at last received his just due. He takes great delight over his new-found celebrity which will give him ample opportunity for skewering other well-known cultural figures for their misperceptions about American literature and African-American identity. In one memorable letter where he relates meeting William Faulkner (not to mention Bernard DeVoto and Archibald MacLeish) while in New York to receive his National Book Award for *Invisible Man*, Ellison tells Murray about his visits to black colleges which gave him a chance to "talk on minority provincialism as a problem for the creative writer" and, eventually, "point out where the so-called New Negro boys crapped up the picture."[9] "I don't know why those guys want to mess with a contentious Mose like me anyway," Ellison declares. "I done told them I ain't no gentleman, black or white, and I definitely ain't colored when it comes to writing" (*Trading* 46). In the succeeding years Ellison would make this claim time and again.

Throughout these letters, Ellison uses what he would often refer to as "the idiom," or the coded language African-Americans created and used to address one other as African-Americans. He speaks in a voice far from the measured, highly literate one that he would use throughout the 1950s and 1960s to dominate panel discussions and impress on others, with limited success, his view of the crucial presence of blackness of American history and identity. Reading a transcript of Ellison discussing the *American Scholar*-sponsored forum on the status of the modern novel from 1955 or his bravura performance at the Southern Historical Association meeting of 1968 where he crossed swords with C. Vann Woodward, Robert Penn Warren, and William Styron, one sees what a truly "contentious Mose" Ellison was and how much he enjoyed correcting and challenging his interlocutors' assumptions about aesthetics and American history from his seemingly unique critical perspective: one who is completely at ease in "the idiom" of black culture yet who was also probably the most well read "classic" author in the history of American literature.

A letter he writes to Murray, dated August 6, 1953 and printed on Harvard "Faculty Club" stationery from the Dana-Palmer House, aptly and comically highlights Ellison's highly ironized sense of his new place in the literary world. "Incidentally," he tells Murray, "we're told that Henry James once lived in this house, which is probably true – I haven't been able to sleep in it" (*Trading* 56). With its finely delivered punch line, this letter, like the rest of his correspondence with Murray, calls to mind a certain laughter in the briar patch, the cackling, whooping sounds of two black men who know they are pulling some kind of joke that never made it to his more measured public lectures. The joke that Ellison and Murray share, among others, is that Ralph Waldo Ellison has taken over the house of James. Ellison is now the turn of the screw, the ghost that neither Henry James nor Ellison's namesake could imagine but who has now arrived and is ready to set some matters straight.[10] If Ellison never completed his college degree at Tuskegee, then *Invisible Man* embodied his scholarly credential to the best (and white) universities in America: only he arrived as a mostly self-taught professor whose experience differed from virtually every one of his students. It was a difference Ellison relished drawing attention to. *I don't know why those guys want to mess with a contentious Mose like me.* When we dispense with the canonical view of Ellison as merely the author of one classic novel and instead understand *Invisible Man* as the first public step of his goal to fulfill his mother's charge that he become a Negro leader, Ellison's post-*Invisible Man* career as a public speaker is as noteworthy as his novel was.

From this perspective, *Invisible Man* was merely Ellison's passport to a career as a Negro leader in which he was as challenging as Douglass, King or Malcom X. Ellison's protagonist rejects the examples of Clifton and Ras, both types of black princes. In the 1960s Ellison looked askance at Malcom X, even if he was happy to acknowledge that he had portrayed a version of Malcom with Ras. Like King, Ellison spent an extraordinary part of his life speaking to skeptical audiences about race. After King and Malcom were murdered, Ellison remained, still with ready access to the college classrooms whose students made up his main audience. How painful and galling it must have been for Ellison to be labelled a white apologist by critics. Only rarely did he hint at the bitterness he had to swallow when, in effect, he was called an Uncle Tom. When critic Robert Stepto and poet Michael Harper asked him in 1976 what he thought of the infamous *Black World* issue devoted to his work, Ellison pointedly replied, "Hell, man, what would you expect? It was obvious that I couldn't have a fair exchange of opinion with those who used the issue to tee off on me, so there was nothing to do but treat them as I had bad dogs and bigoted whites down South: Mentally, I walked away from it" (*Conversations* 330).

In a perceptive 1970 portrait of Ellison, "Indivisible Man," novelist James Alan McPherson captures the conflict Ellison experienced between himself and many African-American readers when he went on campus to defend the universality of his novel in the wake of the Civil Rights movement. "I think what made it hard for him," one young woman tells McPherson, "was that Leroi Jones was coming to Oberlin the next day." Paired off with the militant Jones, whose rhetoric has always emphasized white racism (something Ellison never denied) over American pluralism, Ellison seems to the students old-fashioned and out of date. Another student tells McPherson that while "as an artist the man is beautiful," she cannot mask her disappointment of "hearing him explain the figure in *Invisible Man*. So many concerned blacks had read the plight of the Afro-American into this figure with no face and no name. So many people saw the author riding to champion the cause of the black man. Those same people heard him say that the symbol was representative of a universal man. I found that most disheartening" (*Collected Essays* 379). This anonymous critic nicely identifies the critical conundrum that would frustrate Ellison's career as a public black leader. *Invisible Man* had demanded and even argued for the de facto integration of American society; yet, even as the nation's segregation laws were being eradicated, Ellison was being seen as an apologist for the white society to which blacks had always been denied public access. At Ellison's eightieth birthday, a few weeks before his death, prominent African-American critic Henry Louis Gates, Jr. would tell the *New Yorker*'s David Remnick: "Ellison was shut out, and Richard Wright was elected godfather of the Black Arts Movement of the nineteen-sixties because Wright's hero in *Native Son*, Bigger Thomas, cuts off a white girl's head and stuffs her in a furnace. For Ellison, the revolutionary political act was not segregation; it was the staking of a claim for the Negro in the construction of an honestly public American culture" (*Conversations* 398). Martin Luther King had a similar ambition and he was murdered. Ellison too had to withstand symbolic murder attempts on his career.

As a matter of literary history Gates is probably right. The Oberlin student's remarks from twenty-five years before confirm this. Yet, what conventional literary history has missed is the extent to which Ellison, wearing a mask of universalism, was – to use the vernacular of his letters – bringing the "Mose view" of America to his predominantly white audience. He simply refused to present his hero as a special case, isolated from the main currents of American identity. Reading Ellison's letters from the 1950s, when he was still perceived as an active and unlikely black novelist, it is clear that Ellison's relation to his audience was always confrontational.

Like his invisible protagonist who spoke almost always "as a Negro," Ellison well knew that he was invited to most universities because he was "a mose," an anomaly on the platform, a rarity like Frederick Douglass, W. E. B. Du Bois, and Richard Wright: a Negro who could write and talk better than white men. Ellison seized the opportunity to mix it up on the platform with the other, white, intellectuals. His arguments, so often predicated on personal experience, did not allow him to acknowledge that he was a rarity: like his invisible narrator he "was in the cards, other things having been equal (or unequal)" since Reconstruction (*Invisible* 15).Tellingly, Ellison's letters to Murray reveal that his model as an artist and as a speaker was not the classical black male model for integration, Frederick Douglass, but the great black fighter, Jack Johnson, who caused trouble for defiantly transgressing that most sacred of American racial boundaries, the one that separates black men from white women. He tells Murray

> So just as with writing I learned from Joe [Louis] and Sugar Ray [Robinson] (though that old dancing master, wit, and bull-balled stud, Jack Johnson is really *my* mentor, because he knew if you operated with skill and style you could rise above all that-being-a-credit-to-your-race-crap because he was a credit to the human race and because if he could make that much body and bone move with such precision to his command all other men had a chance to beat the laws of probability and anything else that stuck up its head … here I'll also learn from your latest master strategists, the N.A.A.C.P. legal boys, because if those studs can dry run the Supreme Court of the U.S. and (leave it to some moses to pull that one) I dam sure can run skull practice on the critics. Meanwhile I'm trying to get this dam book done
>
> (*Trading* 132, Ellison's spelling throughout)

This 1956 letter changes how we read not only the Battle Royal chapter but our understanding of Ellison as a public intellectual as well. Letters like this one to Murray suggest how different Ellison was from his protagonist and how the stance that Ellison took in public contrasted with the private feelings that motivated him to risk his identity as a speaker before others. This passage also makes clear that Ellison understood his role as American spokesman to be a kind of extension of the civil rights movement. Running "skull practice" on critics sounds closer to Malcom X, or Ras the Exhorter, than it does to Martin Luther King – then again, as Ellison told one interviewer in the 1950s, he invented the militant Ras the Exhorter character in response to an unpleasant, enraging conversation he once had with a group of whites who wanted to tell him what Negro experience was really like.[11] If Ellison was a classicist, then he was a militant, defiant one whose perspective derives from wide reading and an American experience that was a consequence of his having been born black. The idiomatic language of the private letters enacts precisely the role Ellison would adopt in defining his relationship to American culture and, by extension, that of African-American culture to American culture. Making body and bone move is what Ellison wanted to do to his audience. He wanted to make them over and he wanted to knock them out. Maybe they would get off the floor better Americans; at the very least they would know that something had hit them and perhaps someone, preferably a young black man or woman, would also think that he or she could beat the laws of probability.

To Ellison, the example of Jack Johnson predicted the extraordinary success the NAACP had overturning school desegregation in the courts. He marvels that "those studs can dry run the Supreme Court of the U.S." and force America to accept as real what Ellison in *Invisible Man* presented as persuasive fiction. As a public speaker from the time of *Invisible Man* on, he dramatized a version of what he saw his mother do when she brought the child Ralph and his younger brother to the zoo in Oklahoma City to challenge the just passed Jim Crow laws. Writing for *The New York Times Magazine* in 1989, Ellison recalls that memorable, life-defining trip. After visiting the zoo despite the new laws, a plainclothes policeman shouted at Ida Ellison, "Girl, where are your *white* folks?" She responded defiantly, as the mother does to the butcher in "Boy on a Train." Ellison writes:

> "*White* folks," your mother said. "What white folks? I don't *have* any white folks. I'm a Negro!"
> "Now, don't you get smart with me, colored gal," the white man said. "I mean where are the white folks you came *out* here with!"
> "But I just told you that I didn't come here with any white people," your mother said. "I came here with my boys . . ."
> "Then what are you doing in this park," the white man said.
> And now when your mother answered you could hear the familiar sound of anger in her voice.
> "I'm here because I'm a *tax-payer*, and I thought it was about time my boys have a look at those animals. And for that I don't *need* any *white* folks to show me the way!"
>
> (*Collected Essays* 824)

Ida Ellison's stance reveals uncommon self-reliance and predicts the Rosa Parks bus protest still more than thirty years in the future. Her perceptive young son absorbed the nuances that his mother's protest suggested. Ellison's recollection of this incident seventy-one years after it happened, combined with his use of the second person address, convey powerfully the lasting influence his mother's act had on him. She appears in this recollection as an insuperable force whose strong example would be difficult for anyone to live up to. Yet, Ellison also suggests, that in the face of such strength one has no choice but to try to live up to her. When as an adult he found himself speaking at literary symposia on the "universal" nature of *Invisible Man*, he did so not to express an identity that he accepted and wore as well as he did his fine tailored suits, but to remind his audience that his protagonist was, turning Ida's words into metaphor, a tax-payer whose common Americanness, or humanity, was not open to question.

If Jack Johnson, his mother, and those legal studs could battle racial prejudice so effectively and with such force, then so could he. As the years passed, Ellison remained true to his vision of himself as a Jack Johnson intellectual. Ever the artist, Ellison converted Jack Johnson's power into a mask he could wear to enjoin his audiences to live up to his own ideals of what they should become. His "Commencement Address at the College of William and Mary," given in 1972 but repeated in different forms scores of times to untold numbers of graduates, provides a compelling instance of the leadership role he chose to play as a representative Negro American. Speeches such as this one enacted his answer to the question of "the ambiguity of Negro leadership" that his novel did not provide. Clearly, a rescripting of the occasion he gave to his narrator at the Battle Royal, the address attempts to confront and make a future better than the present. At the College of William and Mary Ellison addresses a privileged, mostly white audience whom he must frame, as King did in his "Letter from a Birmingham Jail," as the "white moderate." Nearly twenty years have passed since those "legal studs" had managed "to dry run" the Supreme Court. With Martin Luther King four years dead and the political party associated with the Civil Rights movement voted decisively out of office, the future probably seemed to Ellison the more likely audience to address than the present.

Ellison begins his address with a characteristic note of high purpose. He informs his listeners that they are "undergoing a rite of passage" and notes that present among them is "a member of the highest court of the land and the governor of the state of Virginia" (*Collected Essays* 407). That is, the occasion is quite serious as it marks one's entry into American society. It is appropriate, Ellison suggests, that these representatives of American justice be present because the graduates cannot understand their rite of passage without acknowledging that they are being initiated in a ceremony that makes them upholders of democracy – potential lawmakers and judges all. Speaking four years after the King assassination, Ellison injects a moment of historical consciousness uncommon to such events. "If," he notes, "we were to go back a few years into the history of mankind, instead of my standing here with my own face exposed, I would be wearing a ritual mask; my role in this ceremony of initiation would require it." He adds, "it is an established part of all such rites of passage that the initiate be made aware that his moment of transcendent glory ... involves the most serious values of the tribe" (407). Of course Ellison is donning a mask of sorts – he is an American who has a privileged view – second sight, as Du Bois might call it – on American history. Ellison never overtly refers to the fact of his racial identity – that he is one of the handful of people present whose face is black. Yet, even if Ellison is what his narrator would describe as an accident of history, the historical fact of his identity as a *black* American is what gives him the authority to be the initiator of this rite. Thus, Ellison defines his role as the one who must confront his audience with painful knowledge. Observing that no initiation is completed without the initiate experiencing pain, he says, "I, I am afraid you are aware, have been given the role of inflicting the pain" (408).

In this speech Ellison subtly and carefully identifies the pain he experienced as what Emerson would have called a representative American, only one who happened to be black. He also tries to transform his personal pain into a collective experience that includes his audience. Ellison openly subjects his audience to a painful rite of history. While he speaks, anyway, they are subject to the same history as he is. He portrays American history as a continuing battle to realize the promises written in "what I speak of as the 'sacred documents' of this nation – the Declaration of Independence, the Constitution, and the Bill of Rights" (408). Ellison invokes the patriotism such an invocation invariably inspires so that he may observe that there "was a flaw in their hopeful project of nation building" that led to a "war of words" until it became a "war of arms" (409). He does not mention slavery or the Civil War, just as he does not refer to the color of his face. He speaks as an American to other Americans, who are, as he says, "A people without memory" (411). *Invisible Man*'s narrator addressed a white audience who laughed at him for letting slip the word "equality"; Ellison addresses an audience whose understanding of "equality" is something he knows that they take for granted. Hence, his role: to inflict the pain of what should be a shared memory. He warns them that their graduation does not mean they "are being paid off" (411). Rather, they are enduring a "rite of preparation" that to be meaningful must acknowledge the blood that was spilled so that they will not have to ask themselves, as their forbears did, "Is the black man an American?" (411). Ellison's perspective does not allow for cults of authenticity, and instead demands that we each accept our full responsibility as Americans, for the promises of equality we repeat to one another, and for the history we share merely by being Americans. Nonetheless Ellison's position as an African-American, his face of color, provides the mask that authorizes him as the master of this ceremony and it is this mask that his audience may finally refuse to see or to wear, symbolically, themselves.

One might say that Ellison's mask is that of the American, that he uses his American mask to efface or at least diminish the threat of African-American identity. However, I think it more apt to say that Ellison's mastery of his African-American identity is what gives him the authority to speak as a representative American to other Americans whom, to be frank, he probably considers his equal in theory only and not in practice.[12] Despite Ellison's very public universalist stance, his letters to Murray could be amusingly chauvinistic about the superiority of his subject – Negro Americans – over conventional, white American life. "Stick to mose, Man. He's got more life in his toenails than these zombies have in their whole bodies," he advises Murray (*Trading* 68). Ellison's *joie de vivre* in being Negro extended to the interpretation of classic nineteenth-century American literature: "Been rereading *Moby Dick* again and appreciating for the first time what a truly good time Melville was having ... The thing's full of riffs, man; no wonder the book wasn't understood in its own time, not enough moses were able to read it!" (170). These letters give us previously unavailable insight into Ellison's aims as a novelist. What comes through here is not the Ellison of the essays, imperious and Olympian, but an Ellison deeply committed to a pre-Civil Rights ethic of African-American life.

Despite the persistent charges that he had become an Uncle Tom, Ellison chose to live his life out in Harlem, among other speakers of "the idiom." We see in his letters to Murray that Ellison equates the idiom with his personal past, the wellspring of his identity. He explains to Murray why he will not take an attractive offer from Brandeis to join their faculty. The prospect of the "congenial atmosphere of the Waltham-Cambridge area" and nice salary notwithstanding, Ellison is reluctant about the prospect of "living in an environment in which there are no Moses" (123). Living in rural New York with Saul Bellow he remarks wistfully that he loves the isolation but that "the only thing that's really wrong with it is that there are no moses to keep me tuned in" (218–19). He feels homesick in Europe, he reports, because "I haven't heard the idiom since Harlem in the fall" (159). Elsewhere he notes, "I just like to hear the idiom" (209). In Rome he confides, "I suspect old Snowden [the cultural attaché] can speak the idiom" (100). Also in Rome, stranded from the idiom, he speaks of jazz, his tapes of Ellington and Basie, as being "my only true atmosphere" (170). After entertaining one evening he is happy his guests leave so he can spend the rest of evening "playing Duke" and could go to bed "feeling a little less lonely. I'd heard the idiom and relived a bit of the past – which is really the same thing" (171).

Throughout his life and career, Ellison's deepest impulses were always rooted in the idiom, that untranslatable aspect of African-American identity out of which Ellison found his voice as an American. There is a poignant moment in one of the letters to Murray where Ellison describes himself as forced to spy as an outsider on a convention of the NAACP.

> I went down to look at the delegates to the N.A.A.C.P. convention yesterday and I must say the mixture is as before–Only now the clothes are more

expensive and there are more young people around. I don't know what I was doing exactly, but it was quite meaningful to simply stand there in the lobby and feel them moving and talking around me. Hell, I know what we want, I just like to hear the idiom. Fifteen minutes in a meeting with some of those studs and I'd want to start a fight, but just seeing them walk and pose and talk and flirt and woof – that's damn pleasant. (*Trading* 209)

Invisible to his peers, Ellison soaks up the idiom, revelling in the nuances of black speech and culture in an environment where being black matters more than being American, even if the meeting he secretly joins looks to be able more fully to express themselves as Americans. Ellison does not need or want to hear the arguments the group presents – indeed, he would only want to argue with them as he did with most black intellectuals in the years after he wrote this 1959 letter. His recollection here conforms to Ellison's well known public arguments that culture matters more than politics and that style prevails over content. It was this experience of having been a Negro, one of a tribe, Ellison spoke out of and tried to protect. Ellison conveys to his friend the distinctiveness of the language he goes there to hear, the fragile sense of a culture whose point of view is not always coincident with being American. What matters here is not their political perspective but their shared experience. He hears in their voices and language, sees in their gestures and style, a shared cultural creation that may even matter more than the "rights" they gather to fight for. Despite whatever political conflict he may have experienced within his group, Ellison could only find his deepest, most private identity within the idiom.[13] One reason it took years for the black folk sources of *Invisible Man* to be widely recognized as an integral part of that novel, despite Ellison himself frequently pointing to them, is because the novel itself seemed to be about breaking out of one's received cultural tradition. The black folk myths were so part of the protagonist's (and Ellison's identity) that they became the air in which the book breathed.

As a novelist and a public intellectual, integration was for Ellison both a social ideal and an aesthetic imperative. He tells Murray, "I knew mose lore yes, but I didn't really know it until I know something about literature and specifically the novel, then I looked at Negro folklore with a shock of true recognition. I was trying to write novels in the great tradition of the novel, not folk stories. The trick is to get mose lore *into* the novel so that it becomes a part of that tradition" (166). Indeed, the courses in American literature that Ellison taught – from Twain and Crane to Faulkner – exemplified Ellison's argument, one that he also makes in his essay "Twentieth-Century Fiction and the Black Mask of Humanity," that "from the late nineteenth century the literary imagination of the Country (the first class imagination, that is) has to smuggle the black man into its machinery in some form, otherwise it can't function" (*Trading* 223). In 1969 he told a gathering of African-American scholars in his "Haverford Statement" that "as a writer who tries to reduce the flux and flow of life to meaningful artistic forms, *I am stuck with integration*, because the very process of the imagination as it goes about bringing together a multiplicity of scenes, images, characters, and emotions and reducing them to significance *is nothing if not integrative*" (*Collected Essays* 429–30; emphasis mine). Yet, in 1953 he had written Murray that "this doggone integration thing maybe is going too fast" (*Trading* 53). He expresses not a fear of integration but of losing his unique identity as a Negro. Ellison's appropriation of the term integration as a motivating literary practice involves not simple elitism but represents a response to what he experienced as the social and personal difficulties of integration. He clearly wanted to pursue the same outcomes that lay behind the political activism of the period but through his own understanding of the politics of art.

The tensions that Ellison experienced between identity and integration were what generated – and what made it impossible to complete – a second novel. Based on the excerpts published as *Juneteenth*, it appears he wanted to write a novel true to the idiom, yet that would also make the idiom the language of all Americans. "I'm planning to get back to my old preoccupation with the ceremonial form of the Negro church," he tells Murray in 1957 at a point when his novel about a Negro preacher was already well launched (*Trading* 171). Perhaps he could not realize his ambition, as it were, to baptize all Americans, white or black, in the life-giving stream of the Negro idiom because, as his letters to Murray often suggest, the idiom could not obviously belong to anyone who did not share its culture and its color. How ironic, then, that his sequel to *Invisible Man* apparently hinges on the failure of its central "white" character to be true to the black people who invented him, as if Ellison felt let down by what happened in American life after *Invisible Man*. Situated in the pre-integration era, the novel explores a self-contained black identity and community crucially at odds with what he preached in his public, American persona. It aimed at an epic expression of specifically African-American experience, written from within "the idiom," and placed in what he called "our kind of time" (*Juneteenth* 130). Seeking a version of what Toni Morrison in *Beloved* (1987) will portray as "Sweet Home," Ellison shows no nostalgia for slavery but pays tribute to an idealized pre-Civil Rights movement African-American identity created out of the shared experience of slavery.[14]

A pivotal exchange between Ellison's central black protagonist, Reverend Alonzo "Daddy" Hickman, and Bliss, the now race-baiting Senator that Hickman raised as a child, conveys a sense of shared identity that is both affirmative and secret, known only to those who have been initiated into its practices. Near death, Bliss is made to recall having participated in the ceremony that celebrated Juneteenth, "back to a bunch of old-fashioned Negroes celebrating an illusion of emancipation, and getting it mixed up with the Resurrection" (116). Bliss remembers that long past ceremony in which he and Hickman would recreate and reenact the history of becoming African-American. Adopting a classic call-and-response even as he talks about the past with Bliss, Hickman prompts the dying Bliss in some ways to participate once again in that ritual celebration. The exchange bursts with eloquence but the effect is a gesture toward a shared, made past, "moving beyond words back to the undifferentiated cry," back to a time when there was no division among African-Americans (117). In this episode, as in *Juneteenth,* Ellison looks to the past as a way to imagine an "undifferentiated cry" that depends on a kind of communal solidarity, an in-group expression nowhere to be found in *Invisible Man* or in Ellison's public speeches, but that Ellison is everywhere looking to go back to in the letters that privately gloss his public speeches, appearances, and writings.

Yet, while Ellison's unfinished novel might well have been quite acceptable within the context of the Black Arts Movement, Ellison's work remained crucially integrationist in the sense that he does not manage to create a truly separate world even within the space of this unfinished fiction.[15] Ellison might have been able to tell such a story had he eliminated white characters from his novel, but at the bitter core of this work is Bliss, a white boy brought up as a black boy who would grow up to exploit and betray those who raised him. Where the passing novel is ordinarily about blacks passing as whites (as in the case of Philip Roth's *The Human Stain,* a novel that I read as a meditation upon Ellison's career), Ellison writes about a white man who thinks he is a black man passing for white. For some readers, passing novels have been about identity theft, the presumption and usurpation at the heart of Roth's fictional imagining of a black character passing for a Jew. In his unfinished second novel, Ellison seems to have portrayed passing as being at the heart of integration, not cultural authenticity. For Ellison this means that the ultimate gesture of integration would be to make American identity continuous with African-American identity: "white" Bliss is the hopeful legacy of the "black" Hickman. Ultimately, though, while Bliss knows that Hickman is "the true father, but black, black," he betrays the identity that his father gives him (117). "Bliss," Hickman asks the unconscious senator, "how after knowing such times as those you could take off for where you went is too much for me to truly understand . . .. I mean the *communion,* the coming together" (133). As an ardent integrationist – in terms of cultural and aesthetic practice – Ellison could not write white characters out of his vision of "that vanished tribe into which I was born: the American Negroes"; more-over, he explored the possibility that white Americans too had been trans-formed by African-American invention. Without Bliss, the conflict between being black and being American would have had no place in the work – the book would have instead truly been a *Juneteenth* celebration of Ellison's "vanished tribe."

Hickman's question to Bliss – which I take to be at the core of the work – is one that Ellison could not answer to his satisfaction since doing so would have placed him at odds with his optimistic and always courageous public stance as a fully integrated American, even if what he stood for seemed to be at best a dream. Ultimately, *Juneteenth* confirms what Ellison's private letters reveal: Ellison could not resolve the conflict between his public pos-itions on art and aesthetic integration and what seem to have been his private attitudes towards identity and community. His unfinished novel portrays how African-American identity and African-American culture must always be understood as the specific creation and in a sense property of African-Americans. It is not that Benny Goodman, for instance, cannot become a great jazz artist (Ellison says he is) but that Goodman's aesthetic achievement cannot allow him to pass for black in American society. This means that Goodman would not have to worry about being harassed by the police or denied job opportunities; more important, from Ellison's perspective, it means that Goodman can never have that unique experience of being an African-American among other African-Americans. This is the special knowledge that Ellison gives Bliss and he betrays it. Ellison never did and perhaps for this reason never published his novel.

In this context, Ellison's apparent failure to make his unfinished novel whole with an artistic vision that was, he said, indivisible from his vision of American life is almost unbearably poignant. In 1954 he breathlessly sends Murray completed passages from his next book: "Here are a few riffs from old Cliofus, who seems on the way to try to out lie Sallywhite. The choc-drinking Charlie character appeared just as I was typing up this copy to send to you, I don't know where the hell Cliofus got him but here he is anyway" (*Trading* 83–4). It is telling that these characters seem to appear not in his copy of the manuscript (and they are not included in *Juneteenth*), but really as riffs that are only improvised in the context of his exchanges with Murray who so clearly connected him to a larger communal idiom and experience. Three years later, he reports, "I've been too busy battling with myself and with this novel-of-mine to get much reading done. I'm going to whip the dam thing but it [is] giving me a tough fight" (165). Indeed, that his next novel was even more than *Invisible Man* obviously concerned with black folklore as a subject unto itself suggests his tragedy may have been that he could not entirely square his experience as a Negro with his experience as an American. In the end his career became a version of the experience he describes in his late essay, "On Being the Target of Discrimination." As a boy, he relates, segregation obligated him one day to turn himself "into a one-man band" (*Collected Essays* 827). On that occasion Ellison had taken out the brass cornet his mother had given him so that he could play, surreptitiously, alongside a group of "men and women postal workers who were playing away at a familiar march" (827). Near where he lived a shining new school had been built that Ellison wanted to attend but was disappointed to learn would be for the white kids only. Ellison describes himself as having been frustrated since memory began that "the prevailing separation of the races made it impossible to learn how you and your Negro friends compared with the boys who lived on the white side of the color line" (826). So young Ellison happily grabs his cornet, hides himself, and plays along with an unsuspecting postal band. In the sound of the music his voice could be heard without drawing attention to the color of his skin. He recalls, "At last by an isolated act of brassy cunning you had become a member of the band" (828). Predictably, given his nature, the young Ellison "grew bold in the pride of [his] sound" and, despite his apparent safe seclusion, makes himself known to the others. "I'll be damn, it's a little nigger," a man exclaims and Ellison's invisible place is exposed (828). Ellison does not tell us when he resumed playing but one suspects it was later that same day, for Ellison never stopped playing his cornet. Even when his playing became novel writing, and then his writing became speaking, he never quit performing a version of the Negro leader his mother wanted him to become. If he had to stand alone while he played his defiant, beautiful tune, he did not seem to mind. He had become used to it.

Notes

1. As Ellison preferred to identify himself as a "Negro," I have used that term rather than the more current designation, African-American, where appropriate. "I'm a Negro, by the way," he says at the 1968 Southern Historical Association meeting, substituting the term for "black." See *Conversations with Ralph Ellison.* Ed. Maryemma Graham and Amrijit Singh (Jackson: University Press of Mississippi, 1995), p, 171. Hereafter cited as *Conversations* in the text.
2. "Boy on a Train." In Ralph Ellison, *Flying Home and Other Stories.* Ed. John Callahan (New York: Random House, 1996), p. 12. Hereafter cited as *Flying* in the text.
3. Lawrence Jackson, *Ralph Ellison: Emergence of Genius* (New York: John Wiley & Sons, 2002), p. 26. Hereafter cited as Jackson in the text.
4. Ralph Ellison, *Invisible Man* (New York: Modern Library, 1992), p. 154. Hereafter cited as *Invisible* in the text.

5. Ralph Ellison, *Juneteenth*. Ed. John F. Callahan (New York: Random House, 1995), p. vii. Hereafter cited as *Juneteenth* in the text.

6. Irving Howe established a critical pattern when he attacked Ellison for betraying the reality of black experience in his fiction in his "Black Boys and Native Sons." Ellison responded with his classic essay, "The World and the Jug." There he argued that his purpose as an artist was to write literature, not sociology, and that *Invisible Man* must ultimately be "judged as art; if it fails, it fails aesthetically." *The Collected Essays of Ralph Ellison*. Ed. John F. Callahan (New York: The Modern Library, 1995), p. 182. Hereafter cited as *Collected Essays* in the text. For Ellison, who viewed art as the supreme and most demanding kind of expression, to be an artist and to be a Negro at the same time was itself a deeply radical act. When the "Black Aesthetic" movement emerged in the late 1960s and early 1970s, Ellison's triumphant "integration" was seen as a cop out, a surrender of black culture to white agendas. *The Black Aesthetic* (Garden City: Doubleday, 1971), edited by Addison Gayle, Jr., typifies this period of Ellison studies. In the 1980s, Houston A. Baker, Jr. in *Blues, Ideology and American Literature* (University of Chicago Press, 1984) and Henry Louis Gates, Jr. in *The Signifying Monkey* (New York: Oxford University Press, 1988) sought to return Ellison to a distinctively African-American tradition of language and attitude. Robert O'Meally's *The Craft of Ralph Ellison* (Cambridge: Harvard University Press, 1980) remains the best study of how Ellison borrowed from the African-American folk tradition. The best discussion of the shifting relationship between Ellison and his black critics is Larry Neal's 1970 personal essay "Ellison's Zoot Suit" in his *Visions of a Liberated Future* (New York: Thunder's Mouth Press, 1989), pp. 30–56. Robert Stepto's *From Behind the Veil* (1979) (Urbana and Chicago: University of Illinois Press, rpt. 1991) contains a probing discussion of Ellison's place in the canon of African-American literature (163–94). In the 1990s Jerry Watts revived the Ellison–Howe debate and judged Howe the winner (*Heroism and the Black Intellectual: Ralph Ellison, Politics, and Afro-American Life* (Chapel Hill: University of North Carolina Press, 1994), while Ross Posnock connected Ellison to an African-American pragmatist tradition of W. E. B. Du Bois and Zora Neale Hurston (*Color and Culture: Black Writers and the Making of the Modern Intellectual* (Cambridge: Harvard University Press), pp. 184–219.

7. See Watts, *Heroism and the Black Intellectual*, p. 116.

8. Actually, his interviews over the years seemed to indicate that working on it was enough. His first serious foray into art was as a musician which, to become accomplished, requires endless practice. It may have been that Ellison, after his great success, preferred practicing for himself than performing for others. "Writing is a discipline. It's not important how much you write" (*Conversations* 383).

9. Ralph Ellison and Albert Murray, *Trading Twelves: The Selected Letters of Ralph Ellison and Albert Murray*. Ed. Albert Murray and John F. Callahan (New York: The Modern Library, 2000), p. 46. Hereafter cited as *Trading* in the text.

10. In 1974 an interviewer asks him, "Why did you choose to write the novel as a first person 'I' narration and perhaps limited view?" Ellison responds: "I felt that I had to test my own abilities, and I wanted to test certain theories of a writer whom I

admire very much and that was Henry James, who felt that Dostoevski was not very much of a novelist because he wrote in the first person, and novels in the first person tend to be great baggy monsters ... So I wanted to see if I could do that" (*Conversations* 263).

11. Ellison had been asked if Ras were based on Marcus Garvey. He answered: "No. In 1950 my wife and I were staying at a vacation spot where we met some white liberals who thought the best way to be friendly was to tell us what it was like to be a Negro. I got mad at hearing this from people who otherwise seemed very intelligent. I had already sketched Ras but the passion of his statement came out after I went upstairs that night feeling that we needed to have this thing out once and for all; then we could go on living like people and individuals" (*Conversations* 17–18). That Ellison's identification with Ras was closer than has usually been allowed is also suggested by the fact that several years before beginning *Invisible Man* he referred to himself in a letter to Langston Hughes as "Mohammed Ras De Terror." See Jackson 215.

12. As Ellison joked to an African-American member of the audience who addressed him at the 1968 Southern Historical Association who had asked him if he had ever considered himself to be invisible, "I am by no means. I was not invisible, and I would think that you, speaking with your inclination, would remember that old joke: the Negro is unseen because of his high visibility" (*Conversations* 170–1).

13. A letter he writes Murray concerning Faulkner's 1956 apology for segregation reinforces this point of view: "[Faulkner] thinks that Negroes simply exist to give ironic overtone to the viciousness of white folks, when he should know very well we're trying as hard as hell to free ourselves thoroughly and completely, so that when we get the crackers off our back we can discover what we (moses) really are and what we really wish to preserve out of the experience that made us" (*Trading* 117).

14. Morrison may have read excerpts of Ellison's work in progress published in the 1965 *Quarterly Review of American Literature* and so been moved to write the great passage in *Beloved* where ex-slave Baby Suggs preaches to her congregation about the necessity of re-claiming their identities after slavery.

15. Harold Bloom has suggested of Ellison that "the final quarter-century of his life (I base this on a number of conversations with him) seemed less shadowed by his inability to finish a second novel that would meet his own high standards than it was by social pressures that could have been relieved only if he had abandoned his own very individual stance." I think his second novel would have been embraced as such a recanting. Harold Bloom, *Genius: A Mosaic of One Hundred Exemplary Critical Minds* (New York: Warner Books, 2002), p. 809.

8

JOHN S. WRIGHT

Ellison's experimental attitude and the technologies of illumination

The year following the 1952 publication of *Invisible Man,* at the presentation ceremony for the National Book Award he had just won, Ralph Ellison told his audience that if he were asked in all seriousness what he considered to be the chief significance of *Invisible Man* as a fiction, he would reply, first, "its experimental attitude" and, second, "its attempt to return to the mood of personal moral responsibility for democracy which typified the best of our nineteenth century fiction."[1] That his first novel had won such an award he acknowledged as a clear sign of crisis in the American novel, a sense of crisis that he and the other "younger novelists" of the time shared.

On the aesthetic level, Ellison's experimental novel had proceeded from his own reaction to a growing uncertainty about the formal possibilities of the novel – an uncertainty that led him to reject both the forms of the "tight, well-made Jamesian novel" and the "hard-boiled novel" of Hemingway, which had been a center of literary revolt among apprentice writers of the 1930s (*Shadow* 178–9). The narrative experiment that Ralph Ellison created to fill the void moved consciously "from naturalism to expressionism to surrealism," from the world of "facts" to the world of dream and nightmare, from the determined to the disordered.

Over the past half century those of us engaged in interpreting *Invisible Man* have devoted no small measure of attention to the musical sources of the book's experimental attitude – to jazz and blues, in particular, in part because of the manifest autobiographical impress of musical experience on Ellison's sensibility. We have searched out, with great industry, the vernacular folk traditions and shape-shifting trickster archetypes that, along with jazz and blues players, seem to embody improvisatory and experimental stances toward life and art. And we have betrayed no sign of shyness in excavating the eclectic mosaic of literary models and movements, "ancestors" and "relatives" that demonstrably helped expand Ellison's sense of aesthetic possibility.

In this context however, Ellison's own frequent, almost incantatory allusions to the primacy of "technique" have perhaps helped reinforce narrowly aestheticist readings of the sources of his experimental attitude. For those of us who have cultivated with determined seriousness such exegeses of Ellison's "technique," there is a joke in this, precisely that kind of wry disjunction between illusion and reality that Ellison routinely turns to comic effect in his fiction and essays.

For if "technique" is, in Kenneth Burke's phrase, a kind of "God-term" in Ralph Ellison's critical vocabulary, this is not, I want to suggest, because of any implied supernatural powers in the how and the what of literary method, style, or manner. Rather it may be because, in Ellison's use, the concept of "technique" has the very potent capacity to suggest both the literal, organizational, procedural part of executing a work of fiction *and* that much broader system of applied sciences and practical arts by which any society provides its members with those things needed or desired – "technology," in other words. Over the course of his career, in critical essays and reviews, in short stories and interviews, in his novel and his novel-in-progress, Ellison used "technique" as a *synthesizing* term, as a way of making connections between the world of art and the world of our mechanized material civilization, *more* insistently than as a set of operations peculiar to literary text-making. And as such, in tracking his allegiances as an artist and a man, we should not be surprised to find his notions of technique often less akin to those purveyed by the autotelic New Criticism promoted in the 1930s and 1940s by John Crowe Ransom, Allen Tate, Robert Penn Warren and company than to the notions of *technics* and *technology* preferred during the same years in the wide-ranging, often highly speculative cultural criticism about science, utopia, architecture, religion, and "the myth of the machine" that Lewis Mumford developed in the series of books that included *The Golden Day* (1924), *Technics and Civilization* (1934), and *Art and Technics* (1952).

Alan Nadel's study of Ralph Ellison and the American canon provides one of the rare explorations of Ellison's connection to Mumford's "neo-technic" terrain; and in a pivotal chapter, Nadel first recaps Mumford's *The Golden Day* as an oversimplified drama of the individual locked in a losing combat with the ascendant machine age, then very deftly reads "Jack-the-Bear's" descent into chaos at a southern bordello dubbed likewise, "The Golden Day," as a punning Ellisonian deflation of Mumford's dismissive treatment of slavery and race as issues in the conflict that led to civil war. Nadel accuses Mumford of writing fiction, not history, in his account of the culture of Emerson, Thoreau, Whitman, Hawthorne, and Melville; and to buttress his reading of Mumford's book as "an ode to a period that never existed," he quotes a letter he received from Ellison himself, excerpted as follows:

It wasn't that I didn't admire Mumford. I have owned a copy of the sixth Liveright printing of THE GOLDEN DAY since 1937 and own, and have learned from, most of his books. I was simply upset by his implying that the war which freed my grandparents from slavery was of no real consequence to the broader issues of American society and its culture. What else, other than sheer demonic, masochistic hell-raising, was that bloody war all about if not slavery and the contentions which flowed there-from? As a self-instructed student I was quite willing for Mumford to play Aeschylus, Jeremiah, or even God, but not at the price of his converting the most tragic incident in American history into bombastic farce. For in doing so he denied my people the sacrificial role which they had played in the drama.[2]

This is classic Ellisonian infighting, and it leaves no doubt about the grounds of difference on which Ellison's send-up of Mumford's Golden Day proceeds. It does not, however, gainsay what Ellison *shares* with Mumford about interpreting the culture of the closing three antebellum decades – their absolute import in shaping American values and literature. Nor does it deny the extent to which Ellison shares Mumford's sense of the *omnipresence* of technology and the machine, and the artist's moral obligation to envision aesthetic possibilities for the machine that will not reinforce the fragmenting, life-denying, dehumanizing conditions created by capitalist technology.

Mumford's notion of the ideal relation between art and technics is in fact closely allied with that revealed in Ellison's work; and it is precisely in Ellison's conceptualization of the "experimental attitude" which culminated in *Invisible Man* that such a relation is most explicitly articulated. "What has been missing from so much experimental writing," he asserted in "Brave Words for a Startling Occasion," has been "the passionate will to dominate reality as well as the laws of art. This will is the true source of the experimental attitude" (*Shadow* 105). And the clues Ellison has given us about its development in his own life direct us first, not to art, but to technology, to the applied sciences, to the systems, mechanical and electrical, whereby the means of transportation and communication, the configuration of the landscape, the very sense of time and space and consciousness were being transformed during the decades of Ellison's boyhood and maturation as an artist.

The very first question of the very first interview framed in *Shadow & Act,* the 1961 exchange titled "That Same Pain, That Same Pleasure," called on Ellison to describe "the way in which you as a Negro writer have vaulted the parochial limitations of most Negro fiction" – a question whose presumptions we hope have withered over the past forty years. Answering that it was "a matter of attitude," and calmly contradicting any assumptions that his own might resemble traditional 'portraits of the artist', Ellison recalled

Like so many kids of the twenties, I played around with radio – building crystal sets and circuits consisting of a few tubes, which I found published in the radio magazines. At the time we were living in a white middle-class neighborhood, where my mother was custodian for some apartments, and it was while searching the trash for cylindrical ice-cream cartons which were used by amateurs for winding tuning coils that I met a white boy who was looking for the same thing. I gave him some of those I'd found and we became friends .... His nickname was Hoolie and for kids of eight or nine that was enough. Due to a rheumatic heart Hoolie was tutored at home and spent a great deal of time playing by himself and in taking his parents' elaborate radio apart and putting it back together again, and in building circuits of his own .... It didn't take much encouragement from his mother, who was glad to have someone around to keep him company, for me to spend much of my free time helping him with his experiments. By the time I left the community, he had become interested in short-wave communication and was applying for a ham license. I moved back into the Negro community and began to concentrate on music, and was never to see him again, but knowing this white boy was a very meaningful experience. It had little to do with the race question as such, but with our mutual loneliness (I had no other playmates in that community) and a great curiosity about the growing science of radio. It was important for me to know a boy who could approach the intricacies of electronics with such daring and whose mind was intellectually aggressive.   (*Shadow* 23–4)

That the impress of technology on consciousness and communion would remain a fixture of his life, and finally effect a fusion with the musical and the literary Ellison had earlier acknowledged in a 1955 piece for *Hi Fidelity* magazine, called "Living With Music." In the course of recalling the intimate battle-history of his inter-apartmental audio system warfare with a musically committed but painfully untalented would-be songster next door, Ellison also recounted his intense re-engagement in the late 1940s with the electronics world that, with a great technological leap forward, suddenly interposed itself between his records, his typewriter, and his ears roughly midway in the course of his long labor with the experimental novel:

I had started music early and lived with it daily, and when I broke I tried to break clean. Now in this magical moment all the old love, the old fascination with music superbly rendered, flooded back .... If I was to live and write in that apartment, it would be only through the grace of music. I had tuned in a [Kathleen] Ferrier recital, and when it ended I rushed out for several of her records, certain now that deliverance was mine.

But not yet. Between the hi-fi record and the ear, I learned, there was a new electronic world ... It was 1949 and I rushed to the Audio Fair ... I had hardly entered the fair before I heard David Sarser's and Mel Sprinkle's Musician's Amplifier, took a look at its schematic and, recalling a boyhood acquaintance with such matters, decided that I could build one. I did, several times before it measured within specifications. And still our system was lacking ... I built a half a dozen or more preamplifiers and record compensators before finding a commercial one that satisfied my ear, and, finally, we acquired an arm, a magnetic cartridge and – glory of the house – a tape recorder. All this plunge into electronics, mind you, had as its simple end the enjoyment of recorded music as it was intended to be heard. I was obsessed with the idea of reproducing sound with such fidelity that even when using music as a defense behind which I could write, it would reach the unconscious levels of the mind with the least distortion. *(Shadow* 193–4)

Here, as part of a pattern we as readers have probably understated over the years, we glimpse Ralph Ellison focused for a moment on the least acknow-ledged corner – revolutionary technological modernity – of what he often posits as a triangular sense of African-American identity, whose complemen-tary corners are the changing fate of being "American," as mysterious and uncertain as that may be, and the "racial predicament," with its complex legacy of oppression, repression, and possibility.

In "Some Answers and Some Questions" posed for the magazine *Preuves* in 1958, he addressed directly the problematic role of modern industrial evolution on the "spiritual crisis of the Negro people of our times," and its potential dangers for the future of a "genuine Negro culture." He saw that role to be as ambiguous in African-American life as in the life of any modern people:

it depends on how much human suffering must go into the achievement of industrialization, upon who operates the industries, upon how the products and profits are shared and upon the wisdom used in imposing technology upon the institutions and traditions of each particular society. Ironically, black men with the status of slaves contributed much of the brute labor which helped the industrial revolution under way; in this process they were exploited, their natural resources were ravaged and their institutions and their cultures were devastated, and in most instances they were denied anything like participation in the European cultures which flowered as a result of the transformation of civilization under the growth of technology. But now it is precisely technology which promises them release from the brutalizing effects of over three hundred years of racism and European domination. Men cannot unmake history, thus it is not a question of reincarnating those cultural traditions which were destroyed, but a matter of using industrialization, modern medicine, modern science generally, to work in the interest of these peoples rather than against them. Nor is the disrup-tion of continuity with the past necessarily a totally negative phenomenon; some-times it makes possible a modulation of a people's way of life which allows for a more creative use of its energies ... One thing seems clear, certain possibilities of culture are achievable only through the presence of industrial techniques.

> It is not industrial progress per se which damages peoples or cultures; it is the exploitation of peoples in order to keep the machines fed with raw materials. It seems to me that the whole world is moving toward some new cultural synthesis, and partially through the discipline imposed by technology.
>
> (*Shadow* 255–6).

However our own experience of machine society may lead us now to evaluate the technological ethos Ralph Ellison embraced at mid-century, his own reflections then seem bound up with those of Lewis Mumford in the same kind of "antagonistic cooperation" that characterizes so many of Elllison's engagements with leading thinkers of the era. Mumford's monumental studies of the development of technology and the history and culture of the city; his extra-academic generalist's readiness to trespass constantly across disciplinary boundaries in the effort to define "organic" connections between different realms of thought and experience; his troubled awareness of the historic abuse of technology and the apparent human inability to control the aggression and power lust that threaten ecological disaster and global conflagration; his utopian strain of belief in the redemptive possibilities of a humane technology mediated by a new "vitalistic," "gestaltic" perception of the "complicated interdependences" of all things – these facets of Mumford's thought seem to resonate on the *cooperative* side of Ellison's intellectual confrontation with the author of *The Golden Day*.

But lest I overstress the convergence, I want to turn for a moment to another point where Ellison's technological ethos and Mumford's ultimately diverge. The impetus of Mumford's career carried him from an early focus as a critic of American literature and the arts – with painting, architecture, and technology as simply *part* of the mix – to ever larger questions of human history and destiny *centered* on the origin, meaning, and potential of technology. The fate of urban culture, the possibility of constructing a global technological utopia that was *not* technocratic, the hopes and frustrations of large-scale urban planning – all impelled Mumford toward a collectivizing, macrocosmic vision that made the specific technology and symbolism of architecture his prime nexus for locating and evaluating the social meanings of the machine.[3]

For Ellison, if frequent forays into the world of cultural criticism inclined him at all toward this grander "organicism," his vocation as a novelist drove him instead to seek the "universal" in the particular, the macrocosm in the microcosm. "More than any other literary form," he argued in 1957 in "Society, Morality, and the Novel," the novel "is obsessed with the impact of change upon *personality* . . . . Man knows that even in this day of marvelous technology and the tenuous subjugation of the atom, that nature can crush him, and that at the boundaries of human order the arts *and* the instruments of technology are hardly more than magic objects which serve to aid us in our ceaseless quest for certainty."[4] It is not then technology as a vast alienating system of machines moving through history with implacable force that preoccupies Ellison. It is technology as an extension of human lives, as something *someone* makes, *someone* owns, something *some* oppose, most *must* use, and *everyone* tries to make sense of. However dreamlike and surreal, the processes of living, through which technology acquires personal and social meaning, are what prevail in Ellison's "experimental attitude." And more than architecture it is the impact on personality of the new technology of *electrification* and the machinery of the Electric Age that defines the crucial contexts of value in his novelistic experiment with the forms of fiction, consciousness, and democracy.

One of the things differentiating *Invisible Man* most dramatically from the other black fictions of its time is this absorption with the immediate effects of the technological environment on the human imagination and spirit, and on the blurring line between reality and illusion, the natural and the artificial – as the "technoscape" replaces the landscape, and as the very nature of human perception is changed by the pervasive presence of the artificial. During the years of Ellisons' literary novitiate, other black writers created fictions rooted in the ethos of blues and jazz – Langston Hughes in *Not Without Laughter*, for instance; other black writers fabricated characters immersed in the tales and trickster traditions of African American oral lore – perhaps none more extensively than Zora Neale Hurston; other black writers like Chester Himes in *If He Hollers* and Richard Wright in *The Long Dream*, brought the world of dreams to center stage; and other writers – here William Attaway's *Blood on the Forge* served as Ellison's reference point – dramatized the epic migration from the feudal southern landscape to the urban, industrial modern north. None, however, attuned these crucial facets of African-American life as consciously as Ellison would to the new world of social and psychic meanings created by technological change; and none attempted to fuse them *all* into the odyssey of a single black personality whose consciousness is mediated pervasively by technology.

In *Invisible Man* the conflicts between personal and public values, between psychic power and political power, between the ethic of material progress and the spiritual potential of the solitary soul, are dramatized through technological experience. From the punning structural and thematic frame appropriated from H. G. Wells's science fiction classic, *The Invisible Man*, to the controlling optical metaphors and hyper-illuminated underground "sound stage" of Jack-the-Bear's monologue-in-flashback, technologically altered perceptions reverberate. The confrontations with human antagonists like the southern white bigwigs at the Battle Royal, like A. Hebert Bledsoe, Mr. Norton, Lucius Brockaway, the Liberty Paints doctors, and the Brotherhood's Jack, reflect the challenges to "natural," autonomous values and self-consciousness presented by the new "artificial" environment of machines and by what Mumford calls the "megamachines" – the machine-like human organizations that convert the "raw material" of humanity into automatons, robots, and "zombies" – as the crazy vet at the novel's "Golden Day" calls Jack-the-Bear. Such "character" as he becomes conscious of emerges from the dramatic series of agons with machines and technology, including the electrified rug, the electric gauge-laden paint boiler, and the electrifying hospital machine that gives him the equivalent of a prefrontal lobotomy. Transported from site to site in his new northern home by electrified streetcars and subway trains, and driven finally underground by the boomerangs of fate, Jack-the-Bear ultimately grapples with the forms and formlessness of his life and identity in the artificial illumination made possible by electrification.

Why electrification and electric machinery more than the other technologies of the time? Let me offer some suggestions, the first of which Ellison understood from deep personal experience. The period from 1880 to 1940, as David Nye's history of the new technology details, was the period when, spurred by startling scientific inventions and an aggressive new social class of entrepreneurial engineers, we embarked upon the vast technological process of "Electrifying America." Americans adopted electrical technologies across a wide spectrum of social, political, economic, and aesthetic contexts, reconfiguring the whole texture of national experience. Electricity changed the appearance and multiplied the meaning of the landscapes of ordinary life, its above-ground and underground transport systems; electricity created new ties between city centers and separated outlying districts like Harlem, created the vast network of electric cables and transformers that made possible assembly-line factories (like Liberty Paints), electrified homes, and the new experience of night space that fascinated painters and photographers and spawned a new species of phantasmagoric public spectacles along the "Great White Way."[5] Electrification created the "mass media" as we know it – the radio, the phonograph, the telephone, the movies – and a newly verbalized entertainment taste for on-stage "live wires," "human dynamos," and "electrifying performances" – the taste that Ralph Ellison, during his boyhood in a small town on the edge of the Oklahoma frontier, was attempting to gratify in the early 1920s by obsessively mastering the techniques and concepts of crystal-set circuitry, vacuum tubes, and winding coils.

The impact of electrification on Ellison's maturing literary imagination, though, had other sources, contemporary and historic. If during Ellison's coming-of-age electricity was, in the public mind, a sign of Thomas Edison's inventive genius and the hallmark of specifically *American* progress, it was also a "mysterious power Americans had long connected [as far back at least as Mumford's mid-nineteenth century Golden Day] to magnetism, the nervous system, heat, power, . . . , sex, health, and light." The Golden Day had been ended, Mumford wrote, by a war "between two forms of servitude, the slave and the machine . . . The machines won; and the war kept on . . . The slave question disappeared but the 'Negro' question remained." Mumford read the era's abolitionism as unenlightened moral righteousness "oblivious to the *new* varieties of slavery . . . practiced under industrialism."[6] But Ellison's own ancestral moorings in the Golden Day inverted Mumford's allegory of dark and light, blindness and sight, and instead read the social crises of the age more in accord with the phalanx of transcendentalist millenarians, social reformers, spiritualists, and abolitionists who heeded Walt Whitman's call to "sing the body electric" as an anthem to the new democratic vistas in which electricity – "the demon, the angel, the mighty physical power, the all-pervading intelligence," one of Hawthorne's characters calls it[7] – the new democratic vistas in which electricity would be bound up with the realm of human spirit more profoundly than the machine ever had.

At the same time that Ellison's moral allegiances to the literary lights of the Golden Day reinforced his allegorical sensitivity to the tropes of electrification, his ties to the Jazz Age artists against whom his own literary experiment had to be defined – Hemingway and Fitzgerald in particular – made the electrified technoscape an almost inevitable site of interpretive confrontation and revision. Ellison's critique of the 1920s' writers resounds throughout his critical essays, but perhaps nowhere more cogently than in the aforementioned "Society, Morality, and the Novel," where he contends that the "organic" moral-aesthetic struggle during the Golden Day against slavery both in *this* world and in the world of spiritual values, had its trajectory broken by the failure of Reconstruction and by the Hayes-Tilden Compromise. The consequent moral evasions and materialism of the Gilded Age, Ellison posits, "prepared for the mood of glamorized social irresponsibility voiced in the fiction of the twenties, and it created a special problem between the American novelist and his audience . . . . [The] novel, which in the hands of our greatest writers had been a superb moral instrument, became morally diffident and much of its energy was turned upon itself in the form of technical experimentation" (*Going* 252). In Hemingway's case, Ellison contends, "the personal despair which gave the technique its resonance became a means of helping other Americans to avoid those aspects of reality which they no longer had the will to face" (*Going* 255). The unfaced and enduring problem of race, and its relationship to the health of democracy, loom largest here in Ellison's mind; and despite that element of Hemingway's "technique" which recognizes that what is left out of a fiction is as important as what is present, the want of a *black* presence in Hemingway's pivotal images of America marks the moral evasion Ellison detected as real, and aesthetically indefensible.

To see F. Scott Fitzgerald in Ellison's eyes requires a closer acquaintance with the "little man at Chehaw Station," the hypothetical cross-bred connoisseur, critic, and trickster whom the Tuskegee concert pianist, Hazel Harrison, foisted on Ellison during his college student days, as the ideal audience and goad for would-be American artists. Internalizing the little man as an alternate authorial persona, Ellison notes that in Fitzgerald's *The Great Gatsby*, the narrator, Nick Carraway, "tells us, by way of outlining his background's influence upon his moral judgments, that his family fortune was started by an Irish uncle who immigrated during the Civil War, paid a substitute to fight in his stead, and went on to become wealthy from war profiteering." Quick to see the symbolic connections between this ancestral moral legacy and Gatsby's illusory rise and fatal end, Ellison's little man represents a possible "saving grace" for both Fitzgerald and his doomed protagonist:

> The little man, by imposing collaboratively his own vision of America upon that of the author, would extend the novel's truth to levels below the threshold of that frustrating social mobility which forms the core of Gatsby's anguish. Responding out of a knowledge of the manner in which the mystique of wealth is intertwined with the American mysteries of class and color, he would aid the author in achieving the more complex vision of American experience that was implicit in his material. As a citizen, the little man endures with a certain grace the social restrictions that limit his own mobility; but *as a reader*, he demands that the relationship between his own condition and that of those more highly placed be recognized. He senses that the American experience is of a whole, and he wants the interconnection revealed. (*Going* 14)

Fitzgerald's failure, however, to incorporate the little man's experience into his own diminishes his fiction for readers of the highest standard, Ellison counsels; and Jay Gatsby, whose murder-by-mistake might have been averted had the black man who witnesses the real driver of the death car *not* been left voiceless and disconnected from the novel's action, pays with his life.

Now, in case it seems that I have strayed too far from Ellison's own electrified technoscape, let me try to make those connections clearer. For both Hemingway and Fitzgerald, as for many of their American peers, electrification helped chart, fictively, "the changes in values and self-perception that came with modernity" (Nye 284). But for them as for writers like

Eugene O'Neill, connections between the modern drama of electrified technological change and the modern drama of race went unperceived. O'Neill, who "electrified" his own career with three "Negro plays" – *Emperor Jones, The Dreamy Kid,* and *All God's Chillun* – also produced a play called *Dynamo* in 1929, in which the stark contrasts between tradition and modernity, between the certainties of Protestant fundamentalism and the morally indeterminate universe of Darwin, Freud, and Einstein, are dramatized onstage in the opposing images of two family homes, one pious and *un*electrified, the other fully electrified and infused with the worship of electricity. The worlds of O'Neill's "Negro plays" and *Dynamo*, however, are mutually exclusive: the characters of the Negro plays kept confined to the expressionist jungle of Jungian primitivism, and the electrified world of *Dynamo* kept imperturbably white.

In Hemingway's work also, electrification takes on broad spiritual and metaphysical import; and one of the classic examples of his style and technique, the much anthologized 1933 story, "A Clean, Well-Lighted Place," deploys electric light not just as a pragmatic substitute for older forms of illumination, but as a sign of the existential force that in a modern world darkened by the loss of meaning, both holds back the void and, within the frame of enveloping spiritual darkness, solidifies and confirms the fragile reality of human existence. Two waiters sit in a Spanish café, one old, one young; one wise but wearied by the ways of the world, the younger one naively confident about his life and its prospects – "I have confidence. I am all confidence," he declares. The older waiter is no longer religious but still seeking human communion, the younger one void of empathy and absorbed in personal pleasure. The two converse about a customer after he leaves, an old man who has recently attempted suicide, and whom the two waiters, at the insistence of the younger, have put out of the bright, cheery bodega so they can close for the night.

Arguing that they should have permitted the customer to stay and to share the café's lighted communion rather than sending him home to drink alone, the older waiter acknowledges that he too is one of those "who like to stay late at the cafe . . . with all those who do not want to go to bed. With all those who need a light for the night." After the young waiter leaves, *he* stays on, reluctant to close, and after asking himself *why* he needs a "clean, well-lighted place," realizes that it offers the aura of order in answer to "a nothing that he knew too well." On his own way home in the darkness, without the light, he holds back the void by reciting a parody of the Lord's Prayer – "Our nada who art in nada, nada be thy name thy kingdom nada thy will be nada in nada as it is in nada" – before retiring sleeplessly to await the light of day.[8]

Like Hemingway and Eugene O'Neill, F. Scott Fitzgerald recognized that the new technology of illumination "was far more than a utilitarian prop for home economics" (Nye 284): electricity confronted the modern world with new ways to express and understand the self. David Nye points to *The Great Gatsby* as a modern fable in which electricity becomes literally a tool of self-creation. Nick Carraway's first images of Gatsby come from the extravagant lawn parties where caterers mount "enough colored lights to make a Christmas tree of Gatsby's enormous garden."[9] The lights conjure up the mood of grand spectacle for Gatsby's guests, who equate the parties with Coney Island amusement. His lights advertise Gatsby's success to the world; and making them more intensely visible makes that success *seem* more real – and more able to fascinate and draw Daisy to him from across the bay. They blaze brighter the closer he comes to regaining her, and brightest on the night a rendezvous is arranged. Gatsby's spectacular lighting asserts the self he has fabricated, multiplies his sense of worth, and answers Daisy's green light flashing at him across the bay. Gatsby *believed* in that green light, Nick Carraway concludes, "the orgiastic future that year by year recedes before us" (182).

By now the reader, I trust, is making connections well ahead of me; so some shorthand should serve to bring me to a close. Ralph Ellison connected himself to Hemingway and Fitzgerald and their Lost Generation peers partly through a counterpointing novelistic sense of mission: "Ours is a task," he wrote, which "whether recognized or not, was defined for us to a large extent by that which the novels of the twenties failed to confront, and implicit in their triumphs and follies were our complexity and our travail" (*Going* 257). In *Invisible Man*, Ellison confronted the modernist tropes of electrification in Hemingway's "A Clean, Well-Lighted Place" and Fitzgerald's *The Great Gatsby* with revisionary narrative riffs bright with comparative implication, and anchored in the particular experience of technology and its social contexts that mark three centuries of African-American life in the alloy bowels of the machine, and that mark black men and women themselves, Ellison reiterated through the years, as, in many ways, hyper-modern, self-fabricated creations as far from the "primitives" of popular stereotype as Lewis Mumford's utopian "neotechnic" age is from the neolithic ooze. Alongside all the other things it would become, *Invisible Man* would also constitute a gloss on the "techniques" and technological consciousness of the American novel from the Golden Day to the Jazz Age and beyond; and Ellison's fictive experiment in "revolutionary technological modernity" would heed carefully the little man at Chehaw Station's goad to incorporate the experience of multivarious "others" into its own, and with the combinatory energy of plural truths, to synthesize new thresholds of consciousness.

The famous framing prologue of Ellison's novel nigrifies, hyperbolizes, and renders comically surreal and ironic the controlling motifs of

Hemingway's "clean, well-lighted place."[10] The social and spiritual assumptions upon which the violence, social cynicism, and understatement in Hemingway's work was based – assumptions rendered questionable to Ellison by his place in the social order – were rejected by his creation of an entirely new kind of figure in American literature: the theory- and concept-toting, gadget-fabricating black "thinker-tinker,"[11] kin to Ford, Edison, and Franklin, he quips, and deft enough with the techniques of electrification to shunt off enough purloined electricity from Monopolated Light & Power's local power station to charge the 1,369 light bulbs he has wired the ceiling of his underground retreat with to "shed light on his invisibility." "Light confirms my reality," Jack-the-Bear tells us, "gives birth to my form" (*Invisible* 6). But the insight that has led him to this consciousness he has won from the master of formlessness, Bliss Proteus Rinehart, that "spiritual technologist" and man of many other parts who, with electrified guitar music and glowing neon signs – dark *green* neon signs – fishes Harlem streetcorners for "marks" ready to "Behold the Invisible" (*Invisible* 495).

Rinehart orchestrates the Ellisonian riff on Gatsby's green light, with the scene of electric illusion moved from Gatsby's hyper-illuminated manicured lawns to Rinehart's Harlem storefront, "where a slender woman in a rusty black robe played passionate boogie-woogie on an upright piano along with a young man wearing a skull cap who struck righteous riffs from an electric guitar which was connected to an amplifier that hung from the ceiling above a gleaming white and gold pulpit .... The whole scene quivered vague and mysterious in the green light" (*Invisible* 376). Both Jack-the-Bear's and Rinehart's "spiritual technologies" suggest one final facet of Ellison's fictive confrontation with the myth of the machine and the forms of the novel that we should bear in mind. The will to personal power and agency that their shared facility with electrical power mirrors manifests itself most directly in Jack's and Rinehart's *inventiveness*, their *ingenuity*. "When you have lived invisible as long as I have, you develop a certain ingenuity. I'll solve the problem," Jack tells us (*Invisible* 7). Unlike Rinehart, "that confidencing sonofabitch" whose own ingenuity knows no moral boundaries, he commits himself to community. And if in projecting himself as a "thinker-tinker" kin to Ford, Edison, and Franklin, we presume *that* community to be something other than his own, Ellison hints at one last underground illumination from his people's underground history. In his prologue, Jack-the-Bear makes a point of having wired his ceiling "not with fluorescent bulbs, but with the older, more-expensive-to-operate kind, the *filament* type. An art of sabotage, you know" (*Invisible* 7).

Ellison *knew* from his early 1940s research and writing labors alongside Roi Ottley, Waring Cuney, Claude McKay and company, for the WPA manuscript project which culminated in the publication of *The Negro in New York* (1967), that despite disclaimers to the contrary,

> the bewildering array of technical inventions, which altered human life within a brief span, found Negroes in the vanguard.... But the machine age, which did so much to bring about divisions in the ranks of labor, put men out of work and caused protest from sections of the laboring population, [and] also brought whites new reasons to bolster their hatred of blacks.... When the third rail was invented and electricity replaced steam on the elevated railways in this city, the white men, who lost their jobs as steam locomotive engineers because of the innovation, heaped all manner of abuse on the whole Negro race because its inventor was a Negro. After its installation, Negroes were not safe on the streets of New York. They were frequently attacked by persons aware only that a new-fangled electric device invented by some "damn nigger" had taken away their jobs. Violence subsided only when the company finally rehired the old engineers and taught them the new job of motormen. The inventor, Granville T. Woods, a native of Ohio, had arrived in New York in 1880 and soon after invented a system by which telegraphing was made possible between trains in motion, technically known as "induction telegraph." During the next thirty years, until he died in New York City in 1910, he perfected twenty-five inventions, ... was employed by Thomas Edison ... and while working at his laboratory ... the American Bell Telephone Company purchased his electric telephone transmitter.[12]

One of Woods's black thinker-tinker peers, Louis Latimer, who as a draftsman made the drawings for the first Bell Telephone from a design by Alexander Graham Bell, superintended the installation of the electric lighting systems in New York City, Philadelphia, several Canadian cities, and London. He became associated with Thomas Edison in 1896 and as a member of the "Edison Pioneers," perfected the carbon *filament*, which made the intense, smokeless, fireless, glowing orange "Edison light" throw off an illumination unlike anything seen before. The spiritual cost of that filament illumination is what Jack-the-Bear's guerrilla war levies against Monopolated Light & Power; and ultimately for him acts of sabotage and the art of illumination become inseparable facets of his own "spiritual technology," a site of one more "electrifying" Ellisonian joke, and evidence that, waking or dreaming, in this writer's world of high fidelity and calculated distortion the ways of invisibility are invariably mysterious, their wonders to perform.

Notes

1. Ralph Ellison, *Shadow and Act* (New York: Random House, 1964), p. 102; Hereafter *Shadow*.
2. Ralph Ellison, quoted in Alan Nadel, *Invisible Criticism: Ralph Ellison and the American Canon* (University of Iowa Press, 1988), p. 158.

3. Robert Casillo, "Lewis Mumford," in *Dictionary of Literary Biography*, vol. 63 (Detroit: Gale Research, 1988), pp. 184–200.

4. Ralph Ellison, *Going to the Territory* (New York: Random House, 1986), pp. 244–6; Hereafter *Going*.

5. David Nye, *Electrifying America: Social Meanings of New Technology* (Cambridge: MIT Press, 1990), p. 51.

6. Quoted in Alan Nadel, *Invisible Criticism*, pp. 88, 90.

7. Clifford in *The House of the Seven Gables*, chap. 17.

8. Ernest Hemingway, "A Clean Well-Lighted Place," in *The Fifth Column and the First Forty-Nine Stories* (New York: Scribner's, 1939), pp. 477–81.

9. F. Scott Fitzgerald, *The Great Gatsby (New York: Scribner's, 1925)*, p. 39.

10. See Robert O'Meally, "The Rules of Magic: Hemingway as Ellison's 'Ancestor,'" *Southern Review* 21 *(1985)*, pp. 751–69.

11. Ralph Ellison, *Invisible Man* (New York: Vintage, 1995), p. 7. Hereafter *Invisible*.

12. Roi Ottley and William Weatherby, eds. *The Negro in New York: An Informal Social History: 1626–1940* (New York: Praeger, 1969), pp. 140–3.

9

SHELLY EVERSLEY

Female iconography in *Invisible Man*

In 1953, one year after the publication of Ralph Ellison's *Invisible Man*, Hugh Hefner launched his men's magazine, *Playboy*. The magazine's centerfold featured a nude Marilyn Monroe posed against a striking red velvet curtain. The photograph was taken in 1949 as Ellison was working diligently on the novel, and it became a quintessential example of American femininity, an icon of American cultural history. As a photographer, art student, and collector of painting and portraiture, Ellison understood the power of visual images. He liked to look at pictures. In his novel, Ellison describes a nude woman that seems to invoke the *Playboy* image: "the red robe swept aside like a veil, and I went breathless at the petite and generously curved nude, framed delicate and firm in the glass."[1] This nameless woman, "acting a symbolic role of life and feminine fertility" (*Invisible* 409), has a sexual affair with the protagonist and she appears in the novel just as invisible man confronts "The Woman Question." Ellison's artful description of the woman's symbolic role, like Monroe's pose, suggests complicity in a well-known and longstanding iconography of female difference and sexual objectification that critics have argued amounts to nothing more than a literary pinup. Ellison also describes the woman as framed by "a life-sized painting, a nude, a pink Renoir," and the narrator sees her nakedness haunted by a shadow. The painting emphasizes the very constructedness of gender difference. As a double, it offers a visual and life-sized reference to the history of female objectification so that Ellison's readers can look at the woman and see the "mirrors of hard, distorting glass" (3) that distort her humanity. The scene provokes in invisible man the sense of "a poignancy," something that forces him to question his reality – "[i]t was like a dream interval" – and most importantly, to question his assumption that invisibility is exclusive to black men (416–17). Here, both the narrator and the woman appear as nameless types. Their mutual and their individual challenge is to achieve an identity, one independent of the stereotypical images that conceal the truth.

At the start of the novel, Ellison's protagonist defines his predicament as one in which "people refuse to see me." His words call attention to the practice of looking as it informs and deforms humanity. The deliberate blindness that reduces humanity to stereotype amounts to an intellectual myopia, what Ellison calls a "construction of the *inner eyes*, those eyes with which they look through the physical eyes upon reality" (3). This metaphor also illustrates the status of women in the novel. Descriptions of Mary Rambo, Sybil, the "magnificent blond" at the Battle Royal, Norton and Trueblood's daughters, as well as the nameless nude framed by a Renoir, reveal concretely the deficiencies within the "*inner eyes*" that the protagonist must also rehabilitate. While they are the most consistent and crucial symbols in *Invisible Man*, women are also "more than symbols."[2] Indeed they become sites of *revelation* that transcend the simple opposition between black and white to offer new complexity to the novel's organizing themes. For this author who maintained a longstanding interest and engagement with the visual arts, telling by words is not enough to recover the humanity of women. As literal description, women cannot expose the social and psychological blockages that explain the gendered particulars that inform their invisibility. And, rather than read the debased iconography of women in the novel as proof of Ellison's "system of essentially androcentric seeing,"[3] a more suggestive approach will regard them as vivid renderings of the logic of invisibility. Fully aware of the universal implications of invisibility's attack on individual humanity, Ellison inserts visual depictions of women into the novel because he seeks a "way of revealing the unseen."[4] In his own introduction to the novel, Ellison describes his objective "to reveal the human complexity which stereotypes are intended to conceal" (xxii), and he argues that " 'high visibility' actually render[s] one *un*-visible" (xv). Consequently, "*un*-visible" women are everywhere in the novel; their stereotypes dramatize, with particular vividness, the most critical moments in the protagonist' s now universal quest for revelation and freedom.

Vision is perhaps the most underexplored aspect of *Invisible Man*. More than a literal question of seeing, the protagonist's life depends on his ability to "learn to look beneath the surface" and discern reality despite "mirrors of hard, distorting glass" (153, 3). Such discernment requires he learn to distinguish salient meaning from stereotype. While critics have discussed the phenomenological implications of Invisible Man's desire to be seen, his desire for social equality, few engage the contradictory significance of what he sees, and more importantly, how he processes the visual image. As John Berger explains, "The relation between what we see and what we know is never settled," since the meaning of what a person sees is mediated by time and space.[5] Invisible man makes this point when he recalls the details of his life experience from his subterranean hole. The reader becomes especially aware of his subjective vision precisely because of his convoluted narration in which the past, his recollection, becomes crucial to the organization of the present time that begins and ends the novel – "the end is in the beginning and the beginning lies far ahead" (6). In this way, Ellison's narrative choices reveal a gap between language and perception – what invisible man sees precedes his words. In an interview, Ellison explains that *Invisible Man* is "about innocence and human error, a struggle through illusion to reality" (*Collected Essays* 219).

Consequently, if the novel's struggle to recognize humanity requires a movement from "illusion to reality," visual depictions of women correspond to a world of illusion that reflect false realities. Ellison writes that "the true artist" must escape anachronism, "a distorted perception of social reality ... that divides social groups along lines that are no longer tenable, while fostering hostility, anxiety and fear" (*Collected Essays* 685–6).[6] The artist's position presents a challenge to the salience of stereotype so that when invisible man looks at women in the novel he confronts the false divisions that breed anxiety and fear. As a result, upon leaving the woman framed by the Renoir, he says: "Between us and everything we wanted to change in the world they placed a woman: socially, politically, economically. Why, goddamit, why did they insist on confusing the class struggle with the ass struggle, debasing both of us and them – all human motives?" (418). His question positions women – especially white women – as markers of privilege ("class struggle") and sexual property ("ass struggle"), so that, as symbolic capital, women become the currency in the false hierarchy of human exchange. The narrator's language indicates a palpable anxiety that can easily be misread as his and Ellison's anachronistic antipathy towards women, but then he notes "the confusion" debases everyone. As the lesson of ambivalence becomes more vivid, the protagonist begins to understand that such divisions are untenable constructions that distort his access to reality. His intellectual "confusion" requires a revolution in his ways of seeing.

The priority Ellison gives to the visual in the novel, especially as it elucidates the process of looking, corresponds to the conditions of his writing. As he composed *Invisible Man*, Ellison worked as a freelance photographer (ix–x). At the same time, he collected photos from *Life* magazine, especially clips from a section called "What's in a Picture." One notable clip, dated April 2, 1951, stands out. It reads: "An event is often seen better in pictures than in actuality. In a picture we can study the facts and details with calm detachment and see things we would have missed had we been there."[7] "What's in a Picture" suggests an important claim about the author's aesthetic priorities. Believing that "[a]n event is often seen better in pictures than in actuality," Ellison presents visual revelation as crucial to deciphering the meaning beyond the literal and beyond "our trained incapacity to perceive the truth." The clip also suggests that the intellectual distance manifest in photography creates a kind of detachment that encourages the potential to see more than surface. In 1946, the same year Ellison began writing *Invisible Man*, he photographed portraits of his friend Albert Murray, and book jacket covers. By 1948 he regularly went out with his friend, the well-known photographer Gordon Parks, taking photographs and developing prints.[8] Parks made such an impression on Ellison, that the novelist modeled his protean character Rinehart after him. In the novel Rinehart's chameleon-like presence inspires the protagonist to ask himself, "What on earth was hiding behind the face of things?" (493). As much as this question applies to Rinehart, it equally applies to the images of women that riddle the novel. And, as invisible man gets closer to self-understanding despite the challenge of mistaking surface for reality, he thinks again of Rinehart: "Could he himself be both rind and heart? What is real anyway?" (498). Reality, as Ellison pictures it, is both the "rind," the immediate surface of things, and the "heart," the more difficult to decipher truths that lie beneath, beyond what the eye can see.

In photography, as in painting, an image becomes intelligible via the manipulation of light.[9] Ellison, a writer, a photographer, and an art student[10] understood the relation between light and intelligibility. Finally conscious of his invisibility, the protagonist understands this insight:

> I now can see the darkness of lightness. And I love light. Perhaps you'll think it strange that an invisible man should need light, desire light, love light. But maybe it is exactly because I *am* invisible. Light confirms my reality, gives birth to my form . . . without light I am not only invisible, but formless as well; and to be unaware of one's form is to live a death . . . that is why I fight my battle with Monopolated Light & Power. The deeper reason, I mean: It allows me to feel my vital aliveness. . .In my hole in the basement there are exactly 1,369 lights . . . Nothing, storm or flood, must get in the way of our need for light and ever more and brighter light. The truth is the light and the light is the truth.
>
> (6–7)

Like any visual artist, invisible man knows that light gives an object its form, as radiation acts on the retina, the optic nerve, literally to make sight possible. Metaphorically, light represents knowledge, or mental illumination. When invisible man declares his mortal dependence on light, he calls attention to the notion of vision as insight, the epistemological depth humanity requires. The protagonist's invisibility stems from the absence of light, the dark benighted thinking that can only see a black man as rind without heart, form without content, a body without the ability to think or to feel. Such stunted thinking undermines the complexity of individual personhood; and, rather than illumination, it projects invisibility, what the protagonist calls "figments of . . . imagination – indeed, everything and anything except me" (3). This epistemological blindness to full humanity stems from a logic that positions black people and women as subhuman, as out of sight. In the novel, "Monopolated Light & Power" thus stands for a metaphorical myopia that pretends to possess exclusive control of the defining features of human actuality, of the truth ("The truth is the light and the light is the truth"). The narrator's underground appropriation of a "Monopolated Light & Power" enacts his dissent from their totalizing control. By avoiding having to pay for the 1,369 lightbulbs that illuminate his hole, the invisible man seeks an independent source of insight.

At the Battle Royal and in his "blind terror" (21), a metaphor of proliferating invisibility, invisible man sees only the image of a "magnificent blonde," her image constructed in the social imaginary. While he has not yet developed insight, he begins to learn its lessons. In this scene that frames the entire novel, the woman – also nameless and "stark naked" – stands before the protagonist, the fearful black boys, and the town's most respected white men. The novel's description frames her visually, and her subjectivity first appears through the male eyes that look at her body. Her humanity seems to disappear as her body submits to the voyeuristic gaze that renders her a pornographic sex object. She is invisible. Her manipulated image presents stereotypes of truth and social authority that rationalize domination over women and black people. For the narrator, however, this woman prompts him to see and feel ambivalence: "I wanted at one and the same time to caress her and destroy her, to love her and murder her, to hide from her, and yet to stroke where below the small American flag tattooed on her belly her thighs formed a capital V" (19). Even as the woman's presence provokes a visceral response, the protagonist's engagement calls attention to her visual and revelatory significance. For instance, the V of the woman's thighs juxtaposed with the American flag signals democratic victory. As Ellison began writing *Invisible Man* at the end of World War II, the United States had defeated totalitarian threats against global humanity. This victory not only positioned the nation as the world's leading democracy, it also promised integration, an honest racial equality that would finally realize the most sacred principles of American freedom. Yet, at the same time, the V between the woman's thighs also represents her gender difference and it reminds the protagonist of women's unequal status. Looking past the symbolic surface of the "magnificent blonde," Invisible Man begins to realize that no victory has been won. Neither the woman nor the man can rely on the national symbols that should, in actuality, indicate their freedoms.

In the segregated United States, a black man's gaze upon a white woman could, in the South, warrant death by lynching. By accepting the risk associated with the deathly potential of looking at a white woman ("[h]ad the price of looking been blindness, I would have looked," he says), invisible man refuses the tyranny of monopolated vision. He rebels against the social order that objectifies him and the woman in order to rethink the unreality that shrouds her appearance. The protagonist looks: "she began to dance . . . the smoke of a hundred cigars clinging to her like the thinnest of veils." The veils and the smoke imagistically emphasize the blinders that make her invisibility possible, and then they invoke another myth, Salome, whose seemingly promiscuous sexuality conceals her gender oppression. Salome's sensual dance allegedly cost John the Baptist his life. But, like the multiple meanings of the V between the blond woman's thighs, Salome's reluctant dance suggests more. In the myth, Salome refuses the persistent and inappropriate sexual advances of the King, her stepfather. Like "the most important men of [invisible man's] town," the king demands that Salome dance. In an act meant to demonstrate his masculine authority, his offer to compensate her for her services is calculated to reduce an independent woman to a possession, as one to be purchased as one would a whore.[11] The parallel between Salome's "Dance of the Seven Veils" and the blond woman's dance calls attention to the links between the myth of a dangerous, forbidden female sexuality and a blind-sighted objectification of women. Salome, like "the magnificent blonde," only *appears* to possess a dangerously seductive power over men.

A chauvinistic power that subjugates women and people of color distorts the protagonist's vision, for in his blindness he mistakes the blonde as a threat to his progress. As invisible man looks at "the magnificent blonde," he sees yet another myth: "She seemed like a fair bird-girl girdled in veils calling to me from the angry surface of some gray and threatening sea" (19). This Homeric and Joycean image invokes a siren, a nymph, part bird and part woman, who lures sailors to their death with her seductive singing. When he finally sees the woman distinct from her mythic sexuality – "I saw the terror and disgust in her eyes, almost like my own terror and that which I saw in the others boys" – he begins to understand their shared subjugation (20). The novel offers no pause, no distinction, between the woman's dance as pornographic entertainment and the boys' fight, the Battle Royal, that immediately follows. This seamlessness depicts their common position in relation to a social authority that falsely constructs their positions as opposites. As the protagonist describes the chaos and the terror of his own fight, like "a joggled camera sweeps in a reeling scene," he reminds the reader of its visual and symbolic resonance. He narrates chromatically – "The room went red as I fell" – and invisible man invites the reader to see, with "inner eyes," the importance of his struggle in relation to women who, shrouded in myth, also struggle with the burden of invisibility (20). Invisible man's red room predicts retribution and earth shattering revelation, as does the ominous red moon that is present in the Salome myth.[12]

The narrator's blindness and his insight in relation to the blonde woman initiates his education in invisibility. As he becomes aware of the distinction between formal education and the kind of knowledge that affords insight, invisible man recalls the images that inspire his illumination. He wonders whether the statue of the College Founder presents a "witnessing of revelation or a more efficient blinding," and in his resistance to blindness he becomes an intellectual. His "mind's eye" demands that he seek answers to his questions, "Why? And how? How and why?" (36). In another instance of the visual serving as a catalyst for revelation, the protagonist describes cinematically his encounter with Mr. Norton, a white benefactor of the Negro college. "As I drove," he recalls, "faded and yellow pictures of the school's early days displayed in the library flashed across the screen of my mind ... photographs ... of people who seemed almost without individuality ... the figures in the photographs had never seemed actually to have been alive, but were more like signs or symbols one found on the last pages of the dictionary" (39). Pictures flash across the "screen" of the protagonist's mind like projections in a slide-show. His description of the photographs suggests the opacity of blank-faced people who, in representing "signs or symbols," provide the key to deciphering a "sphinxlike" code. The mystery includes the enigma of Mr. Norton, "a symbol of The Great Traditions" (37), specifically the white paternalism that honors "time, custom and our trained incapacity to perceive the truth" and forecloses the pre-invisible man's ability to actually see. Most important, Mr. Norton declares his role as benefactor by way of his obligation to "construct a living memorial" to his daughter (45). The man's dead daughter becomes the myth that organizes his philanthropic intentions. "She was a being more rare, more beautiful, purer and more perfect and more delicate than the wildest dream of the poet ... a perfect creation, a work of purest art ... a personality like that of some biblical maiden," he tells the protagonist (42). No longer a person but "a work of purest art," the nameless daughter becomes an abstraction, "a *being*" without humanity, a fantasy that defines Mr. Norton's false sense of reality. In his loss and longing, Mr. Norton projects an hallucinatory immediacy onto the photograph of his daughter that he carries in his wallet, speaking of her as if still alive: "[h]er beauty was a well-spring of purest water-of-life, and to look upon her was to drink and drink and drink again" (42). Upon looking at her picture, invisible man "almost dropped it," not because of its "perfection," but because of its similarity to "the magnificent blond" (42). "I seemed to remember her, or someone like her, in the past," he says, reminding the reader of the female images that recur throughout the novel (43).

For invisible man, the virginal picture of the girl presents a reversed image, a negative, of the Battle Royal's "whore." Mr. Norton's possession, "framed in engraved platinum," brings to mind King Herod's desire for his stepdaughter, a parallel that echoes the scene from the protagonist's past as well as the mythical history that clouds his vision in the present (42). He "almost dropped" the photograph because the image of the girl haunts him, directing invisible man toward what Roland Barthes calls a "blind field" since it prompts other memories (such as the "magnificent blond") and it creates sensory and intellectual discomfort.[13] In looking at the now dead, virginal girl, invisible man remembers a certain violence – a pornographic objectification – that in its invisibility, he shares with the real and mythical women he meets on his journey toward self-discovery. Norton's erotic and urgent desire for an unreal woman resonates beyond this father–daughter relation since Mr. Norton implicates invisible man, the school, and the social progress of black people in the girl's image: "You are bound to a great dream and to a beautiful monument" (43). The mystery of this transgressive desire remains unfocused until Mr. Norton and invisible man meet Jim Trueblood, a black sharecropper, whose incestuous impregnation of his daughter brings to the surface the chaos beneath Norton's desire. Trueblood's admission, "sometimes a man can look at a little ole pigtail gal and see him a whore," invokes the picture of the virginal girl that resonates in the narrator's memory of the "magnificent blonde" (59). As images, women can represent whatever a metaphorically blind man sees. And, while Trueblood's ability to "see" a whore in a girl – his daughter – resonates for Mr. Norton, Trueblood acts on his short-sighted desire masked as a dream.

"You have looked upon chaos and are not destroyed!," Norton exclaims upon hearing confirmation of Trueblood's transgression (51). Notably, his surprise stems not from Trueblood's action, but from his escape from punishment. Incest has not destroyed the man who has not only "looked upon chaos" but partaken of it. In his discussion of this incident in the novel, Houston A. Baker, Jr. argues the "status of the farmer's story as a commodity cannot be ignored," that Trueblood's situation "can be viewed as a capitalist's dream. And if such results can be achieved without fear of holy sanction, then procreation becomes a secular feat of human engineering." Baker's cogent reading of the commodity exchange crucial to this pivotal scene recognizes the profit a patriarchal, capitalist culture understands in the legacy of heirs. He contends that if Mr. Norton had had the courage to believe that he could also escape retribution for such actions with his own daughter, the millionaire might have enacted his own "incestuous domination [of his family] as a productive unit, eternally giving birth to new profits."[14] Although Baker exposes the critical parallels between Trueblood and Norton's incestuous and capitalist ambition, he misses the point about their ambition's object. It is not merely the story as commodity that cannot be ignored; it is the images of women, one black the other white, that become the glaring commodities from which both men enjoy profit. Ignoring the female images that instigate the episode as well as the poignant communion between Norton and Trueblood, Baker focuses on the incident as an artful exploration of black male sexuality even as he notices Trueblood's "firm possession of all his 'womenfolks'" (Baker 180), and Norton's eyes "blazing … with something like envy and indignation" (51). Ellison's narrator watches Norton give Trueblood a hundred dollar bill, and his comment on this exchange of female imagery is telling: "I saw him removing a red Moroccan-leather wallet from his coat pocket. The platinum framed miniature came with it, but he did not look at it this time" (69).

The failure to risk looking at women occludes their humanity. Ellison purposely crafts female presences in the novel in relation to manipulations of light so that, on first glance, readers only see a form without substance, highly visible objects without meaningful significance. But, with closer scrutiny, they become a cogent lesson in illumination: now visual and at the same time "*un-visible*," women in the novel demand the kind of engagement that inspires discomfort, a discomfort now understood as the revelation of truth invisible man associates with light. In his journey toward insight and self-discovery, the protagonist must confront and engage their symbolic illumination. His describes the nude woman framed by a Renoir as "the kind of woman who glows" (409), and the light heightens the visual effect of her symbolic character as it delineates the contours of her particularly gendered invisibility. As their sexual tension increases, invisible man notices a slight anomaly of color in the woman "with raven hair in which a thin streak of white had begun almost imperceptibly to show." This black and white detail suggests the binary logic of race and gender difference that also mirrors the thinking that cannot imagine insight. At the same time, it reverses the color imagery of Liberty Paints – the streak of white subtly contaminates the "pure" blackness of her "raven hair." And, like the moment of terror at the Battle Royal, the protagonist admits, "she was so striking I had to avert my somewhat startled eyes," and his gaze returns to the painting (411). In his discussion of the female nude in the visual arts, Berger explains that their recurring presence has become the criteria in which "women have been seen and judged as sights" (Berger 47). Gender difference, based on a notion of masculinity as power and agency, defines women as objects, most "particularly an object of vision," a "sight" that ultimately divides her subjectivity into two parts in which she simultaneously watches herself even as she is accompanied by an image of herself. She is always aware of being looked at by a spectator. By looking, invisible man risks confrontation with the "chaos" that comes with insight.

At the center of the novel, the protagonist encounters a black woman, Mary Rambo. He meets her just after he leaves the Liberty Paints factory hospital. Some critics have argued that the narrator looks at Mary only as a stereotypical mammy, "with echoes of Sambo," whom the protagonist sees "not as a person" but only as "a link between past and future" (Sylvander 79). Because Mary nurtures the narrator back to health, many critics read her as a striking example of Ellison's limited view of women. Anne Folwell Stanford, for instance, contends that Mary's nurturing presence in the novel refuses to acknowledge diversity among black women by presenting her on the moral high ground of a "madonna/whore duality" (Stanford 118). But, as Claudia Tate notes, Mary "is not bound by this stereotype," but rather she "sets the tone as well as determines the idiomatic language for the novel." As the protagonist's surrogate mother – not his mammy – she nurtures not the master's white child, but a black one.[15] To reduce Mary to stereotype ignores the force of Ellison's aesthetic commitment as well as what I am arguing is the revelatory potential of the *"un-visible."* Mary escapes stereotypical objectification not only because of the crucial wisdom she imparts to the narrator ("Don't let this Harlem git you. I'm in New York, but New York ain't in me, understand what I mean? Don't git corrupted"), but also because she exercises her insightful ability to *see* the humanity in an invisible man (255). The narrator first encounters her as an abstraction, a disembodied voice, "And the big dark woman saying, *Boy, is you all right, what's wrong?* in a husky contralto" (251). He falls asleep "in the echo of her words," and when he awakens, he "saw her across the room" (253). His vision seems to render her like the nameless woman shadowed by the Renoir, as "a sight," objectified as the reflection of stereotype. But, in a challenge to the authority of a masculinist view, in what bell hooks calls an "oppositional gaze," Mary returns his look and sheds passive objectification:[16] "Then I realized that through [her] glasses still slanted down, the eyes were no longer focused on the page, but on my face and lighting with a slow smile" (253). The "lighting" of her eyes focused on his face suggests Mary's independent illumination, one not determined by a monopolated light. In Ellison's short story, "Out of Hospital and Under the Bar," readers see an even better picture of Mary's complexity and her insight. In this earlier draft, not included in the final edition of *Invisible Man*, Mary sees the protagonist confined in the hospital. Upon looking at him, he explains "she tried seriously to communicate with me."[17]

Mary and invisible man's potential "seriously to communicate" seems to emphasize the possibility of meaningful and sympathetic exchange between individuals. This potential also appears within his encounter with the woman framed by the Renoir: "the sensed possibility of a heightened communication." Concerning their encounter, he says it was "as though the discordantly invisible and the conspicuously enigmatic were reaching a delicately balanced harmony" (411). Here, the woman, "enigmatic," and the man, "invisible," share a self-awareness of the paradoxical conditions of their objectifications. Their "harmony" reveals what Hortense J. Spillers calls "the damaged humanity of an acquisitive culture"[18] in which this white woman and this black man see their stereotypes as their only assets in a short-sighted human exchange. This acknowledgment becomes a crucial detail of their interaction and it forces the reader – who also becomes a viewer – to seek the truths concealed by images. For Ellison, the possibility of "heightened communication" between two "*un-seen*" individuals foregrounds the visual and discursive power that reduces women to one-dimensional surfaces. And by framing the woman in the visual, the narrator illustrates the disturbance of his insight, "[m]y vision seemed to pulse alternately clear and vague." His inability to focus calls attention to the woman's invisibility and also reveals the narrator's metaphorical blindness. The woman's debasement as sexualized commodity barely comes into focus for the protagonist as the "dim light from the hallway filters into the darkness of the room." This filter of light illuminates, however briefly, the protagonist's consciousness ("my mind revolved," he says) by presenting him with a new way of seeing (417). A sliver of light penetrates his darkness and it creates an epistemological uncertainty that must come as he learns to see. "I didn't know whether I was awake or dreaming," he says in a surreal sequence that mirrors the dream that prompts Trueblood's transgression. The narrator recounts the image of a white man acknowledging – with indifference – their post-coital, interracial moment. "It was strange," he recalls, noting the uncertainty that forces him to question his reality. "I wanted to linger there, experiencing the sensation of something precious perilously attained too late and now to be lost forever – a poignancy" (417).

More than sex, the narrator's feeling of an inscrutable sensation of "a poignancy," defines invisible man's encounter with the enigmatic woman. Barthes writes, "A photograph's *punctum* is that accident which pricks me (but also bruises me, is poignant to me)" (27). Framed by the visual, invisible man's poignancy is the unspeakable, unfocused accident of "a heightened communication." The poignancy he feels recalls the narrator's response to Mr. Norton's photograph of his daughter – "I almost dropped it" – and it becomes especially disconcerting. Since his intimacy with an enigma represents something he cannot grasp, he cannot confirm its reality. For Barthes, this poignancy offers "a power of expansion. The power is metonymic" so that invisible man's experience of looking requires a "thinking eye" which forces him to "add something" (Barthes 45) and discover a way to articulate his experience. Like Ellison's narrator's "inner eyes," Barthes's Spectator's eyes and mind focus on the "something" in the image he can neither name nor identify. In order to articulate the meaning of what they see and feel, Barthes and Ellison's spectator must think and act. Poignancy thus depends on imagination as the ability to integrate form ("the rind") and substance ("the heart").

"The Woman Question" foreshadows the poignancy of the encounter between "the discordantly invisible [man] and the conspicuously enigmatic [woman]" framed by a Renoir painting. The woman's spectacular, sexualized persona brings into focus the very specularity of the black man's impotent position in relation to the monopolated light that can never render his person three dimensional. The white woman, like the black man, functions for the Brotherhood as an icon of their exclusive power. Even as the Brotherhood pretends inclusiveness, they rely on hierarchy of race and gender which hobbles their ability to discern a full picture of humanity. Wondering if he has been made "the butt of an outrageous joke" in the eyes of the Brotherhood, invisible man understands his assignment as spokesman for women's rights as a punishment (407). In yet another echo of the Battle Royal scene, he tries to convince himself that the white male power brokers acknowledge his ability so much that his assignment reflects their endorsement. He tells himself, "by selecting me to speak with its authority on a subject which elsewhere in our society I'd have found taboo, weren't they reaffirming their belief both in me and in the principles of Brotherhood, proving that they drew no lines even when it came to women?" (408). But of course lines have been drawn; the boundaries created breed what Ellison calls "social anachronism . . . that imbalance in American society which leads to a distorted perception of social reality" (*Collected Essays* 685). Brother Jack's reductive pamphlet on "The Woman Question" illuminates this anachronistic simplicity with which the Brotherhood perceives any kind of difference. Their decision to couple their surface commitment to political questions of gender (women) with race (invisible man) reinforces – via sexual taboo – those "anachronisms" and the false social divisions they produce. Women and people of color thus figure as the light and shadows that lend the Brotherhood its form. Invisible man must, therefore, change his perspective and utilize all of his senses in order to discern what these prevailing images might reveal.

When asked about her husband's plan for social change in the Brotherhood, Sybil, the next white woman who inadvertently instructs invisible man on the contours of false images, responds with a spectacular insight: "Georgie's blind 'sa mole in a hole 'n doesn't know a thing about it" (524). George, Sybil's husband, cannot see social equality. According to the man's wife, his blindness is his representative problem: "Men have repressed us too much," she says. "We're expected to pass up on too many human things" (519). Her use of the term "repression" does not only describe a masculinist refusal to acknowledge women as an equal part of the conscious world. It also echoes the Vet's declaration of "that great false wisdom taught to slaves and pragmatists alike" (95), that, for him, emerges ultimately from a blindness he calls "repression": "He registers with his senses but short-circuits with his brain," he says. Invisible man has "learned to repress not only his emotions but his humanity" (94). Like the Veteran-doctor, Sybil perceives "repression" as a social sickness that replaces reality with false images. The problem allows for men like her husband, Mr. Norton, "the most respected men of the town," and even invisible man to mistake myopia for clear vision. Relegated to the social unconscious, women, according to Sybil, are pushed beneath the surface and locked in distortion and unreality. It is no wonder that invisible man meets Sybil at a party in a building called "the Chthonian," a word relating to the underworld, as in infernal. Unlike invisible man's self-determined subterranean hole, the Chthonian underworld literally exists in the world above ground, in the social world where actual women appear as unreal images.

Invisible man's encounter with Sybil signals the penultimate moment of revelation that not only drives the protagonist underground, but also prompts his desire to articulate the double-consciousness that emerges from epistemological blindness. The two participate in a flirtation that depends on their symbolic statuses – "just the type of misunderstood married woman" and "Brother Taboo-with-whom-all-things-are-possible" (515, 517). Plotting revenge on the Brotherhood, the narrator intends to seduce the lonely woman in order to secure restricted information to which her husband, George, has access. At the same time, Sybil encourages the encounter so that she can confirm her fantasy of a black rapist. In their interaction invisible man finally sees a symbolic and "a very revolting ritual" and he asks whether Sybil's face displays "horror" or "innocence," an ambivalence that emerges from the "obscene scheme of the evening" (517). His question reveals his desire for answers, not sex. Now, near the end of his journey, he sees a woman with whom he communicates; or, at least, she communicates something to him. Her articulation of the contours and the logic of negation prompts the protagonist to think; his next step requires action.

Unlike earlier instances of chaos that begin with unreal depictions of women, this time invisible man lands in Harlem during a riot that "sounded like a distant celebration of the Fourth of July." The narrative describes a new level of perception: "there was a sudden and brilliant suspension of time" and "then time burst" at the very moment in which a black community takes action against the inequality that has repressed their humanity (535). This moment signals – both visually and literally – a declaration of independence marked by illumination. And, seeking a reason for the cause of the people's action, the protagonist hears an explanation that implicates his "revolting ritual" with Sybil: "they said a white woman set it off by trying to take a black gal's man ... She was drunk" (541). Whether the unacknowledged Sybil inspires the chaos remains unclear but prophetic; the anachronistic notion that a drunk white woman could instigate a riot in a black community exposes the damaging effects of false perceptions. It confuses "the class struggle with the ass struggle" even as it anticipates parallels between race and gender inequities. As invisible man moves through the scene of chaos, he learns to see the surreal contradictions of everyday life. On top of a milk wagon, for example, he sees "a huge woman in a gingham pinafore ... drinking beer from a barrel which stood before her ... she bowed graciously from side to side like a tipsy fat lady in a circus parade, the dipper like a gravy spoon in her enormous hand" (544–5). The black woman, under the guise of symbolic mammy, does not offer a picture that would reconcile her stereotype with her behavior. Rather than nurture, she destroys, "she laughed and drank deeply while reaching over nonchalantly with her free hand to send quart after quart of milk crashing into the street." Here, this enigmatic woman's actions repudiate her "mammy" image so as the narrator looks, he asks "Why was I torn?" (545). Now "torn," the man feels the poignancy of ambivalence and contradiction – a revelation mediated by false images of women – that send him running underground toward hibernation, "a covert preparation for a more overt action" (13). He thinks, "the mind that conceived a plan of living must never lose sight of the chaos against which that pattern was conceived" and he pursues a plan of confronting the chaos he now associates with revelation. His experience among invisibles has awakened his "sense of perception," and he finally declares, "I'm invisible, not blind" (576).

Notes

1. Ralph Ellison, *Invisible Man* (New York: Vintage Books, 1995), p. 416. References hereafter in text.
2. Carolyn W. Sylvander, "Ralph Ellison's Invisible Man and Female Stereotypes," *Negro American Literature Forum* 9:3 (Autumn 1975) , p. 79.
3. Anne Folwell Stanford, "He Speaks for Whom? Inscription and Reinscription of Women in *Invisible Man* and *The Salt Eaters*," *The Critical Response to Ralph Ellison*, Robert J. Butler, ed. (Westport, CT: Greenwood Press, 2000), p. 124.
4. Ralph Ellison, *The Collected Essays of Ralph Ellison* (New York: Modern Library, 1995), p. 690. References hereafter in text.
5. John Berger, *Ways of Seeing* (London: British Broadcasting and Penguin Books, 1972) , p. 7.
6. This statement appears in his essay "The Art of Romare Bearden."in *Collected Essays*.
7. "Photography," 1937–55, 1984, n.d. Ralph Ellison Papers. Box 27. Library of Congress, Washington, DC.
8. Lawrence Jackson, *Ralph Ellison: Emergence of Genius* (New York: John Wiley and Sons, Inc., 2002), p. 376.
9. In photography, the artist must subtract light in order for an image to appear on film; in painting, the artist must add light to a canvas so that the viewer can discern the image. Thanks to photographer Matthew Rodgers and painter Robert Sciasci for pointing out this detail.
10. In addition to his well-known study of music, Ellison maintained a longstanding interest in the visual arts. Ellison studied art in college, and upon his arrival in New York, he began to study sculpture under Augusta Savage at her well-known Harlem Community Art Center. He maintained a lifelong friendship with painter and collage artist, Romare Bearden, whom he met at Charles Seifert's Ethiopian Art School; and he later became the first student of Richmond Barthe, a man many argue is the United States' greatest African-American sculptor. See *Ralph Ellison: Emergence of Genius*, pp. 164–7.
11. In the New Testament, Salome is the daughter of Queen Herodias and step-daughter to King Herod Antipas. John the Baptist condemns Salome's mother's marriage to Herod, her first husband's brother. Herod holds John the Baptist prisoner, but he is afraid to kill him since many think John a man of God. Herod also lusts for his young stepdaughter, so on his birthday he asks her to dance for him. She declines; but, when Herod offers her anything in his kingdom in exchange for the dance, she accepts. Upon concluding her seductive dance, "The Dance of the Seven Veils," she asks for John the Baptist's head delivered to her. Fearfully and reluctantly, Herod honors her wish, and Salome delivers the head to her mother. See Mark 6: 14–29. For centuries many have represented Salome as the original femme fatale, a symbol of the erotic and dangerous woman. See paintings such as "The Dance of Salome" by Benozzo Gozzoli (c. 1461–81), and "Salome with the Head of John the Baptist" by Carlo Dola (c. 1600). Oscar Wilde's controversial one act tragedy (first published in 1893), suggests that Herod's lascivious looks and his sexual desire for his stepdaughter, coupled with Iokanaan's (John the Baptist's) scorn for Salome and her mother ("By women came evil into this world" [22]), position Salome as

the subject and object of a more general masculine contempt for women. See Aubrey Beardsley and Oscar Wilde, *Salome: A Tragedy in One Act* (New York: Dover Publications, 1967). German composer Richard Strauss was so moved by Wilde's account of Salome (who is unnamed in the biblical story), that he composed the opera, *Salome*, first performed in Dresden in 1905.

12. In Wilde's account of Salome's story, Iokanaan's death also marks the appearance of a blood red moon. In the Bible, a red moon represents the realization of the prophecy of Revelation: "the moon turned red as blood all over, and the stars of the sky fell onto the earth ... For the Great Day of his retribution has come ..." See Revelation 6: 12–17.

13. Roland Barthes, *Camera Lucida: Reflections on Photography*.Trans. Richard Howard (New York, Hill and Wang, 1981), pp. 57–8.

14. Houston A. Baker, Jr., *Blues, Ideology and Afro-American Literature* (Chicago and London: University of Chicago Press, 1984), p. 192.

15. Claudia Tate, "Notes on the Invisible Women in Ralph Ellison's *Invisible Man*," *Speaking for You: The Vision of Ralph Ellison*, ed. Kimberly W. Benston (Washington, DC: Howard University Press, 1990), p. 168.

16. bell hooks, *Black Looks: Race and Representation* (Boston: South End Press, 1992), p. 115.

17. Ralph Ellison, "Out of the Hospital and Under the Bar," *Soon, One Morning: New Writing By American Negroes 1940–1962*, ed. Herbert Hill. (New York: Knopf, 1963), p. 244.

18. Hortense J. Spillers, *Black, White, and in Color: Essays on American Literature and Culture* (Chicago and London: University of Chicago Press, 2003), p. 79.

10

KENNETH W. WARREN

Chaos not quite controlled: Ellison's uncompleted transit to *Juneteenth*

One of the stranger documents among Ralph Ellison's published works is the essay "Tell It Like It Is, Baby," which he began writing while in Rome in 1956 but left uncompleted for almost a decade until he published it in the centenary issue of *The Nation* in 1965.[1] What prompted the essay was a letter to Ellison from a boyhood friend, Virgil Branam, who had written to express outrage at the defiance of southern senators in the face of the US Supreme Court's *Brown* v. *Board of Education* ruling. In March of 1956 twenty-two US senators from southern states, led by Strom Thurmond of South Carolina, signed and circulated a "Southern Manifesto," in which, among other things, they embraced *Plessy* v. *Ferguson* with the claim that the 1896 ruling had become "a part of the life of the people of many of the States and confirmed their habits, traditions, and way of life." The manifesto concluded with the senators vowing to reverse the decision of the US Supreme Court in Brown.[2] Troubled by this open defiance, Branam, one of Ellison's long-time correspondents, wanted to know what sense the famous novelist could make of the events roiling the American scene.

Ellison recalls that Branam's letters always contained "a trace of mockery, directed at my odd metamorphosis into a writer, which is meant to remind me whence I come" (*Collected Essays* 29). Clearly, Ellison seems quite open to the provocation represented by Branam's missive. Not only did the vernacular phrasing of Branam's prose find its way into the title of the piece, but a passage from the letter also stands as the essay's epigraph. Even so, despite Ellison's insistence that he is merely attempting to respond to a down-home demand, the essay itself is anything but a down-home exercise. On the contrary, Ellison has constructed a complex dream vision into which he enfolds a variety of disparate elements that include autobiographical reminiscences (specifically, the death of his father), the assassination of Abraham Lincoln, snippets of American intellectual history, and references to popular culture, all of which he leavens with Freudian symbolism in an attempt to reflect the "barely controlled chaos" enveloping him as he worked on his second novel. But if his lived chaos was at least somewhat controlled, it was Ellison's estimation that the article, even with the lengthy interval between conception and fulfillment, fell short of even this minimal containment. Winding to a conclusion he declares, "So I confess defeat, it is too complex for me to 'tell it like it is'" (*Collected Essays* 46).

Ellison does not, though, allow his admission of defeat with his essay to translate into pessimism about his efforts with his novel-in-progress. In the essay's last sentence Ellison tells Branam and his other readers, "Following my defeat with the essay, I returned to my novel – which, by the way, has as its central incident the assassination of a Senator" (46). The irony here, of course, is that while Ellison did manage, however unsatisfactorily, to complete the essay he began in 1956, he never finished the novel that might have redeemed what he regarded as the essay's conceptual failure. Yet if "Tell It Like It Is, Baby" represents Ellison's reflections on what happens "when a Negro American novelist tries to write about desegregation," the difficulties he faced in finishing the essay might offer some insight into the problems that plagued his famously unfinished novel (31). That is, the incomplete transit from *Invisible Man* to the second novel, understood as Ellison's unsuccessful attempt to negotiate the difference between writing about segregation and writing about desegregation, reflects the extent to which the Negro American novel as a cultural project was tied to the Jim Crow era – the period Ellison describes as having been conjured from "the horror generated by the Civil War and the tragic incident [Lincoln's assassination] which marked the reversal of the North's 'victory,' and which foreshadowed the tenor of the ninety years to follow" (30). Thus, while the Negro American novel at its best – and *Invisible Man* may be the genre's apotheosis – was at once a testament to the rich and variegated humanity achieved by the Negro within, and despite, the strictures of segregation, it also had to be an eloquent indictment of the nation's continued failure to welcome the Negro into the polity. Notwithstanding Ellison's apparent dissent from Irving Howe's contention that a Negro could not "put pen to paper . . . without some impulse to protest, be it harsh or mild, political or private, released or buried," the truth was, as Ellison admitted, the Negro novelist (and his novel) was "a product of the interaction between his racial predicament, his individual will, and the broader American cultural freedom in which he finds his ambiguous existence."[3]

Tellingly, Ellison insists that the Negro's "racial predicament" remained, despite the pattern of northward migration, southern in character. The novel of desegregation was therefore obliged to "regard, in all its tortuous ambiguity, the South" and the "clusters of conflicting images" through which that region was constituted (31). The south of which Ellison writes in this essay is defined in the first instance not by the history of slavery but rather by the post-Reconstruction era and the nation's commitment to Jim Crow, which he refers to as "hellish." We live, Ellison laments, in a state of "equivocation . . . (born of the Hayes-Tilden Compromise of 1877 and faintly illumined by the candle of liberty) . . . It is the candle alone which guides us through the chaos and when the candle flickers we're in the dark" (*Collected Essays* 32). And while the Brown decision should have put an end to that equivocation, southern resistance continued, creating the momentary descent into darkness that gives rise to Ellison's essay: "And so in the Roman dark I dreamed"(32).

The Negro novel, then, was a form born of this state of equivocation, written to fan the candle of liberty into a steady flame. Ellison, to be sure, bridled at any suggestion that those elements of the American experience associated with the Negro were nothing more than reactions to racial domination. In his review of Gunnar Myrdal's *An American Dilemma* he asks rhetorically, "But can a people . . . live and develop for over three hundred years simply by *reacting*? Are American Negroes simply the creation of white men, or have they at least helped to create themselves out of what they found around them?"[4] But the implied affirmation of some measure of black cultural autonomy, which itself assumed that the reproduction of Negro culture (of the Negro himself) was only partly a response to Jim Crow, also suggested that the transition from segregation to desegregation, while powerfully unsettling, would not mark the terminus of a cultural order. Moreover, given that Jim Crow required whites to deny the "true interrelatedness of blackness and whiteness," the discovery and affirmation by whites of their identity with the Negro and his culture would in all likelihood touch off a social revolution. And yet, taken together, "Tell It Like It Is, Baby" and *Juneteenth* testify to Ellison's sometimes profound reservations about the cultural project he spent most of his creative life advocating. That is, the two works suggest that even if it were possible in an era of desegregation to keep Negro culture recognizably Negro, it still might not be true that wresting from white culture an admission of its own blackness might not contribute to social revolution.

The bulk of "Tell It Like It Is, Baby" narrates a dream that fairly bristles with symbolism ready-made for psychoanalytic interpretation. Ellison in fact concludes the essay by providing just such an interpretation, which I'll touch on shortly, as it is an interpretation that seeks to conceal as much as it reveals. The dream commences with Ellison's memory of himself as a boy walking on a brilliant spring day made slightly grotesque by an overabundance of catalpa worms being voraciously consumed by a host of birds. "The worms were everywhere, the walk smeared green and white with their pulp and skin." And Ellison recalls trying "to avoid both worms and smears" as he walked. And yet mitigating his disgust at the display of smeared worms is his "expectation of some pleasantness, some long looked for reward" which he then realizes derives from the fact that he "was going to see my father."

This mingling of disgust and anticipation plays out on a scene of degraded phallic images where it seems almost impossible for the boy to avoid participating in an avian orgy of castration – a series of attacks which are at this point rendered more sickening than sinister because the narrative at first emphasizes the "relentless" worms and not the voracious, consuming birds. Correspondingly the descriptive stress comes down on the boy's inability to keep from stepping on the worms or the smears. He cannot but do the thing he most wishes to avoid, and therefore he cannot avoid the guilt triggered by his actions. In short order, then, the "certain joy" he experiences when he thinks he sees, "under the high archway of worm-damaged leaves a tall, familiar man coming toward me," changes almost immediately into an encounter with the uncanny, as the familiar man becomes a racially ambiguous "stranger wearing a dull black and gray diamond-checked suit" who regards the boy with an "accusatory" stare. The boy then loses sight of the man when a "mirror or window paned nearby sent the sun glaring into my eyes" (32–3).

The scene then changes and the boy finds himself "walking through an arcade lined with shops and on into an old street-car terminal." From there he enters a great public square where once again he is confronted with degraded phallic imagery, this time in the form of an equestrian military statue whose rider displays an "expression of victory ... on his bronze face, despite the fact that his saber had lost three-fourths of its blade." And once again the degraded phallus is associated with the stranger/father who comes into the boy's line of sight, "Gazing upward past [the statue's] head, I saw on the balcony of a building across the square the man who had stared; now, accompanied by a mysterious woman, he was looking toward me" (33). The man and the woman then engage in a cryptic conversation about the boy, who is suddenly transported to Washington DC just after the Civil War, where he catches a glimpse of the body of "a tall man who seemed familiar: there was something about the way the disarranged sheet draped the toes of his shoes" (34).

This familiarity precipitates a scene of déjà vu as the young Ellison moves "forward with a feeling of dread, thinking, 'It's happening again'" (35). Given the immediate post-Civil War setting, we might expect the "it" to refer to the Lincoln assassination, so that the face of the man lying before him will be that of the slain President. Instead, Ellison is transported to the hospital room where he saw his father for the last time, and once again the young boy must say goodbye as his father is being taken away on a "cold white metal" hospital bed. This extended scene is, in reality, three scenes in one. The first is the moment before his father is taken into the operating room when parents and son are together. The second is the brief instance when Ellison claims to have caught a last glimpse of his father, and the third actually occurs well after the fact when Ellison's mother recalls for her son the traumatic details of the days following her husband's death.

The second of these moments occurs when the door of the operating room opens briefly to reveal the older man

> *lying in a great tub-like basin, waiting to be prepared for his last surgery. I could see his long legs, his knees propped up and his toes flexing as he rested there with his arms folded over his chest, looking at me quite calmly, like a kindly king in his bath.* (35)

But while Ellison recalls that his father "*had looked at me and smiled,*" Ellison's mother "*wouldn't believe that I had seen him*" (35). And if the final, benevolent smile clearly reflects the boy's desire to believe this incident had happened, of greater importance than the accuracy of the son's memory is the ambiguous role of the mother. Here the role of the mother is to undermine the last pleasant exchange between father and son, at once echoing the effect of the disparaging comments uttered earlier by the woman who had appeared with the stranger on the balcony in the square ("he's not the one"), and also anticipating the last of the three scenes when, well after the death scene, Ellison's mother recalls for her son the stinking, decaying body of the dead father/king: "*Years later ... my mother had said that difficulties with money and the weather caused his body to be withheld from burial until it stank in the dark back room of the funeral parlor.*" [5] The intrusion of death and decay into the fecundity of midsummer (Ellison's father died on July 19) repeats the dream's first worm-infested scene and threatens to blight the young manhood of the son. And yet while Ellison refers to sociological formulas by which his father's death would have left his elder son "*fatally flawed and doomed – afraid of women, derelict of duty, sad in the sack, cold in the crotch, a rolling stone in social space, a spiritual delinquent, a hater of self – me in whose face his image shows?*" Ellison insists that the reality was otherwise: Counterintuitively, his mother's disturbing memory enables Ellison to imbibe the certainty that his father "*only perished, he did not pass away.*" As a result, Ellison describes himself as a recipient of both his parents' "*values and their love*" (36).

In the strange logic of the dream, however, this moment of familial redemption cuts immediately back to the Lincoln assassination where Ellison is transformed into "a child again and dressed in the one-piece garment of a young slave." He watches as the president's funeral procession transmutes into a "carnival, an *Oktoberfest,* a Mardi Gras, with the corpse become the butt of obscene jokes" (37). The young Ellison and "four ragged Negro men" who are pressed into service to carry the body are the only people in attendance who show any respect for Lincoln. The rest form a mob that engages in acts of ritual humiliation of the body. They call the dead president a coon and, in an act of symbolic castration, they cut up his clothing for souvenirs. A woman with "heavily powdered breasts which ... kept flipping out of her low-cut bodice and tossing about like two bloated, moon-mad, oxygen-starved flounders" puts on Lincoln's stovepipe hat and dances suggestively. In the meantime a beer-drinking man "who resembled Edmund Wilson" forces a tin bucket onto Lincoln's head, "clamping the wire handle beneath the bearded chin" after which, the body is brought to rest before the "austere shaft" of the Washington Monument. There the four men who had been carrying Lincoln are beaten and "sent fleeing into the darkness" (40). The young Ellison, however, is made to stay and watch the rest of the horrific spectacle, in which the corpse is exposed to the hysterical laughter of a "thin granddame" who screamed "like a great tropical bird"; the mock sympathy of a man "who looked oddly like Mr. Justice Holmes"; and a contest among the rabble "to see who could kick the corpse into the most fantastic positions, standing it on its head, doubling it over, twisting it in the cordwood postures of Dachau."

The young Ellison's reactions and thoughts punctuate the nightmare vision. At first, the spewing of racial epithets at Lincoln's body undermines the boy's sense of his own humanity. He wonders, *"And how can I be me, if Old Abe be a 'coon,' ... and how can I be a slave or even human?"* (38). As the horrific scene plays out before him, however, Ellison realizes that the sense of humiliation and embarrassment he shares with the abused corpse has been, throughout the dream, mitigated by his refusal to believe that "the President was actually dead. He isn't dead: I wouldn't have it so" (42). Ellison writes,

> So I could not believe Mr. Lincoln dead. Thus, in the dislocated, is-and-isn't world of dream, I felt that the President bore his indignities out of a temporary weakness incurred by his wound or out of war weariness – even out of a saint-like patience, out of a hero's grace before the mob's wild human need. It was as though the noisy desecration of his body was being accepted as he had accepted the tragic duty of keeping the country unified even through an act of fratricidal war ... he is not tolerating the mob's outrages out of the insensitivity of death, but submitting willingly to them out of the most sublime and tragic awareness of the requirements of his fated role. (42–3)

Ellison tells us, however, that his consoling vision of the return of the king who brings salvation and restoration to his troubled land is rooted in a prior denial: to this point Ellison has refused to believe that his own father is actually dead. Beguiled by a "recurring fantasy in which, on my way to school of a late winter day I would emerge from a cold side street into the warm spring sun and there see my father, dead since I was three, rushing toward me with a smile of recognition and outstretched arms." This fantasy, Ellison realizes, had "held off" through his childhood "the processes of time and the cold facts of death" (42).

Suddenly then, the point of the dream seems to be clear. Ellison must finally face the death of his father as fact without the consolatory cover of myth. And as if to drive home this point, Lincoln's corpse rapidly decomposes into "an advanced state of putrefaction" achieving a monstrous bloated shape that causes the President's underwear to resemble "the Michelin trademark," a mundane image that seems to deny the possibility of transcendence. The effect on Ellison is immediate: "Death undeniable looked out at me, the sublime mocking its earthly shell" (43). And yet despite Ellison's wishes, this realization does not end the mob's fixation on the corpse. They persist in their desecration, but when a man attempts to remove the misshapen underwear, "a sound like a fusillade of shots ripped the air" precipitating a scene that echoes the frenzied feast of worms with which the dream opened:

> and a dense cloud of gray, slime-drenched birds burst up from the earth on swift metallic wings and attacked the onlookers with feet of fire. Screaming with pain, they burst apart like an exploding grenade, turning to claw at one another as they milled wildly about. And in the confusion I was pinned against the monument, burned by the flying slime. (43)

The four Negroes who had initially carried the body then return and prepare to inter the corpse, at which point Ellison's status as mere spectator is momentarily underscored as the "scene became a scene on a movie screen, which I was watching from a distance and with a feeling of utmost clarity, as though I grasped the mystery of all experience." But before Ellison is able to utter any words attesting to this clarity, this spectatorial distance collapses, and Ellison is whisked to the graveside where the Negroes beckon him to look into the hole in which he sees an interracial "multitude" as they sit "at a table making a ghoulish meal of some frightful thing that a white sheet hid from view." Then just as something appears to be stirring beneath the sheet, Ellison at last awakens, and is only able to calm himself by remembering and reciting the "compassionate words uttered by Lincoln at Gettysburg" – a memory aided by Ellison's ability to recall Charles Laughton's recital of the Address in the film, "Ruggles of Red Gap" (45).

The over-the-top imagery of the dream, with its obsessive repetition of scenes of the death and defilement of the father, its insistence on the impotence of the son, and its haunting by birdlike devouring women possibly indicates that Ellison is playing some sort of trick on the reader, leaving an obvious interpretive trail that will turn out to be a false one. Yet the interpretation that Ellison himself offers after telling his reader that he had "fallen asleep reading Gilbert Murray's chapter on 'Hamlet and Orestes,'" is rather straightforward, although Ellison protests that in regard to the dream, Murray's text "would seem to shed no light at all." Even so Ellison goes on to note

> A possible relationship between my dream and a pattern of classical tragedy: the hero-father murdered (for Lincoln *is* a kind of father of twentieth-century America), his life evilly sacrificed and the fruits of his neglected labors withering some ninety years in the fields; the state fallen into corruption, and the citizens into moral anarchy, with no hero come to set things right.　　(46)

But by this point in the essay Ellison has already discounted some of the real world correlatives for his dream. The figure who looked like Mr. Justice Holmes "only resembling him and the man in the long gray coat only *looking* like Mr. Edmund Wilson" (45). Despite this discounting, the appearance in the dream of both Edmund Wilson and Justice Holmes seems apt, as both men could indeed be charged with abetting the neglect of Lincoln's labors. In *Giles* v. *Harris* (1903) when blacks in Alabama challenged their disenfranchisement under the Alabama state constitution, Holmes's opinion effectively limited the power and will of the federal government to redress state-sanctioned injustice. Holmes held that

> If the conspiracy and the intent [to disfranchise] exist, a name on a piece of paper will not defeat them. Unless we are prepared to supervise the voting in that state by officers of the court, it seems to us that all that the plaintiff could get from equity would be an empty form. Apart from damages to the individual, relief from a great political wrong, if done, as alleged, by the people of a state and the state itself, must be given by them or by the legislative and political department of the government of the United States.[6]

As for Wilson, his 1962 study, *Patriotic Gore*, paints an unidealized, and strangely pro-southern portrait of the Civil War in which he likens the Confederacy to the states of eastern Europe and central Asia that had been incorporated into the Soviet Union or drawn into its sphere of influence and laments the "premature enfranchisement of the Negroes."[7] Characterizing Lincoln as an "uncompromising dictator" on the order of Bismarck and Lenin, *Patriotic Gore* rereads the motives of nations at war as enacting in human terms neither more nor less than the zoological phenomenon of "a primitive organism called a sea slug ... gobbling up smaller organisms through a large orifice at one end of its body."[8] Given the acts of voraciousness everywhere in evidence in Ellison's essay, Wilson's conviction that geopolitics can be likened to hungry organisms attempting to consume all other organisms, even those only slightly smaller than themselves, might indicate *Patriotic Gore* as a source text for the imagery of Ellison's dream, preoccupied as it is with acts of consumption. Yet *Patriotic Gore*'s publication date in 1962 would mean that the Wilson-like figure in the dream was added when Ellison went back to the essay several years after his initial attempt to write. Likewise even the Holmes look-alike may not have been in the first version of Ellison's 1956 Roman nightmare. Instead, the provocation that may have led to inclusion of this image was the violent attack on Civil Rights marchers on the Edmund Pettus Bridge in Selma, Alabama in March 1965, which led Congress to debate and pass the Voting Rights Act signed into law by Lyndon Johnson on August 6.

And yet even if these antagonists manqué could make an appearance only well after the night of Ellison's 1956 dream, their belated inclusion oddly underwrites the accuracy of Ellison's initial sense of his dream's significance: "more dismaying than having such events erupt one's dream life was that no living hero or surrogate had appeared to play Anthony to Lincoln's Caesar" and that even "the villains were less than individualized" (45). The absence or inadequacy of a surrogate or successor turns out to be the deep provocation of the dream. For a writer struggling to produce a second novel in the wake of having written a book that had almost immediately been proclaimed a classic, the failure of a successor to appear would resonate on several levels: the question of how the son might rise to the stature of the slain father/king would be inseparable from the question of how a second novel might rival the "classic" status of the first.

Characteristically, then, the text that Ellison says "would seem to shed no light at all" on Ellison's dream – Gilbert Murray's chapter on "Hamlet and Orestes," – from Murray's book *The Classical Tradition in Poetry*, turns out to be quite illuminating. Murray's chapter explores what he terms an "unconscious tradition in poetry [that] reaches further back into the past, than any deliberate human imitation."[9] Focusing on character-typology in both *Hamlet* and *Orestes*, and focusing for both plays on the traditional sources that gave rise to the classic texts themselves, Murray attempts to understand these similarities as the result of something other than authorial intention. Instead these repetitions mark "a great unconscious solidarity and continuity, lasting from age to age, among all the children of the poets."[10] Murray surmises that artistic genius probably stems from the ability to stir or move the "stream" of "desires and fears and passions, long slumbering yet eternally familiar, which have for thousands of years lain near the root of our most intimate emotions and been wrought into the fabric of our most magical dreams"[11]

The subject of the intimate and magical dream that haunts *Hamlet* and *Orestes* is the plight of the son whose father, the king, has been murdered by a kinsman who then himself marries the queen. The story of the murdered king, according to Murray, is part of "the world-wide ritual story of what we may call the Golden-Bough Kings," and is also, of course, the myth that had underwritten many of the masterpieces of high modernism. And as we have already seen, Ellison's reading of his dream had emphasized the novelist's roles as the son, not only of his own father, but of Lincoln as well, overwhelmed by his inability to act in any way that might restore either the dignity of the slain king or the disorder of the state. What effect could Ellison as a novelist, working in a form that many scholars had declared defunct, have on a nation still at war with itself over the status of the Negro?[12]

Arguably, then, as a window onto the task that Ellison set for himself in writing the second novel, "Tell It Like It Is, Baby" – filtered through Gilbert Murray's reading of *Hamlet* and *Orestes* – reveals the composing process for the second novel to have been an extended effort to discover whether or not the elements of classical tragedy could be produced from the ninety-year history of post-Civil War American society. Ellison had banked heavily on the idea that the tragic mode for American literature could be found only behind the comic mask that American society had imposed on the Negro.[13] Thus, the burden he placed on himself was to start with the comic elements of the Negro's position in American society in the twilight of the Jim Crow era and to extract from those elements the features that Gilbert Murray had deemed basic to all classical tragic literature. Accordingly, *Juneteenth*, in a somewhat vestigial fashion, puts in play various aspects of the King cycle. The death and birth of the Golden Bough Kings resurfaces as the religious con routine orchestrated by Reverend Hickman. In this routine the Reverend Alonzo Hickman's young charge, Bliss, himself a boy preacher who may or may not have any direct black ancestry and who later becomes the race-baiting Senator Sunraider, rises dramatically from his coffin, as if from the dead. Ellison then uses one of these episodes to introduce the mythic Queen figure into the story. Just after Bliss has been "resurrected" by Hickman a white woman bursts into the Juneteenth service claiming to be Bliss's mother. The disruption forces Hickman to tell Bliss something about the woman's past, and in trying to abate the young boy's rising tide of curiosity, Hickman dismisses her as suffering from a delusion, "Well, she thought she was some kind of queen."[14] Even the figure of the Fool, which Gilbert Murray includes as a common feature of this myth, makes an appearance as the blackface clown who troubles the young Bliss at the circus.

But at the center of the story is the slaying, or the attempted slaying, of the king. *Juneteenth* commences with the arrival of the Reverend Hickman and his congregation in Washington DC in an attempt to prevent Bliss's (now Senator Adam Sunraider's) unacknowledged son from killing his father. The Senator's racist secretary refuses to allow Hickman to see Bliss, and her intransigence permits the assassination attempt to go forward, and the Senator is gunned down on the floor of the Senate. Only after the wounded Senator calls for Hickman from his hospital bed is the Reverend reunited with his former protégé. Through the shared reminiscences of the two men, as the wounded Senator drifts in and out of consciousness, we begin to piece together Bliss's biography. The boy's realization, after his tumultuous emergence from the coffin at the Juneteenth service, that he is at least partly if not all white had precipitated an emotional crisis that derailed him from the tracks laid down by Hickman. As indicated in Ellison's notes for the novel, "Bliss's coffin is a threshold, a point between life and death. Note that after its symbolism of rebirth (Christian) he does indeed find rebirth – but in an ironic reversal he becomes white and anything but the liberator he was being trained to become."[15]

The liberator, of course, is Abraham Lincoln, who haunts this novel as he pervasively haunts "Tell It Like It Is, Baby." After having been rebuffed in their first attempt to see Sunraider, the Negro congregants and Hickman are "seen praying quietly within the Lincoln Memorial" where "an amateur photographer, a high-school boy from the Bronx" snaps their picture, thinking they made a "'good composition . . . I thought their faces would make a good scale of grays between the whites of the marble and the blackness of the shadows" (*Juneteenth* 9). With the photographic documentation of the Civil Rights movement in venues like *Life* magazine as an obvious referent, *Juneteenth* seeks to sear into the mind's eye of its reader a liberatory American iconography of white shading into gray and from there into black. When later in the novel, we view up close the encounter between the Negroes and the Lincoln Memorial, Ellison treats the moment with the intensity and reverence associated with a religious experience. The statue, like the corpse in the dream, is not dead – "the stone seemed to live and breathe, then, its great chest appearing to heave as though, stirred by their approach it had decided to sigh in silent recognition of who and what they were and had chosen to reveal its secret life" (280). A woman among the group responds as if she has seen the living Lincoln and not merely his representation, "'Oh, my Lord! Look, y'all, it's him! It's HIM!' her voice breaking in a quavering rush of tears" (281). Hickman, likewise moved, preaches a sermon. His mind preoccupied with Bliss, Hickman compares the white president, who had become "*one of us*," with the boy who though raised among Negroes, had become their sworn demagogic enemy. Overwhelmed by the irony, and sitting in the shadow of Lincoln, Hickman muses sadly, "*And to think ... we had hope to raise ourselves that kind of man*" (283).

The question at the heart of Ellison's unfinished novel was, why would someone who didn't have to be a Negro choose to become "one of us"? Bliss's tortured career was intended as an answer because the alternative to becoming "one of us" was self-destruction and self-denial. The signatories of the 1956 Southern Manifesto, who were leading their states into bloodshed and chaos on behalf of an impossible purity, were ample evidence of the cost of that alternative. The question, however, went even deeper. If even those whites like Bliss, who had, so to speak, imbibed Negro culture with their mother's milk (Faulkner, who had dedicated *Go Down, Moses* to his Negro nursemaid, had disappointed Ellison with his recent reactions to desegregation) could go so far awry, where was the evidence that somewhere in the experience of being Negro lay the key to claiming the full measure of our humanity?

Ellison struggled with *Juneteenth* as the legal pillars of Jim Crow America were being progressively demolished and as the scene of struggle shifted from southern states to northern cities. The 1967 fire that destroyed the manuscript Ellison claimed to be near completion makes it impossible to say with any certainty how he would have resolved imaginatively all of the problems he set for himself if the novel had been published later that decade. One wonders, though, if they could have been resolved. By foregrounding the stark irony of Bliss's apostasy, the novel had taken the risk of denying the redemptiveness of the very force that Ellison's position depended on – the power of the Negro's voice and culture. Only by transforming Bliss's sham resurrections into the real thing could Ellison have achieved some narrative resolution. But such a resolution, given the continued racial turbulence during that period, could only have been factitious. And it may have been Ellison's awareness of this fact that forestalled any conclusion and kept the novelist reworking and reworking his never-completed opus, which had, fatally it seems, demonstrated the futility of its resolution in the very imagining of its premise.

Notes

1. See John Callahan's introductory note, p. 27 of *The Collected Essays of Ralph Ellison* (New York: The Modern Library, 1995). Cited in the text as *Collected Essays.*
2. "The Southern Manifesto," from the *Congressional Record*, 84th Congress Second Session, vol. 102, part 4 (March 12, 1956). Washington, DC: Governmental Printing Office, 1956, 4459–60, rpt.http://www. strom. clemson. edu/strom/manifesto. html
3. Quoted in Ralph Ellison, "The World and the Jug," in *The Collected Essays of Ralph Ellison*, pp. 158 and 160.

4. Ralph Ellison, "An American Dilemma: *A Review*," in *The Collected Essays of Ralph Ellison*, p. 339.

5. Lawrence Jackson writes that Lewis Ellison "was buried four days after his death." See *Ralph Ellison: Emergence of Genius* (New York: John Wiley and Sons, 2002), p. 21.

6. *Giles v. Harris*, 189 US 475 (1903).

7. Edmund Wilson, *Patriotic Gore: Studies in the Literature of the American Civil War* (New York: Farrar, Straus, and Giroux, 1962), p. xxii.

8. Ibid., p. xi.

9. Gilbert Murray, *The Classical Tradition in Poetry*, The Charles Eliot Norton Lectures (Cambridge, MA: Harvard University Press, 1927), p. 205.

10. Ibid., p. 237.

11. Ibid., p. 239–40.

12. In a letter to Albert Murray written from Rome in April of 1956, Ellison complains of having to leave "old Bliss and Cliofus and Severn and Love [characters from *Juneteenth*] to deal with The Novel and those who say the form is dead. Fuck Trilling and his gang]," Ralph Ellison, letter to Albert Murray, April 4, 1957. Rpt. In *Trading Twelves: The Selected Letters of Ralph Ellison and Albert Murray*. Ed. Albert Murray and John F. Callahan (New York: The Modern Library, 2000), p. 157. The article Ellison mentions is most likely "Society, Morality, and the Novel" rpt. in *Collected Essays*, pp. 694–725.

13. Ralph Ellison, "Twentieth-Century Fiction and the Mask of Humanity," in *Collected Essays*, p. 89.

14. Ralph Ellison, *Juneteenth, A Novel*. Ed. John F. Callahan (New York: Random House, 1999), p. 204. Cited as *Juneteenth* in the text.

15. Ralph Ellison, "Notes," *Juneteenth*, p. 357.

II

ROSS POSNOCK

Ralph Ellison, Hannah Arendt and the meaning of politics

Bringing Ellison and Arendt together could well comprise a chapter on yet another failed interaction between black and Jewish intellectuals.[1] After all, on the two occasions when Ellison publically mentions Arendt it is in a less than favorable light. At the start of "The World and the Jug," his compelling skewering of Irving Howe, Ellison remarks that Howe's earlier critique of Ellison is "written with something of the Olympian authority that characterized Hannah Arendt's 'Reflections on Little Rock'" in the Winter 1959 issue of Howe's *Dissent*.[2] Ellison is referring to her notorious misreading of black parents' attempts at integrating segregated grade schools as a parvenu effort at social climbing. Ellison's phrase "Olympian authority" should not be construed as a compliment; it is his sarcastic euphemism for the arrogance of those such as Howe and Arendt "who would tell us the meaning of Negro life" without ever bothering "to learn how varied it really is." "Evidently Howe feels that unrelieved suffering is the only 'real' Negro experience, and that the true Negro writer must be ferocious" (*Collected Essays* 159).

Howe received a very public chastisement from Ellison; Arendt was luckier. Ellison critiqued her presumptions ("Hannah Arendt has failed to grasp the importance of the *ideal*" of "sacrifice" among "Southern Negroes") not at length in an essay but briefly in the course of an interview with Robert Penn Warren, in *Who Speaks For the Negro?*[3] In reply, Arendt sent Ellison a private letter in which she acknowledged her grievous misreading: "It is precisely this ideal of sacrifice which I didn't understand" and she withdrew her charge of parvenu social behavior on the part of black parents.[4] What Ellison pinpoints as Arendt's myopia regarding ideals is, we shall see, a weakness that her critics expound upon and one that *Invisible Man*, in the importance it places on affirming "principle," will resolve.

Parvenu, along with its opposed and honorific paired term pariah, correspond, respectively, to the distinctions in Arendt's major work, *The Human Condition*, between the social and the political and between behavior and action. In sum, social behavior is antithetical to political action. As Hanna

Pitkin observes, social behavior embodies "the parvenu way of thinking, seeing, and conducting oneself" – through deference, status seeking, and rigorous self-interest – and amounts to the failure to act where action is demanded, the absence of politics where politics is demanded.[5] Arendt's reliance on pariah and parvenu, rooted in her personal and generational ordeal of German/Jewish social and political tensions surrounding assimilation, were terms she employed for better and for worse throughout her life. In the case of Little Rock it was surely for the worse since she failed to see that black parents had defied or escaped the pariah/parvenu model, being neither obsequious nor proudly marginal. Rather than acting as social climbing "parvenus," as Arendt had assumed, black parents demanded that their children have equal access to education as a civic entitlement not stratified by race. Acting in effect as "political beings" (Ellison's phrase to which we will return) these parents regarded access to culture as a political matter rather than one of social status. They deliberately put their children through a "rite of initiation," said Ellison, one that required they "face the terror and contain the fear" of public exposure as they risked the disdain of both blacks and whites (quoted in Warren 344).

Ellison, in effect, shows Arendt's parvenu/pariah dichotomy to be a limited analytical tool for political understanding. To be a "conscious pariah," Arendt implies, is the only politically responsible stance of the intellectual. It requires heroic defiance that refuses to assimilate to the status quo. The conscious pariah scorns the desperate striving and deference toward one's social superiors displayed by his fellow outsider, the parvenu. For Arendt, this obsequiousness dooms the parvenu to conformity, self-estrangement, and political irrelevance. Yet the defiant marginality chosen by the intellectual as conscious pariah more than a little resembles (or mimes) the arrogance of aristocratic "Olympian authority" (to borrow Ellison's phrase). This is an irony that the political philosopher Judith Shklar once adroitly clarified. As Shklar noted, Arendt's very choice of the word parvenu has significance: "it is *the* classic snob word, which is thrown at the *bourgeois gentilhomme* by the aristocrats whom he tries to join...That she should have used the word for assimilated Jews tells us a good deal about Arendt. The pariah is so sure of her superiority that she no longer wishes to make efforts to join the larger society...she has in fact absorbed the attitude of its upper class [so] completely."[6] Ellison's critique of the "Olympian authority" of Howe and Arendt contains an analogous irony, for Ellison has often been accused of a similar detachment. Like Arendt, Ellison occupied an uneasy, ambiguous stance as insider and outsider.

Perhaps because of their sharp differences over Little Rock, discussion of these two figures has been absent until very recently.[7] Reducing the

Arendt/Ellison connection to this disagreement disguises the actual, surprising grounds of their affinity: an effort to revitalize politics as creative action in public, a commitment sustained while remaining skeptical of political ideologies preaching radical social change.

In Ellison's famous essay "The World and the Jug" he speaks of the liberating effect of reading in college Marx, Freud, Hemingway, T. S. Eliot, Pound, and Stein: "books which seldom, if ever, mentioned Negroes were to release me from whatever 'segregated' idea I might have had of my human possibilities." These lines are part of our canonical image of Ellison. Less familiar and seldom quoted is what occurs a few sentences later when, in referring to the momentous reading experience mentioned above, he remarks: "Indeed, I understand a bit more about myself as a Negro because literature has taught me something of my identity as a Western man, as a political being" (*Collected Essays* 164).

To explore what Ellison means by "political being" and how his understanding informs *Invisible Man* are tasks that continue to be necessary, for, as the 1999 CUNY "Ellison and American Culture" conference made clear, suspicion from leftist critics of the novelist as a- or anti-political remains strong.[8] Ellison, I would argue, is preoccupied in *Invisible Man* with the political, but this preoccupation is not immediately accessible because it takes the form of a double irony: he reveals how and why activity that imagines itself strenuously, radically "political" (the Brotherhood) is actually anti-political. And he discloses that those who are said to have "plunged outside history" and been relegated to oblivion ("History has passed them by," to borrow the words of Brother Jack) are actually potentially effective political actors.[9] In short, Ellison seeks to defamiliarize our received ideas of the political.

My thesis is that Ellison's 1952 novel constructs the political in ways that bear striking comparison with Arendt's epochal redescription of the political six years later in *The Human Condition* (1958). Bringing these texts together may at first seem anomalous, not least because in the 1960s they enjoyed nearly antithetical reputations among those on the left. Arendt's book, along with her *On Revolution* of 1963, inspired some in the civil rights struggle and especially those in the Free Speech Movement in Berkeley.[10] Like many of the intellectual leaders of the New Left, Arendt rejected both Marxism (for its fetish of labor and its determinism) and liberalism (for its valorizing of the private and minimizing of politics). She insisted on the possibility of recovering human action in the face of the increasing "world alienation" characteristic of modernity – man's withdrawal from the public realm, a retreat underwritten by equating freedom with freedom from politics.[11]

As a prime exemplar of "world alienation" one might easily nominate Ellison's protagonist domiciled underground where, after nearly 600 pages, he reluctantly concludes that he has "overstayed" his "hibernation" (*Invisible* 581). By the late 1960s many readers had lost patience with such a (seemingly) temporizing stance; black nationalists held Ellison's novel up to scorn, condemning it as quietist and elitist. Reading Ellison and Arendt together helps recover not only the complicated status of hibernation – that, as Ellison's narrator notes early on, "hibernation is a covert preparation for a more overt action" – but foregrounds what readers often ignore: the catalytic effect upon the narrator of witnessing the "overt action" of a group in Harlem acting in concert to end inhuman living conditions (*Invisible* 13). Seeing near the novel's end this organized collective "capable of their own action" inspires his fragile hope that until the "world" is put in a "straitjacket, its definition is possibility" (548, 576).

Ellison, like Arendt, reanimated the possibility of political participation during a postwar period when the very notion of meaningful agency had been cast into doubt by the trauma of totalitarianism. A flight from politics into the consolations of self-cultivation became one response among intellectuals to Nazism and Stalinism, some justifying it by believing that "an end to ideology" (in Daniel Bell's famous phrase) was imminent with the Allied victory. Belief in "the end to ideology" crystallized for many New York intellectuals their migration from a youthful embrace of Marxism in the 1930s to a cold-war embrace of literature as an end to politics. Ellison, a socalled "cousin" in the *Partisan Review* family (as Bell called Ellison and James Baldwin) is of course typically seen as having traveled this road from Marxist idealism to political disenchantment and aesthetic refuge, and hence is set in company with Lionel Trilling and others as a quintessential cold-war high modernist.[12]

In order to complicate this received wisdom let us return to Ellison's statement quoted earlier: "Indeed, I understand a bit more about myself as a Negro because literature has taught me something of my identity as a Western man, as a political being." Challenging the modernist tendency to oppose literature and the political, Ellison implicitly here declares their affinity. The political and the aesthetic are realms of freedom, of release from the confinement of "segregation" anchored in the deadly reductionism of race. Belief in literature as unraced, and hence a paradigm of political equality, has a distinct genealogy in African-American intellectual history; its *locus classicus* is Du Bois's "kingdom of culture" where one "sits with Shakespeare and he winces not."[13] Ellison points to an analogous kingdom, one where "political being" flourishes in an unraced realm of universalism, equality, and impartiality. Envisioning the political as unraced is a notion that stretches back to the foundations of Western thought, to Aristotle and his germinal conception of politics as a distinct human activity expressed in citizenship, in civic participation that emerges only when a social order no longer depends on blood, "on the observation of hierarchical rules pertaining to household, family, clan, and tribe."[14] The political idea of civic particip-ation requires that we see people in terms of membership rather than in terms of where they come from or what they look like. The *politikos* refers to those men of various origins and social standing who leave the household realm of necessity to engage in rational debate and judgment.

Ivan Hannaford, whose important study *Race: The History of an Idea in the West* (1996) I have been quoting, argues that race is an antonym to the classical ideas of politics, the principles of civil association. The history of race thinking involves the dissolution of this antithesis, the transmogrifi-cation of historical political communities into nations and races whose "tests of true belonging were no longer decided on action as a citizen but upon the purity of language, color, and shape" (Hannaford 14). Hannaford names Arendt as a prime influence. This makes sense given that *The Human Condition* sets forth a group of terms, appropriated from Aristotle, that are grounded in the opposition between realms of necessity and freedom. Necessity includes the household and private life (which, in Arendt's notor-ious equation, comprises the social or society itself, where the possibility of action is excluded and instead members are "'normalize[d]'" and taught to "behave") and is set against the realm of freedom exemplified by the polis as the public arena of political activity (*Human* 37–8). Those marooned in the realm of economic necessity and excluded from speaking the language of politics were dubbed, according to Hannaford, *ethnos*, the root of ethnic. These provincials, also known as *barbaros*, are embedded in nature, confined to a tight circle of blood relations, reliant on the habits and folkways of forefathers (Hannaford 21).

The *ethnos/politikos* distinction is useful in understanding Ellison's cri-tique of 1970s black nationalism as captive to "blood magic and blood thinking" at the expense of the political (*Collected Essays* 505).[15] The distinction also speaks to a period of American history crucial to Ellison. In the wake of post-Civil War Reconstruction's collapse, the black American was forced to the ethnic province. The effacement of blacks from public political life froze them in the ghetto of group identity. Embedded in Nature, they were Negroes rather than Americans. After 1877, Ellison notes, "the whole focus upon the relationship of black people and their culture to the broader culture was sort of shut down" (*Collected Essays* 376). With this termination vanished the ideal of the political as civic association unan-chored to origin, replaced by any number of ideologies of unfreedom, including the rise of positivist social science and its arsenal of absolute distinctions and neat schematisms – all inimical to literature and to the classical sense of the political. "Sociology" is usually Ellison's covering term of disdain for these discourses of discipline and obedience. Nurturing opposite impulses is the worldly imperative of civic life where the "common interests" of "art and democracy" converge in the "development of conscious, articulate citizens," as Ellison remarked in 1980 (*Invisible* xx).

The philosophical and historical elaboration of this convergence is a central concern of Arendt's political theory. Understood as words and deeds of participatory, public display, the political activity of citizenship produces or discovers self-knowledge not in advance but "in the flux of action and speech" amid "sheer human togetherness" (*Human* 161, 160). As self-disclosure to others, the practice of the art of civic association thus requires communication through the "public use of one's reason," (in Kant's famous phrase that Arendt cherished) and thereby resists the tilt toward privatism and subjectivism encouraged by "world alienation." Adapting in her final book Kant's analysis of taste for political aims, Arendt makes aesthetic, reflective judgment – the capacity to discern and honor the particular within the universal – into a model of critical thinking whose political power is founded on the ability to free the particular from the domination of the universal when the latter has reified into the unthinking inertia of general rules and habit. In sum, the act of judgment, for Arendt the most political of our mental capacities, injects the possibility of change, and is at the heart of communication, of thinking in public, while constituting the boundary where aesthetics and politics meet.

Change, in turn, is founded on action, and in action man reveals a capacity for initiating new beginnings, what Arendt calls "natality." Hence "initiative, an element of action, and therefore of natality, is inherent in all human activities. Moreover, since action is the political activity par excellence, natality, and not mortality, may be the central category of political, as distinguished from metaphysical, thought" (*Human* 11). Arendt emphasizes action's spontaneity, its recalcitrance to rule or prediction, its character of "startling unexpectedness," precisely the quality that has traditionally aroused the disdain of philosophy (157). In stressing how open-ended action is, Arendt complicates the traditional equation of freedom with sovereignty, for action involves "the simultaneous presence of freedom and non-sovereignty, of being able to begin something new and of not being able to control or even foretell its consequences" (211).

In conceiving action as a decentering force outside the framework of teleology, as unconditioned by goals or consequences, ungrounded in reason or nature, Arendt has always invited controversy. In an influential judgment, for instance, Martin Jay described her as an existentialist romantic and irrationalist whose celebration of action for its own sake possesses a kinship with fascist aesthetes like Ernst Junger. In a more moderate revision, Jay has recently remarked: "when you privilege initiatory, agonistic action and spontaneous, independent judgment, above principles, norms, logical arguments, and substance, you don't always get what you bargained for."[16] Rush Limbaugh, says Jay, shares Arendt's performative notion of politics. Other commentators find compelling her deconstruction of action's traditional reliance upon the idea of finality and praise her aesthetic approach to action as worthy of a postmodern Nietzschean *avant la lettre*.[17]

Whether one censures or praises Arendt, the deliberateness of her carefully reckless devotion to action is remarkable and demands accounting. Her commitment to action responds to historical crises (including two world wars) that have sapped human beings' trust in their own creative will and persuaded them of their alleged helplessness and lack of responsibility. It responds to the impoverishment of action – reduced to work under capitalism, to labor under communism. And it responds to a social reality increasingly legislated, on both sides of the cold war, by mandates of technocratic efficiency. In such a world, says Arendt, the "greatest evil" is that "committed by Nobodies ... by human beings who refuse ... to be persons" (quoted in Pitkin 185). In response Arendt would reinstate natality with Emersonian ardor. She calls it the "miracle that saves the world, the realm of human affairs, from its normal, 'natural' ruin." Only the full experience of the capacity for the action "can bestow upon human affairs faith and hope" (*Human* 222).

I have called Arendt's fervent hymn to action Emersonian. Man had become the "dwarf of himself," declared Emerson, and urged as an antidote action that would somehow adhere to "the strong present tense" and remain always "experiment" rather than calcifying into "sacrament." Emerson's very devotion to action produced fear of its fragility; you act "at your peril," he warned. "Men's actions are too strong for them."[18] Although Emerson did not equate action with the political, and was more concerned than Arendt about action's paradoxical elusiveness, both are adamant about exploding the "mischievous notion that we are come late into nature; that the world was finished a long time ago" (Emerson 65). It is not surprising, then, that Arendt has affinities to Emerson's heirs, William James and John Dewey and their philosophy of action known as pragmatism. While Arendt never mentions her contemporary John Dewey, his recovery of the concepts of democracy and experience from the condescension of Western thought is clearly congruent with her own effort to reverse philosophical rationalism's devaluation of politics and action. Her argument that, starting with Plato, the Western philosophic tradition is uneasy and suspicious about action for exposing "the frailty of human affairs," and seeks escape from it in the concept of rule and in administration ("the solidity of quiet and order"), strikingly parallels Dewey's critique in *Experience and Nature* of rationalism's disdain for the messy incalculability that inhabits both experience and democracy (*Human* 198). Dewey's esteem for this messiness leads him, like Arendt, to embrace the hazards of the initiatory: "each individual," says Dewey in 1930, "that comes into the world is a new beginning; the universe is, as it were, taking a fresh start in him and trying to do something, even on a small scale, that it has never done before."[19]

Belief in the freshness of beginning opens a space for action by lightening the burden of the past and its accumulated weight of resentments and neglects. This belief would hold especial attraction to the poor and the enslaved, those sequestered in darkness, who historically have most suffered what Arendt calls "the insult of oblivion."[20] They are "excluded from the passion for distinction ... that can exert itself only in the broad daylight of the public" (*Revolution* 70). Arendt is paraphrasing John Adams's great passage in "Discourses on Davila" on the psychic agony of the poor – their "intolerable" awareness of being "wholly overlooked," of being "only not seen" (69).

Action can begin to redeem the "insult of oblivion" suffered by those consigned to invisibility because action "is never possible in isolation; to be isolated is to be deprived of the capacity to act ... action and speech are surrounded by and in constant contact with the web of the acts and words of other men" (*Human* 167). Like natality, action attests to "the boundlessness of human interrelatedness," a fact that provokes the "never entirely reliable" sanctions of laws and territorial boundaries (170). Their status is always frail precisely because "no such limiting and protecting principles rise out of the activities going on in the realm of human affairs itself" (170). Arendt's lyric evocation of action's unconditioned, spontaneous fertility ("action has no end") stresses the helplessness of law and rule to offset action's "inherent unpredictability" (209, 171). The risk and danger inherent in action is precisely what helps create and sustain a life lived in freedom. This life is threatened by any social order bent on eliminating the living ferment and self-disclosure of deeds, be it by the rule of bureaucratic rationality or ideologies of determinism.

Seeking relief from the "insult of oblivion" and release from the Marxist necessitarianism that is Brotherhood's creed, Ellison's protagonist declares: "I believe in nothing if not action" and defines his "hibernation" as temporary, a "preparation for more action" (*Invisible* 13). In the very act of putting his story down on paper, he reflects on what he has learned:

"Without the possibility of action, all knowledge comes to one labeled 'file and forget,' and I can neither file nor forget" (579). But can he forgive? And what is the relation of forgiveness to the possibility of action? Just as Ellison pursues these matters in the final pages of *Invisible Man*, they are paramount for Arendt in *The Human Condition*.

"Without being forgiven," writes Arendt, "released from the consequences of what we have done, our capacity to act would, as it were, be confined to one single deed from which we could never recover; we would remain the victims of its consequences forever" (*Human* 213). Something of this realization of threatening paralysis informs Ellison's speculations in his novel's epilogue on the need for affirming the "principle" of democracy if not its historical practice. "I sell you no phony forgiveness," says the narrator, explaining that his attitude toward his country is not a simple matter of optimism or conformity but rather one of self-conscious "division" – he loves and hates, says yes and no, denounces and defends (*Invisible* 580, 579). He denounces, he explains, because, "though implicated and partially responsible, I have been hurt to the point of abysmal pain, hurt to the point of invisibility. And I defend because in spite of all I find that I love. In order to get some of it down I *have* to love . . . so I approach it through division"(580). A "phony forgiveness," evidently, would forfeit the embrace of contraries and simply say yes; but having said just this for too long he "became ill of affirmation" (573). What he learns is that a genuine forgiveness says yes while it embraces division by making distinctions between political principles as abstract ideals and their particular enactments. As if preserving Arendt's logic while reversing her terms of critical judgment (which, as I have noted, liberate the particular from the universal when the latter congeals into a locus of routinized unthinking), Ellison's narrator honors the universal, distinguishing it from the degradations of historical particularity.

He is led to honor it by ruminating one final time about his grandfather's dying words (be a "spy in the enemy's country . . . live with your head in the lion's mouth. . .agree 'em to death and destruction" (*Invisible* 16)). At last the protagonist realizes that grandfather's directives do not urge duplicity so much as flexibility, a suppleness that can be translated into a political lesson: "that we were to affirm the principle on which the country was built and not the men, or at least not the men who did the violence . . . because he [grandfather] knew that the principle was greater than the men . . . .Was it that we [black people] of all, we, most of all, had to affirm the principle, the plan in whose name we had been brutalized and sacrificed . . . Or was it, did he mean that we should affirm the principle because we, through no fault of our own, were linked to all the others in the loud, clamoring, semi-visible world" (574).

To "affirm the principle" of constitutional democracy and democratic equality in their universality and abstraction is, in effect, to forgive, that is, to see beyond the particular blinders of race and history, beyond the accumulated horrors inflicted in the name of white supremacy for the sake of starting anew. If one did not affirm release "from the consequences of what we have done" (Arendt) one would fail to open up "the possibility of action" (Ellison), and would have to "'file and forget'" the "principle" and continue "being the mere pawns in the futile game of 'making history'" (*Invisible* 575). Loyalty to the abstraction, then, is what liberates action, releases us from the past. This is the same logic that Emerson ratified when, in seeking to rally the flagging efforts of anti-slavery partisans, he praised the "Abstract! The more abstract the better ... The Declaration of Independence is an abstraction."[21]

Ellison, in sum, revises Arendt in two ways: by releasing the universal from the domination of the particular and by bringing the force of abstract "principle" together with natality and forgiveness. He insists on the galvanizing power of "ideal [s]" (in this case democracy), a recognition that Arendt later in the decade in their disagreement over Little Rock would fail to appreciate: "it is precisely this ideal of sacrifice which I didn't understand," to recall her acknowledgment to Ellison. Like natality and forgiveness, action on behalf of political ideals permits the possibility that those reduced to being pawns might overcome their sense of helpless oblivion and resentment in action's surge of fresh initiative. Forgiveness "is the exact opposite of vengeance, which acts in the form of re-acting against an original trespassing, whereby far from putting an end to the consequences of the first misdeed, everybody remains bound to the process, permitting the chain reaction" of violent retribution (*Human* 216). Vengeance is, of course, the temptation of those who are the pawns of history, as we shall see, but Ellison will complicate Arendt by depicting vengeance as also capable of creating a redemptive beginning.

What are the obstacles to the creative action of politics? Invisible Man offers a clue when he affirms in the prologue his belief in action "despite Brother Jack and all that sad, lost period of the Brotherhood" (*Invisible* 13). In opposing "action" to the political activism of Brotherhood, Ellison posits a tacit distinction that deserves explicit articulation. What Ellison keeps tacit here becomes a major chord later in the novel – how Brotherhood's scientistic logic of historical inevitability ("we are champions of a scientific approach to society") and its mantra of discipline and sacrifice smother the contingency and spontaneity of actual political action – and hence its very creativity – by harnessing it to an absolute called History (with a capital H). This word is one that members of Brotherhood (another inert slogan) endlessly intone as if they control it as one would "a force in a laboratory experiment" (*Invisible* 441). Marxism's necessitarianism, expressed, for instance, in Brother Jack's casual remark that "individuals don't count" for they are "incapable of rising to the necessity of the historical situation" (291) paradoxically makes its political goals profoundly anti-political in the Ellisonian and Arendtian sense.

This discovery repeatedly crystallizes for Invisible Man late in the novel, first in the epiphanies he has in the aftermath of Tod Clifton's death about those "men of transition" "too obscure for learned classification," who "plunge" "outside the groove of history," and then in his participation in the Harlem riot near the novel's close (439, 440, 443). During this latter episode, the narrator stumbles upon a group of men, led by the compelling, taciturn Dupre. The group is bent on "fixing to do something that needs to be done" and to do it with organization and the right tools (542). After getting flashlights and buckets of oil, Dupre and his men carefully soak their despised "deathtrap" of a tenement with kerosene, empty the building of tenants and then calmly, methodically, torch it: "my kid died from the t-bees" in there, remarks Dupre as the flames begin to leap (547). Observing Dupre's determined actions on behalf of community renewal, invisible man recognizes a new kind of leader: "he was a type of man nothing in my life had taught me to see, to understand, or respect, a man outside the scheme till now ... What would Brother Jack say of him?" (547).

What makes Dupre unprecedented is his redemption of the "insult of oblivion" (to borrow Arendt's phrase), an act that places him outside the "futile game of 'making history'" where one is merely a pawn in the hands of white power brokers (575). Instead of making history, i.e., assimilating to Brotherhood's grand narrative, Dupre emerges as a political actor whose speech and deeds bring into being a collective intervention, unveiling the "web of human relationships" latent in the sufferings of those in the Harlem tenement (*Human* 163). This disclosure exhilarates the narrator: "I was seized with a fierce sense of exaltation. They've done it, I thought. They organized it and carried it through alone; the decision their own and their own action. Capable of their own action" (*Invisible* 548). This action gives birth to the possibility of something new – the destruction of dehumanizing conditions. The fire not only opens a space for change, long promised but never delivered by Brotherhood, but renounces the passive, private suffering that is the lot of the invisible – those "excluded from the light of the public realm" (*Revolution* 69).

The actions of Dupre and his group perform something akin to the "cultural work of the inarticulate" that Nancy Ruttenburg has recently identified with what she calls "democratic personality," a mode of public life "not affiliated with the rationality of modern liberalism" but instead the eruption of uncontainable utterance in persons without a public voice within the culture.[22] The collective action in Harlem also recalls how Arendt describes the initial stirring of revolutionary spirit, the "lost treasure" that gives birth to an impromptu and usually short-lived form of voluntary association that Arendt, in *On Revolution*, names the council system, a participatory alternative to the party system. The council, the ground floor level of an increasingly larger system of political representation, is born from below in the neighborhood solidarity of ordinary people rather than imposed on the masses from above by a government or by a party program controlled by elites. Although Arendt praised the power of the American tradition of nonviolent civil disobedience, she did acknowledge that the ghetto violence could serve to dramatize grievances and bring them to public attention (Young-Bruehl 415). The riots of the late 1960s, she notes in *On Violence*, are "articulate protests against genuine grievances," but she hesitates to decide whether they are the "beginnings of something new" – a revival of the "faculty of action in the modern world" – or merely expressions of severe frustration and hence "the death pangs of a faculty that mankind is about to lose."[23]

As the narrator's "exaltation" about Dupre suggests, this political action will eventually inspire his own aesthetic action. But first Invisible Man will enter the chaos of the Harlem riot to settle accounts with Brotherhood's mirror image opposite – the black nationalism of Ras, who, along with Brother Jack, is the main political agent of "blindness" (*Invisible* 559). Soon after Dupre and his men have completed their work, the narrator is pursued by Ras on horseback and spear in hand, intent on killing him as a "Betrayer!" and "Uncle Tom" (557). After Ras's spear misses its target, Invisible Man returns it, catching Ras in mid-shout, "ripping through both cheeks" (560). "It was as though for a moment I had surrendered my life and begun to live again," reflects the narrator as he watches Ras being impaled (560). This violent rebirth confirms the initiatory power in action's uncontainable velocity. The percussive rhythm of eruptive action – the torching of the tenement, the spearing of Ras – will catalyze an aesthetic natality. When the "night of chaos" ends in his discovery of a vacant refuge in a basement, the narrator will begin putting it all down on paper in a sustained bout of self-disclosure.

In his aesthetic action, Invisible Man will at once honor Dupre and complicate his action by fusing his incendiary refusal to suffer intolerable injustice to a commitment to forgiveness by way of affirming the abstract principle of justice. This stance of division marks the novel's uneasy political resolution, one whose rejection of Marxism and nationalism does not lead, as most critics would have it, to a simple embrace of cold-war liberalism.

Instead, Ellison is skeptical of reformism (he mocks the liberal paternalism of Mr. Norton and of young Emerson) while affirming liberalism's foundations in universal principles. But he qualifies his assent to this Enlightenment creed in his belief that a "plan of living must never lose sight of the chaos against which that pattern was conceived" (580). The narrator's respect for chaos breeds awareness of the insufficiency of liberal reason, for the latter is founded on a rationalism that is anti-political insofar as it would domesticate action by binding it to teleogical restraints of previously formulated rules and goals. Believing with Dewey and Arendt that chaos inhabits certainty, Ellison's protagonist stakes the horizon of possibility, both aesthetic and political, on nothing more or less than commitment to action. Its unpredictable energies comprise the burden (for "he who acts never quite knows what he is doing") from which action "draws its very strength" (*Human* 209). From the point of view of philosophic liberalism, which depends on keeping experience (including the aesthetic qualities of spontaneity and action) separate from non-empirical political principles of equality and justice, Ellison is an existentialist anarchist or romantic and the Dupre episode should be read as cautionary, proof of the violence produced by bringing together the aesthetic and political. If political theorists have recently been seeking to end the centuries old enmity between romantic and liberal sensibilities (the project, for instance, of Nancy Rosenblum's *Another Liberalism*) *Invisible Man* may not offer much encouragement. Devoted to "division," the novel makes the irreconcilability of the romantic and liberal a source of dynamism.[24]

The novel's embrace of instability wreaks havoc with any effort to allegorize *Invisible Man*. Yet one version of an Arendtian allegory – reading the narrative's trajectory as an evolution from parvenu to pariah – would at first seem promising since, as the narrator says in the Epilogue, "after years of trying to adopt the opinion of others I finally rebelled. I am an *invisible* man." But the next sentence disturbs the suggestion that he becomes a conscious pariah: "Thus I have come a long way and returned and boomeranged a long way from the point in society toward which I originally aspired" (573). Blurring together coming and returning, this sentence scrambles linearity and mocks any trajectory staked on the teleology of the bildungsroman, be it progress from delusion to enlightenment or from parvenu to pariah. Refusal of unequivocal or linear progression underwrites how the narrator figures his aesthetic and political stance. It is comprised not of simple antagonism or opposition to his country, which would require a fixed point of reference, but partakes of incessant, contradictory movements of coming and returning and boomeranging (including the overlap of pariah and parvenu) to and from his original point of aspiration. This very waywardness produces or, more precisely, constitutes invisibility as a condition of constant and turbulent motion – "I couldn't be still even in hibernation" – as if the narrator takes his cue from Emerson's remark that "the voyage of the best ship is a zigzag line of a hundred tacks" (266). The insistence on a zigzag line, what Ellison calls "approaching it through division," permits Invisible Man to step outside "the narrow borders of what men call reality" and outside of what philosophy calls Reason, keeping open a space of invention and freedom he variously names chaos, possibility, imagination (576).

These elements comprise, as we have seen, vital attributes of the creative public action that is the political and the aesthetic. This linkage has the virtue of retiring the idealist dichotomy that sets the political against the aesthetic, a familiar habit of mind all too alive in the still canonical conviction that a flight from the political characterizes Ellison's thought. Ellison insists on crucial connections too seldom made today – between, for instance, ideals and their enactments, principles and practices. And he and Arendt also challenge factitious distinctions all too abundant in contemporary discourse, especially the postmodern reflex of assuming that the particular and universal, difference and identity, can be thought apart, and pitting one against the other in endless variations of a morality play featuring the beleaguered particular as the frail but noble victim of the imperial, devouring universal. Liberation from the inertia of binaries begins for Arendt and Ellison in never forgetting that "to *think* is the faculty of mysteriously combining the particular and the general."[25] This commitment to honoring both terms generates, among other things, the precariously balanced, irreducibly paradoxical, remarkably fertile relation to the political that Ellison and Arendt share.

Notes

1. They do in fact appear together in a chapter – in Emily Budick's 1998 book *Blacks and Jews in Literary Conversation* (Cambridge University Press, 1998).
2. Ralph Ellison, *Collected Essays.* Ed. John Callahan (New York: Random House, 1995), p. 156. Hereafter cited in the text as *Collected Essays.*
3. Robert Penn Warren, *Who Speaks for the Negro?* (New York: Vintage, 1966), p. 343. Hereafter cited in the text as Warren.
4. Quoted in Elizabeth Young-Bruehl, *Hannah Arendt: For Love of the World* (New Haven: Yale University Press, 1982), p. 316. Hereafter cited in the text as Young-Bruehl.
5. Hanna Pitkin, *The Attack of the Blob: Hannah Arendt's Concept of the Social* (University of Chicago Press, 1998), pp. 180, 182. Hereafter cited in the text as Pitkin.
6. Judith Shklar, *Political Thought and Political Thinkers* (University of Chicago Press, 1998), p. 363.

7. Two recent essays, one by Danielle Allen, the other by Kenneth Warren, consider the Arendt/Ellison connection in ways distinct from my own approach. See Danielle Allen: "Law's Necessary Forcefulness: Ralph Ellison vs. Hannah Arendt on the Battle of Little Rock," *Oklahoma City University Law Review* Fall, 2001: 857–95; and Kenneth Warren, "Ralph Ellison and the Problem of Cultural Authority," *Boundary* 2 30:2 (Summer 2003): 157–74.

8. See Edward Rothstein's account: "Faced With 'Parvenu' or 'Pariah,' Ellison Settled on 'Artist.'" *The New York Times* May 15, 1999: A19.

9. Ralph Ellison, *Invisible Man* (New York: Vintage, 1989), p. 291. Hereafter cited in the text as *Invisible*.

10. See *Seeds of the Sixties*, A. Jamison and R. Eyerman (Berkeley CA: University of California Press, 1993), p. 53.

11. Hannah Arendt, *The Human Condition* (New York, Doubleday Anchor, 1958), p. 231; *Men in Dark Times* (Harmondsworth: Pelican, 1975), p. 12. Hereafter cited in the text as *Human* and *Men* respectively.

12. See, for instance, Thomas Schaub's *American Fiction in the Cold War* (Madison: University of Wisconsin Press, 1991). For a more nuanced political reading of Ellison see Miele Steele, "Metatheory and the Subject of Democracy in the Work of Ralph Ellison." *New Literary History* 27: 3 (1996): 473–502.

13. W. E. B. Du Bois, *Writings* (New York: Library of America, 1986), p. 365.

14. Ivan Hannaford, *Race: The History of an Idea in the West* (Baltimore: Johns Hopkins University Press, 1996), p. 10. Hereafter cited in the text as Hannaford.

15. I discuss this point in *Color and Culture: Black Writers and the Making of the Modern Intellectual* (Cambridge: Harvard University Press, 1998), pp. 16–18.

16. Martin Jay, "Reflective Judgments by a Spectator on a Conference that is Now History." In *Hannah Arendt and the Meaning of Politics*. Ed. Craig Calhoun and John McGowan. (Minneapolis: University of Minnesota Press, 1997), p. 349.

17. For an account of Arendtian action that in effect rebuts Jay's critique of her alleged groundlessness see Pitkin 198–200. See also Kirstie McClure, who defends Arendt's preference for "common sense" derived from experience rather than the axioms of apriori "logic." A consequence is Arendt's willing "violation of proprieties" of political judgment when such judgment is construed as a "process of reasoning from principles, a process requiring clear definitions and consistent logic." For Arendt, in contrast, political argument derives from particular examples and depends on narration. Kirstie McClure, "The Odor of Judgment: Exemplarity, Propriety, and Politics in the Company of Hannah Arendt." In *Hannah Arendt and the Meaning of Politics*. Ed. Craig Calhoun and John McGowan (Minneapolis: University of Minnesota Press, 1997), pp. 77–8. Dana Villa usefully shows how radical is Arendt's account of action by setting it in the context of intellectual history. See his *Arendt and Heidegger: The Fate of the Political* (Princeton University Press, 1996).

18. Ralph Emerson, *Essays and Lectures* (New York: Library of America, 1983), pp. 46, 481, 749. Hereafter cited in the text as Emerson.

19. Quoted in Hans Joas, *The Creativity of Action* (University of Chicago Press 1998), p. 141.

20. Hannah Arendt, *On Revolution* (New York: rpt. Penguin, 1990), p. 69. Hereafter cited in the text as *Revolution*. Kimberley Curtis's book makes the

"insult of oblivion" central to her study of aesthetic experience and Arendtian politics. See Kimberley Curtis, *Our Sense of the Real: Aesthetic Experience and Arendtian Politics* (Ithaca: Cornell University Press, 1999).

21. Ralph Waldo Emerson, *Journals and Miscellaneous Notebooks*. Vol. 14, *1854–61*. Ed. S. Smith and H. Hayford (Cambridge MA: Harvard University Press, 1978), pp. 420–1.

22. Nancy Ruttenburg, *Democratic Personality* (Stanford University Press, 1998), p. 3.

23. Hannah Arendt, *On Violence* (New York: Harcourt, 1970), pp. 77, 83–4.

24. See Nancy Rosenblum, *Another Liberalism* (Cambridge MA: Harvard University Press, 1988).

25. Hannah Arendt, *Lectures on Kant's Political Philosophy* (University of Chicago Press, 1982), p. 76.

12

ERIC SUNDQUIST

Dry bones

Presenting Bernard Malamud the Gold Medal for Fiction from the American Academy of Arts and Letters in 1983, Ralph Ellison spoke of him, a fellow "minority" artist, in terms characteristic of his own self-presentation: "While remaining true to his own group's unique perception of experience, [the minority writer] is also goaded to add his individual voice to the futuristic effort of fulfilling the democratic ideal ... sometimes in making his own segment of experience available to all he manages to reduce our social confusion to forms of lucid insight."[1] Malamud calculated the advantage in similar terms. Being a minority can be a kind of "lucky break" for a writer, he argued at the height of Black Power, since his subject matter comes to him "'hot,' surcharged – call it the emotionalization of history." Although their collective experience might therefore provide African-Americans some artistic advantage, as it once did Jews, however, the risk for young writers is that they will produce "little more than agit-propaganda." Placing Ellison at one end of the aesthetic spectrum and James Baldwin somewhere in the middle, Malamud asked about Leroi Jones (Amiri Baraka), "what has he accomplished by hating half the human race?"[2]

Malamud paid a more profound tribute to Ellison's liberalist aesthetic by writing aspects of it into the plot of *The Tenants* (1971), a brutal inquiry into art at a moment of racial crisis which unfolds as an argument between the Jewish writer Harry Lesser, who proclaims the universality of art's "sacred cathedral," and the black writer Willie Spearmint, who embraces the militant aesthetic espoused by Baraka and others in the Black Arts movement. Dismissing Harry's universalism as the product of his white brain, Willie plunges deeper and deeper into the stark polarizations demanded by the nationalist agenda, which reaches its logical endpoint in the fragmentary manuscript of his poem entitled "Manifested Destiny":

> black, white, black, white, black, white, black, white
> (go to bottom of page) ...

BLACKBLACKBLACKBLACKBLACKBLACKBLACKBLACK
(make five pages of this)...
BLACKNESSBLACKNESSBLACKNESSBLACKNESS
(This is the rest of the book)...[3]

In his allusion to the preacher's riff in the Prologue to *Invisible Man* – "Brothers and sisters, my text this morning is the 'Blackness of Blackness'"[4] – Malamud reduced the galvanizing voice of the African-American sermonic tradition that set the stage for Ellison's encyclopedia of vernacular improvisations to its purest form of tribalism. In Willie's incantations of the holy word BLACK, what Ellison valued in the Negro as the "keeper of the nation's sense of democratic achievement, and the human scale by which would be measured its painfully slow advance toward true equality,"[5] is stripped down to monotonal paralysis.

The acrimonious dialogue between Harry and Willie that structures *The Tenants* also incorporates, while transforming, Ellison's famous exchange with Irving Howe. Inspired by the radicalism that Ellison had disavowed after an early flirtation and promoting Richard Wright's politicized naturalism as the only authentic black aesthetic, Howe thought it imperative that the black writer, motivated by a "pain and ferocity that nothing could remove," speak "from the black wrath of retribution."[6] Ellison's rejoinder in "The World and the Jug" (1964) took Howe to task for assuming that black art could be nothing but the "abstract embodiment of living hell" and charged him with practicing his own brand of segregation: "I found it far less painful to have to move to the back of a Southern bus...than to tolerate concepts which distorted the actual reality of my situation or my reactions to it."[7] Ellison objected not to acknowledging race and racial grievance as defining facts of culture but to elevating them into an ideology. "Exiled in our own land," he said in a coda to his debate with Howe, appearing as part of a 1967 interview, black writers have too often been in such haste to express their anger and pain that they have allowed "the single tree of race to obscure...the magic forest of art."[8]

In returning the interlocutors to their more customary positions – in *The Tenants* it is Willie Spearmint who perfects Howe's aesthetic of black authenticity, while Harry Lesser espouses a feeble version of Ellison's universalism – Malamud's spoof of the debate took account of the sharp antagonism Ellison faced during the 1960s and 1970s from those who found in his integrationist idealism the antics of an Uncle Tom. "The Negro artist who is not a nationalist at this late date is a white artist, even without knowing it,"[9] proclaimed Baraka. Although he would later reverse course by writing what is arguably the most important essay on *Invisible Man*, "Ellison's Zoot Suit," Larry Neal succinctly asserted that, for black youth of the day, the experiences of Ellison's protagonist lacked recognizable relevance: "We know who we are, and we are not invisible, *at least not to each other*. We are not Kafkaesque creatures stumbling through a white light of confusion and absurdity. The light is black . . . as are most of the meaningful tendencies in the world."[10] No wonder their high stakes aesthetic argument at length drives Harry Lesser and Willie Spearmint to mutual homicide: "Lesser felt his jagged axe sink through bone and brain as the groaning black's razor-sharp sabre, in a single boiling stabbing slash, cut the white's balls from the rest of him."[11]

Although tempers had cooled a generation later, Ellison's novel proved a no less valuable touchstone when Philip Roth imagined his protagonist's tragedy in *The Human Stain* (2000). Coleman Silk, an aging classics professor and former dean of the faculty at a small New England college, is brought to ruin by an innocent query about students absent from his class – "Does anyone know these people? Do they exist or are they spooks?"[12] When it turns out that the students, unbeknownst to Silk, are black, he is condemned by his colleagues and driven from his job for an insult he could not have intended. As we come to discover, of course, Silk is a very light-skinned black man masquerading as a Jew. Having elected in 1953 to short-circuit the historical process of ethnic assimilation, Silk turns black emulation of Jews into a virtual parody of them. In accord with the Greek tragic structure underlying Roth's novel, however, Silk is able only to redirect, not dictate, his fate. His classroom query leads inexorably to his being killed as "a Jew" at the hands of a deranged Vietnam veteran.

In Silk's fatal spooks remark, Roth included within his inadvertent epithet the more subtle declaration with which Ellison opened *Invisible Man*, one year before Coleman Silk chose to be seen as not black: "I am an invisible man. No, I am not a spook like those who haunted Edgar Allan Poe; nor am I one of your Hollywood-movie ectoplasms. I am a man of substance, of flesh and bone, fiber and liquids – and I might even be said to possess a mind." In choosing to pass, Silk thus counters, without completely canceling, the predicament of Ellison's hero, who lives as though "surrounded by mirrors of hard, distorting glass" so that others see only "my surroundings, themselves, or figments of their imagination – indeed, everything and anything except me."[13]

In transgressing primordial racial boundaries, making himself an alien to his own "race" and electing membership in another, Coleman Silk flips Norman Mailer's libidinous fantasy of the hipster as "white Negro" upside down. (Mailer "thinks all hipsters are cocksmen possessed of great euphoric orgasms and are out to fuck the world into peace, prosperity, and creativity," said Ellison in a letter to Albert Murray. "The same old primitivism crap in a new package."[14]) He thus enacts the transformation Roth once described in his own fantasy of "magically becoming totally the other, all the while retaining knowledge of what it was to have been one's original self, wearing one's original badges of identity."[15] But Silk, too, lives and dies amid mirrors of hard, distorting glass, as much caught up in the "stranglehold of history that is one's own time" as was Invisible Man in the age of Jim Crow. His act of passing amounts to a preemptive renunciation of the shibboleths of diversity, which now rise up to destroy him – "only a label is required. The label is the motive. The label is the evidence. The label is the logic."[16]

Roth's tribute to Ellison derived likewise from a moment in his early career when he, like Ellison, had been attacked for not toeing the line of racial chauvinism in the stories collected in *Goodbye, Columbus* (1959). Grilled by an audience at Yeshiva University for having depicted characters, said his critics, who confirmed anti-Semitic stereotypes, the young Roth was pleased to find himself defended by fellow panelist Ellison, who instructed the audience "through examples drawn from *Invisible Man* and the ambiguous relationship that novel had established with some vocal members of his own race."[17] In defending his artistic freedom to explore, rather than simply condemn, caricatures spawned by prejudice, Roth responded instinctively to Ellison's desire to be free of communal prescriptions of racial identity. Here and elsewhere, he adapted to his own purposes Ellison's lesson in "Change the Joke and Slip the Yoke" (1958) that "the Negro's masking," very much "in the American grain," must be understood as a manipulation of assigned roles motivated "not so much by fear as by a profound rejection of the image created to usurp our identity."[18] The self-making of self-masking, said Ellison in numerous ways on numerous occasions, constitutes the high art of American individualism.

Ellison might have shared Roth's fantasy of self-transformation enacted in the character of Coleman Silk, but Silk's secret, as well as the tragic shape of Roth's novel, depends on the fact that Silk has the option of a particular kind of masking unavailable to Ellison's Invisible Man or Ellison himself. To cite a source resonant in the postwar dialogue about race in which Ellison and Roth were both steeped, Gunnar Myrdal's *An American Dilemma* (1944), the African-American's badge of identity is "fixed to his person much more ineffaceably than the yellow star [was] fixed to the Jew during the Nazi regime in Germany."[19] Far from invisible in a world governed by the "one-drop rule," according to which any fraction of "black blood" prescribes one's racial identity, the Negro could never remove the star of blackness, and even those who passed might at any moment be unmasked. The Black Arts alternative was to embrace the one-drop rule, to require allegiance to the community of color as the only avenue to power. In the inquisitorial world of identity politics portrayed by Roth a generation later, this inversion in the law of ethno-racial identity had become generalized, often as academic policy and certainly as academic fashion.

Ellison looked upon this spectacle with detached bemusement, as one may infer from his 1977 assessment of the vogue of ethnocentrism in "The Little Man at Chehaw Station":

> The proponents of ethnicity – ill concealing an underlying anxiety, and given a bizarre bebopish stridency by the obviously American vernacular inspiration of the costumes and rituals ragged out to dramatize their claims to ethnic (and genetic) insularity – have helped give our streets and campuses a rowdy, All Fool's Day, carnival atmosphere. In many ways, then, the call for a new social order based upon the glorification of ancestral blood and ethnic background acts as a call to cultural and aesthetic chaos. Yet while this latest farcical phase in the drama of American social hierarchy unfolds, the irrepressible movement of American culture toward the integration of its diverse elements continues, confounding the circumlocutions of its staunchest opponents . . . Where there's a melting pot there's smoke, and where there's smoke it is not simply optimistic to expect fire, it's imperative to watch for the phoenix's vernacular, but transcendent, rising.[20]

Because American culture, on closer examination, was and always had been truly a multinational, multiethnic kaleidoscope, those who wished to keep the culture and the canon uncontaminated – "KEEP AMERICA PURE WITH LIBERTY PAINTS," begins a sequence burlesquing white supremacy in *Invisible Man* – were doomed to fail. By the same token, Ellison hopefully speculated, the delusion of "blood magic and blood thinking,"[21] whether it be Afrocentrism or some other beguiling mystification of identity, would sooner or later be subsumed into the phoenix of dynamic heterogeneity.

As the era of strict ethnocentrism recedes from view, Ellison will surely be proved right. It may be, however, that his acuity will finally lie as much in his criticism and its prophecy as in his fiction. Overt hostility towards Ellison subsided, and *Invisible Man* never lost its easily won place of respect in the canon. Still, as it was displaced first by *Their Eyes Were Watching God* and then by *Beloved* as the one African-American novel everyone should have read, *Invisible Man* began to seem time-bound rather than timeless. Readers stipulated that it was a masterpiece, like *Moby-Dick*, and then neglected to read it. Despite the outpouring of attention to Ellison that followed his death in 1994, the subsequent publication of collections of short fiction, essays, and letters, the fiftieth anniversary of *Invisible Man*, and the inevitably unsatisfactory appearance of his long-awaited second novel in truncated form as *Juneteenth* (1999) – despite all of this, Ellison remains a problem.

With the eventual publication of a scholar's edition of *Juneteenth*, including more manuscript materials and documentation of Ellison's processes of composition, readers and critics will be able to decipher for themselves the novel(s) that might have been, an enterprise certain to govern commentary for many years to come. The textual uncertainties of famous posthumous works such as *Billy Budd* and *The Last Tycoon*, which may be said to have climaxed rather more understandable authorial trajectories, will likely pale by comparison to the thorny issues presented by Ellison's unfinished corpus and the enigma of his stymied career. The loss of a substantial part of his novel-in-progress in a fire in 1967 was harmful, of course, but it does not explain the erosion of imaginative force that turned Ellison into the most highly esteemed disappointment in the history of American literature, apparently unable to match the stratospheric fictive standard set by *Invisible Man*.

Perhaps the explanation is to be found in Ellison's preoccupation with craft, with the "possession of technique," wherein lay "the writer's greatest freedom," as he argued in "Hidden Name and Complex Fate" (1964).[22] Given the episodic structure of *Invisible Man*, whose rehearsal of modern black America's coming of age provided an outline to be filled in by an astute novelistic autobiographer, it may be that Ellison became trapped in virtuosity, producing all manner of scintillating improvisations without finding a way to bring into coherent narrative form the word music he heard in his head.

Was he forecasting his own troubled career in his 1962 postmortem for Charlie Parker? Borrowing from ornithological characterizations of the mockingbird, Ellison found in Bird a style "characterized by velocity, by long-continued successions of notes and phrases . . . by mocking mimicry of other jazzmen's styles, and by interpolations of motifs from extraneous melodies, all of which added up to a dazzling display of wit, satire, burlesque and pathos." Lionized as "a suffering, psychically wounded, law-breaking, life-affirming hero," said Ellison, Bird found his greatest audience not among blacks but among white hipsters, "a ravenous, sensation-starved, culturally disoriented public" before whom he "died slowly (like a man dismembering himself with a dull razor on the spotlighted stage) from the ceaseless conflict from which issued both his art and his destruction."[23] The painful compositional regimen that led to *Juneteenth*, evidenced by whatever archive of notes, phrases, motifs, and extraneous melodies we are eventually given to pick over, would make Ellison himself into the sacrificial figure, not a cultural outlaw wrecked by drugs, to be sure, but a perfectionist devoured at last by the stern discipline of his art and the insatiable expectations of his audience.

Proposing an alternative anxiety of influence, Norman Podhoretz has concluded that Ellison could never finish his second novel because

Faulkner "had invaded and taken him over."[24] Faulkner the stylist looms over all writing in his wake, no doubt, and Faulkner the racial moralist searched out profound complexities in the sectional history of slavery and Jim Crow on a scale that might disable many successors, but Faulkner and Ellison, for all they shared, stood at last on opposite sides of the color line. It was not simply a social judgment but an artistic one that Ellison was making when he ridiculed Faulkner's public opposition to desegregation: "Faulkner has delusions of grandeur because he really believes that he invented these characteristics which he ascribes to Negroes in his fiction and now he thinks he can end this great historical action just as he ends a dramatic action in one of his novels with Joe Christmas dead and his balls cut off by a man not nearly as worthy as himself."[25]

Yet the appeal to Faulkner's intimidating example is not entirely misleading. Whereas Faulkner "thinks that Negroes exist simply to give ironic overtone to the viciousness of white folks," Ellison continued, "we're trying to free ourselves; thoroughly and completely, so that when we['ve] got the crackers off our backs we can discover what we . . . really are and what we really wish to preserve out of the experience that made us."[26] This was the essence of *Invisible Man*. Composed at a time when the drift toward *Brown v. Board of Education* in constitutional law and public policy was apparent, but when the end of Jim Crow could hardly have been predicted with any confidence, *Invisible Man* is the novel of segregation par excellence. Despite Ellison's panoramic exposition of the resources of African-American cultural life, the novel's unnamed protagonist reaches the end of his tale without clearly having articulated an answer to the glaring question put to him, whether in fact or hallucination, as he lies on the operating table following his accident at the Liberty Paints factory: "WHAT . . . IS . . . YOUR . . . NAME? . . . WHO . . . ARE . . . YOU?" Upon waking up from what seems his near lobotomy and castration, the protagonist makes an affirmative but inherently circular supposition that reigns over the novel through the very end: "When I discover who I am, I'll be free."[27]

His maturation as a writer, Ellison said in introducing *Shadow and Act* (1964), required a long struggle "to stare down the deadly and hypnotic temptation to interpret the world and all its devices in terms of race."[28] His liberal idealism to the contrary, however, race could not be transcended until the question of identity was answered. But the question of identity could not exclude the premise of race. At once evanescent and monstrous, something akin to a device whose countervailing forces of rotation, torque, and balance produce a gravity-defying mechanical operation, the "Negro problem," as he enclosed it in quotation marks in "Beating That Boy" (1945), was always the existential motive within Ellison's "gyroscope of irony."[29]

Like all writers, Ellison belonged to his historical moment, and one may ask if this was not finally his artistic trap. While all around him African-Americans took on new names and categorically rejected the label of "Negro" – "there is no 'Negroland,'" argued Richard B. Moore, only a continent whose "record of history bears out a glorious past and a mighty history of achievement for the peoples of Africa"[30] – Ellison remained immersed in "the golden age, the time past" of the Negro problem. Although his terminology slowly adjusted to the times, he never really became, in his fictive imagination, "African-American," let alone "black" in the sense demanded by Black Power ideologues. As he might have put it, however, this was no darky act. *Brown* v. *Board of Education* and the Civil Rights Act of 1964, he wrote, "provided the stage upon which they [Negroes] could reveal themselves," and even in his minstrel's mask, adorned in a costume that mimicked the "sacred" red, white, and blue of the American flag, the "Negro" was "an inseparable part of the national iconography."[31] Connoting cultural vitality and communal integrity, "Negro" was for Ellison both a term of art and a term of respect, as one may witness in the dedication of *Juneteenth*: "To That Vanished Tribe into Which I Was Born: The American Negroes."

The wistfulness here is unmistakable. "American Negroes" vanished into new names, new meanings. But they vanished, too, into a moment of history to which Ellison, even as events of the civil rights era and the post-civil rights era transpired, returned obsessively, as though trying to fix the inchoate meaning of freedom. Whereas *Invisible Man* made "poetry out of being invisible," as Ellison said of Louis Armstrong in the novel's Prologue,[32] his subsequent writing dwelled time and again on the passage to visibility. Alongside his periodic short stories, quasi-fictional tableaux embedded in his essays took up the hazards of desegregation when the "Negro" removed his mask. In "Tell It Like It Is, Baby," for example, Ellison described a personal nightmare dating to 1956, provoked by the southern campaign against *Brown* v. *Board of Education*, in which his own dead father merged with the body of Abraham Lincoln, and Ellison, "fallen out of time into chaos," took on the role of a young slave powerless to stop a white mob's carnivalesque desecration of the corpse of the president, "the old coon." In "An Extravagance of Laughter," a Jim Crow bus ride, "as unpredictable as a trip in a spaceship doomed to be caught in a time warp of history," became a dramatic metonym. Outside "the scenery flashed and flickered, but [the Negroes] themselves remained, like Zeno's arrow, ever in the same old place," playing out their roles "like figures in dreams" until at last "a single tired Negro woman refused to go on with what had now become an unbearable farce."[33]

The present-day action of *Juneteenth*, which pivots historically on the attempted assassination of Adam Sunraider, a race-baiting New England

senator, deals with just this problem circa 1955 – the year of the implemen-
tation decree in *Brown* v. *Board of Education*, with its notorious concession
to the South that desegregation was to be undertaken "with all deliberate
speed"; the year Rosa Parks refused to give up her bus seat to a white man;
the year an unknown minister named Martin Luther King, Jr., was elected
president of the Montgomery Improvement Association; the year Emmett
Till was lynched in Mississippi. Much of the novel, however, tells the earlier
story of the one-time jazz trombonist Alonzo "Daddy" Hickman raising up
the mysterious "white" boy Bliss to be a Negro preacher like himself. In Bliss,
Hickman had hoped to create the new Abraham Lincoln, a white-black
leader capable of "speaking for our condition from inside the only acceptable
mask."[34] Instead, Bliss becomes Adam Sunraider, his gift of oratory dedicated to the destruction of black dreams rather than their fulfillment.

Building a novel around Juneteenth festivities was perfectly congruent with
Ellison's perspective on race. Based on news of freedom that reached Texas
slaves only on June 19, 1865, two and a half years after the Emancipation
Proclamation, the celebration's inherent belatedness has at least two evident
meanings in Ellison's reflection on the nation's long-delayed engagement with
the "horrible serpent…coiled up in [the] nation's bosom," as Frederick
Douglass had described slavery.[35] Despite emancipation in one century and
desegregation in the next, freedom has not yet arrived, and never will, if racists
like Adam Sunraider prevail. More to Ellison's point, however, blacks, still
acting like slaves, have not yet realized in what ways they are already at liberty.
Since "this society is not likely to become free of racism," he wrote in another
note for his uncompleted work, "it is necessary for Negroes to free themselves
by becoming their idea of what a free people should be."[36]

We will never read the second novel Ellison wrote, a work known to those
close to him in privately rendered performance but to the public only in the
imperfect record of John Callahan's devoted reconstruction. Privileged to
have such a private reading, James Alan McPherson heard a combination of
Count Basie, early minstrelsy, and black Baptist preaching through which
Ellison intended nothing less than "to solve the central problem of American
literature." In reinventing "a much broader and much more diverse world for
those who take their provisional identities from groups," McPherson sur-
mised, Ellison was trying at once to include race and transcend it, "trying to
Negro-Americanize the novel form, at the same time he was attempting to
move beyond it."[37] Even so, Ellison seemed ambivalent about his creation –
at once amused to perform Daddy Hickman's set pieces and yet in thrall to
his voice. Recounting a reading of his work-in-progress at Bard College,
where he was teaching in the late 1950s, Ellison compared Hickman's
cadences to those of Mahalia Jackson. "You would have laughed your ass

off to see that old downhome Moses rhetoric work," he wrote to Albert Murray. "It's not too difficult to observe [a similar effect] when Mahalia cuts loose at such places as Newport... but it's more difficult to reduce Hickman's sermons to mere entertainment; that old bastard knows how to get under even so initiated and tough a skin as mine."[38]

It is therefore not surprising that the most polished but problematic section of the novel is the tour de force dialogic Juneteenth sermon preached by Hickman and Bliss, the core of which first appeared as the short story "Juneteenth" in 1965. The chapter begins with the wounded and semi-delirious Adam Sunraider thinking back to "a bunch of old-fashioned Negroes celebrating an illusion of emancipation, and getting it mixed up with the Resurrection, minstrel shows and vaudeville routines."[39] Ellison's rendering of the Juneteenth revival, as Robert Stone has noted, is essentially sacramental in nature.[40] There is no gainsaying the seriousness of the theme or the brilliance of the writing, but the scene nevertheless comes perilously – and, it would seem, self-consciously – close to extravagant parody. The rhythms of the sermon, Ellison reminded himself in a note about the scene, "should feed back one upon the other proving not only perspectives in incongruity, but ironies, and some measure of comedy."[41] No sample can capture the effect of the whole, whose totalizing power depends as well on its aural dimensions. To the extent that it is the centerpiece of *Juneteenth*, however, the scriptural basis of the sermon may suggest why Ellison was unable to assemble his array of passages and chapters into a living novel.

Hickman starts by invoking one of African-America's oldest tropes: "the Hebrew children have their Passover so that they can keep their history alive in their memories – so let us take one more page from their book and, on this great day of deliverance, on this day of emancipation, let's us tell ourselves a story." The antiphonal preaching of Hickman and Bliss then proceeds through an extended exposition of diasporic dispossession that plays continually upon another metaphor borrowed from Jewish tradition, the "scattered" people, and in a crescendo of incantation ultimately unfolds into an allegory derived from Ezekiel's Valley of Dry Bones (Ezekiel 37: 1–14) in which the Negro people are raised up from captivity in the Babylon of America:

> Like seed, Rev. Bliss; they scattered us just like a dope-fiend farmer planting a field with dragon teeth!
> Tell us about it, Daddy Hickman.
> They cut out our tongues...
> ...They left us speechless...
> ...They cut out our tongues...
> ...Lord, they left us without words...

...Amen! They scattered our tongues in this land like seed...
...And left us without language...
...They took away our talking drums...[...]

Ho, chant it with me, my young brothers and sisters! Eyeless, tongueless, drumless, danceless, songless, hornless, soundless, sightless, wrongless, rightless, motherless, fatherless, brotherless, sisterless, powerless...
Amen! But though they took us like a great black giant that had been chopped up into little pieces and the pieces buried; though they deprived us of our heritage among strange scenes in a strange weather; divided and divided and divided us again like a gambler shuffling and cutting a deck of cards; although we were ground down, smashed into little pieces, spat upon, stamped upon, cursed and buried, and our memory of Africa ground down into powder and blown on the winds of foggy forgetfulness [...] Ah, but though divided and scattered, ground down and battered into the earth like a spike being pounded by a ten-pound sledge, we were on the ground and in the earth and the earth was red and black like the earth of Africa. And as we moldered underground we were mixed with this land. We liked it. It fitted us fine. It was in us and we were in it. And then – praise God – deep in the ground, deep in the womb of this land, we began to stir! [...]
Amen. Like the Valley of Dry Bones in Ezekiel's dream. Hoooh! We lay scattered in the ground for a long dry season. And the winds blew and the sun blazed down and the rains came and went and we were dead. Lord, we were dead! Except...Except...

The nerves of organs and limbs are joined together, one by one, and the body of the dead Negro people is resurrected:

...Amen, stirring, and right there in the midst of all our death and buriedness, the voice of God spoke down the Word...
Crying Do! I said, Do! Crying Doooo –
– these dry bones live? [....]
And did our dry bones live, Daddy Hickman?

Ah, we sprang together and walked around. All clacking together and clicking into place. All moving in time! Do! I said, Dooooo – these dry bones live!

Reborn into a new sense of time and nation, a new rhythm of history and culture, these black people became Americans – not yet African-Americans, still Negro Americans, but in that role the truest measure of the nation's hard struggle to realize its own ideals of justice and equality: "They can curse us and kill us but they can't destroy us all. This land is ours because we come out of it, we bled in it, our tears watered it, we fertilized it with our dead. So the more of us they destroy the more it becomes filled with our spirit of redemption."[42]
Especially in its entirety, the revival sermon is writing of exceptional power and grace. Ellison surely knew, however, that he was dealing with a

cliché, not just in the taut, paradoxical mixture of holiness and theatricality that he borrowed from black sermonic conventions and their tradition of literary transfiguration – witness Hurston's variations on the Reverend C. C. Lovelace's sermon in *Jonah's Gourd Vine*, for example – nor just specifically in the Valley of Dry Bones, one of the most often utilized allegories in the tradition.[43] He was dealing with a metaphor and potentially a cliché for his own career. The "jazz-shaped" culture of black Americans, Ellison wrote with curiously distended syntax in "What America Would Be Like Without Blacks" (1970), had enlivened the "dry bones of the nation" with their "tragic knowledge" that democracy's true subject was "not simply material well-being but the extension of the democratic process in the direction of perfecting itself." It was they, therefore, who best defined the nation's political ideals: "by the irony implicit in the dynamics of American democracy, they symbolize both its most stringent testing and the possibility of its greatest human freedom."[44] The sermon dramatizes the essay, just as the essay glosses the sermon, each of them dramatizing the inescapable, salvific "Negro-Americanizing" of the nation. But more than twenty years after the essay and close to thirty years after the short story "Juneteenth" – not to mention the fact that Ellison began his new novel while still completing *Invisible Man* – the work-in-progress remained a scattered chaos of organs and limbs. The dry bones did not live.

There is more to *Juneteenth* than the revival performance by Hickman and Bliss, of course, and it may be that the extensive manuscripts Ellison left behind, along with previously published but unincorporated Hickman episodes such as the dazzling "Cadillac Flambé," in which a black man protests Sunraider's racist oratory by ostentatiously setting his Cadillac ablaze on the senator's lawn, will bear out his continued genius. We will be left, in any event, to contemplate what never came to be. Whether he was paralyzed by the conundrum of how Bliss the Negro savior had become Adam Sunraider the white supremacist, or because, as the years went by, it became harder and harder to plunge "back into the shadow of the past where time hovers ghostlike," as he described the novelist's obligation in *Shadow and Act*,[45] Ellison was unable to solve his own "Negro problem."

Even if all his manuscripts had gone up in flames, however, Ellison would still be the author of one of the very best novels in all of American literature and one of the most important essayists in the modern world. Every word he wrote repays attention. He remains the most acute analyst of the American riddle of race, and it may turn out, in fact, that the dilemma of his career, which might be said to mirror the dilemma of the nation, will be his most revealing addition to that achievement. The finished and the unfinished, the act and the shadow, are his marvelous legacy.

Notes

1. Ralph Ellison, "Presentation to Bernard Malamud of the Gold Medal for Fiction" (1983), *The Collected Essays of Ralph Ellison*, ed. John F. Callahan (New York: Modern Library, 1995), pp. 466–7.
2. Bernard Malamud, "Jewishness in American Fiction," in Alan Cheuse and Nicholas Delbanco, eds., *Talking Horse: Bernard Malamud on Life and Work* (New York: Columbia University Press, 1996), pp. 141–2; Malamud, "On Subject Matter," ibid., p. 115.
3. Bernard Malamud, *The Tenants* (1971; rpt. New York: Penguin 1972), pp. 42, 154–5; my ellipses.
4. Ralph Ellison, *Invisible Man* (1952; New York: Random-Vintage, 1989), p. 9.
5. Ralph Ellison, "Perspective of Literature," *Going to the Territory* (New York: Random House, 1986), p. 335.
6. Irving Howe, "Black Boys and Native Sons," *Dissent* 10 (Autumn 1963): 354.
7. Ralph Ellison, "The World and the Jug," *Shadow and Act* (New York: Random House, 1964), pp. 112, 122.
8. Ellison, "A Very Stern Discipline," *Going to the Territory*, pp. 278, 282.
9. Amiri Baraka, "Black Art, Nationalism, Organization, Black Institutions" (1969), in *Raise, Race, Rays, Raze: Essays Since 1965* (New York: Random House, 1971), p. 98.
10. Larry Neal, "And Shine Swam On," in Larry Neal and Leroi Jones, eds., *Black Fire: An Anthology of Afro-American Writing* (New York: Morrow, 1968), p. 652. Cf. Neal, "Ellison's Zoot Suit," in Kimberly W. Benston, ed., *Speaking for You: The Vision of Ralph Ellison* (Washington, DC: Howard University Press, 1987), pp. 105–24.
11. Malamud, *The Tenants*, p. 173.
12. Philip Roth, *The Human Stain* (Boston: Houghton Mifflin, 2000), p. 6.
13. Ellison, *Invisible Man*, p. 3.
14. Ralph Ellison, letter of September 28, 1958, in *Trading Twelves: The Selected Letters of Ralph Ellison and Albert Murray*, ed. Albert Murray and John F. Callahan (New York: Modern Library, 2000), p. 195.
15. Philip Roth, "After Eight Books" (interview with Joyce Carol Oates), *Reading Myself and Others* (New York: Penguin, 1985), p. 109.
16. Roth, *The Human Stain*, pp. 336, 290.
17. Roth, *The Facts: A Novelist's Autobiography* (1988; rpt. New York: Penguin, 1989), p. 128.
18. Ellison, "Change the Joke and Slip the Yoke," *Shadow and Act* (New York: Random House, 1964) p. 55.
19. Gunnar Myrdal, *An American Dilemma: The Negro Problem and Modern Democracy*, 2 vols. (1944; rpt. New Brunswick, NJ: Transaction, 1996) I: 117.
20. Ellison, "The Little Man at Chehaw Station," *Going to the Territory*, pp. 21–2, 38.
21. Ellison, *Invisible Man*, p. 196; Ellison, "The Little Man at Chehaw Station," p. 21.
22. Ralph Ellison, "Hidden Name and Complex Fate," *Shadow and Act*, p. 163.
23. Ralph Ellison, "The Golden Age, the Time Past," *Shadow and Act*, p. 205; "On Bird, Bird-Watching, and Jazz," *Shadow and Act*, pp. 223, 227–8.

24. Norman Podhoretz, "What Happened to Ralph Ellison?" *Commentary* 108 (July–August 1999): 56.
25. Ellison, letter of March 16, 1956, *Trading Twelves*, p. 117.
26. Ibid.
27. Ellison, *Invisible Man*, pp. 240–3.
28. Ellison, "Introduction," *Shadow and Act*, p. xix.
29. Ellison, "Beating That Boy," *Shadow and Act*, p. 95.
30. Richard B. Moore, *The Name "Negro": Its Origin and Evil Use*, ed. W. Burghardt Turner and Joyce Moore Turner (1960; rpt. Baltimore, MD: Black Classics Press, 1992), pp. 46–7.
31. Ellison, "If the Twain Shall Meet," *Going to the Territory*, p. 102; Ellison, "Change the Joke and Slip the Yoke," p. 49.
32. Ellison, *Invisible Man*, p. 8.
33. Ellison, "Tell It Like It Is, Baby" (1965), *Collected Essays of Ralph Ellison*, pp. 32–45; Ellison, "An Extravagance of Laughter," *Going to the Territory*, pp. 155–6.
34. Ralph Ellison, *Juneteenth: A Novel*, ed. John F. Callahan (New York: Random House, 1999), p. 271.
35. Frederick Douglass, "The Meaning of July Fourth for the Negro," speech of July 5, 1852, in *The Life and Writings of Frederick Douglass*, 5 vols., ed. Philip S. Foner (New York: International Publishers, 1975), II, 201.
36. Ellison, *Juneteenth*, p. 356.
37. James Alan McPherson, "Indivisible Man" (1970), in *Conversations with Ralph Ellison*, ed. Maryemma Graham and Amrijit Singh (Jackson: University Press of Mississippi, 1995), p. 191.
38. Ellison, letter of June 27, 1959, in *Trading Twelves*, p. 205.
39. Ellison, *Juneteenth*, p. 116.
40. Robert Stone, "Ellison's Promised Land," *New York Review of Books* 46 (August 12, 1999): 18.
41. Ellison, *Juneteenth*, p. 352.
42. Ellison, *Juneteenth*, pp. 117–30 passim. All elisions are Ellison's except those marked with brackets.
43. Robert G. O'Meally, *The Craft of Ralph Ellison* (Cambridge, MA: Harvard University Press, 1980), pp. 133–8; Eric J. Sundquist, *The Hammers of Creation: Folk Culture in Modern African-American Fiction* (Athens: University of Georgia Press, 1992), pp. 49–91.
44. Ralph Ellison, "What America Would Be Like Without Blacks," *Going to the Territory*, pp. 110–12.
45. Ellison, "Introduction," *Shadow and Act*, p. xix.

SELECTED BIBLIOGRAPHY AND SUGGESTIONS FOR FURTHER READING

Primary Works

Novels

Invisible Man. New York: Random House, 1952 (30th Anniversary Edition, New York: Random House, 1982).
Juneteenth. New York: Random House, 1999.

Collected short fiction

Flying Home and Other Stories, edited by John F. Callahan. New York: The Modern Library, 1995.

Collected nonfiction

The Collected Essays of Ralph Ellison, edited by John F. Callahan. NewYork: The Modern Library, 1995.
Going to the Territory. New York: Random House, 1986.
Shadow and Act. New York: Vintage Books, 1964.

Letters

Trading Twelves. The Selected Letters of Ralph Ellison and Albert Murray, edited by Albert Murray and John F. Callahan. New York: The Modern Library, 2000.
"'American Culture Is of a Whole': From the Letters of Ralph Ellison," edited by John F. Callahan, *New Republic* 220: 9 (March 1, 1999): 34–49.

Interviews

Conversations with Ralph Ellison, edited by Maryemma Graham and Amrijit Singh. Jackson: University Press of Mississippi, 1995.

Secondary Works

Collections of essays

Benston, Kimberly W., ed. *Speaking for You: The Vision of Ralph Ellison.* Washington DC: Howard University Press, 1987.

Bloom, Harold, ed. *Ralph Ellison.* New York: Chelsea House Publishers, 1971.

Hersey, John, ed. *Ralph Ellison: A Collection of Critical Essays.* Englewood Cliffs, NJ: Prentice Hall, 1974.

O'Meally, Robert G., ed. *New Essays on Invisible Man.* New York: Cambridge University Press, 1988.

Parr, Susan Resnick and Pancho Savery, eds. *Approaches to Teaching Ellison's Invisible Man.* New York: Modern Language Association, 1989.

Reilly, John, M., ed. *Twentieth Century Interpretations of Invisible Man.* Englewood Cliffs, NJ: Prentice Hall, 1970.

Special Issues of Journals

Carleton Miscellany 18 (1980).

Boundary 2 30: 2 (2003).

Books

Eddy, Beth. *The Rites of Identity: The Religious Naturalism and Cultural Criticism of Kenneth Burke and Ralph Ellison.* Princeton, NJ: University Press, 2003.

Jackson, Lawrence. *Ralph Ellison: Emergence of Genius.* New York: Wiley and Son, 2002.

Nadel, Alan. *Invisible Criticism: Ralph Ellison and the American Canon.* Iowa City: University of Iowa Press, 1988.

O'Meally, Robert G. *The Craft of Ralph Ellison.* Cambridge: Harvard University Press, 1980.

Porter, Horace. *Jazz Country: Ralph Ellison in America.* Iowa City: University of Iowa Press, 2001.

Sundquist, Eric. *Cultural Contexts for Invisible Man.* Boston: St. Martin's Press, 1995.

Warren, Kenneth. *So Black and Blue: Ralph Ellison and the Occasion of Criticism.* Chicago: University of Chicago Press, 2003.

Watts, Jerry Gafio. *Heroism and the Black Intellectual: Ralph Ellison, Politics, and Afro-American Life.* Chapel Hill: University of North Carolina Press, 1994.

Parts of Books and Chapters in Books

Baker, Houston A. Jr. *Blues, Ideology, and Afro-American Literature: A Vernacular Theory.* Chicago: University of Chicago Press, 1984.

Byerman, Keith. *Fingering the Jagged Grain: Tradition and Form in Recent Black Fiction.* Athens: University of Georgia Press, 1985.

Callahan, John F. *In the African-American Grain: The Pursuit of Voice in Twentieth Century Black Fiction*. Urbana: University of Illinois Press, 1988.

Cheng, Anne Anlin. *The Melancholy of Race: Psychoanalysis, Assimilation and Hidden Grief*. New York: Oxford University Press, 2000.

Dixon, Melvin. *Ride Out the Wilderness*. Urbana: University of Illinois Press, 1987.

Gates, Henry Louis, Jr. *Figures in Black: Words, Signs, and The Racial Self*. New York: Oxford University Press, 1989.

Gates, Henry Louis, Jr. *The Signifying Monkey: A Theory of African-American Literary Criticism*. New York: Oxford University Press, 1988.

Harper, Michael S. and Robert B. Stepto, eds. *Chant of Saints: A Gathering of Afro-American Literature*. Urbana: University of Illinois Press, 1979.

Harper, Philip Brian. *Framing the Margins*. New York: Oxford University Press, 1994.

Murray, Albert. *The Omni-Americans*. New York: Vintage, 1988.

Scruggs, Charles. *Sweet Home: Invisible Cities in the Afro-American Novel*. Baltimore: The Johns Hopkins Press, 1993.

Smith, Valerie. *Self-Discovery and Authority in Afro-American Literature*. Cambridge: Harvard University Press, 1987.

Stepto, Robert B. *From Behind the Veil: A Study of Afro-American Narrative*. Urbana: University of Illinois Press, 1979.

Tanner, Tony. *City of Words*. New York: Harper and Row, 1971.

Warren, Robert Penn. *Who Speaks for the Negro?* New York: Random House, 1965.

Articles

Abrams, Robert E. "The Ambiguities of Dreaming in Ellison's *Invisible Man*." *American Literature* 49 (Jan, 1978), 592–603.

Allen, Danielle. "Ralph Ellison and the Tragicomedy of Citizenship." *Raritan* 23: 3 (Winter 2004), 56–74.

Anderson, Jervis. "Going to the Territory." *New Yorker*, 22(Nov. 22, 1976), 55–108.

Baker, Houston. "To Move Without Moving: An Analysis of Creativity and Commerce in Ralph Ellison's Trueblood Episode." *PMLA* 98(Oct. 1983), 828–45.

Benston, Kimberly. "Ellison, Baraka, and the Faces of Tradition." *Boundary* 2: 6 (Winter 1978): 333–54.

Dickstein, Morris. "Ralph Ellison, Race, and American Culture." *Raritan* 18: 2 (Spring 1999): 30–50.

Foley, Barbara. "Ralph Ellison as Proletarian Journalist." *Science and Society* 62: 4 (Winter 1998/1999), 537–56.

Foley, Barbara. "From Communism to Brotherhood: the Drafts of *Invisible Man*." In: *Twentieth-Century Americanisms: The Left and Modern Literatures in the United States*. Ed. Bill V. Mullen and James Smethurst. Chapel Hill: University of North Carolina Press, 2003.

Forrest, Leon. "Luminosity from the Lower Frequencies." *The Carleton Miscellany* 18: 3 (Winter 1980), 89–97.

Frank, Joseph. "Ralph Ellison and a Literary 'Ancestor': Dostoevski." *New Criterion* (Sept. 1983), 140–52.

Harris, Trudier. "Ellison's Peter Wheatstraw: His Basis in Folk Tradition." *Mississippi Folklore Register* 6 (1975), 117–26.

Howe, Irving. "Black Boys and Native Sons." In: *A World More Attractive* (New York: Horizon Press, 1963), 98–122.

Hyman, Stanley Edgar. "Ralph Ellison in Our Time." *The New Leader* 47:22 (Oct. 26, 1964), 21–2.

Kent, George. "Ralph Ellison and the Afro-American Folk and Cultural Tradition." *CLA Journal* 13:3 (March 1970), 265–76.

Lewis, R.W. B. "The Ceremonial Imagination of Ralph Ellison." *Carleton Miscellany* 18:3 (Winter 1980), 34–8.

McPherson, James Alan. "Indivisible Man." *The Atlantic* 226: 6 (Dec. 1970), 45–60.

Neal, Larry. "Ellison's Zoot Suit." *Black World* 20: 2 (Dec. 1970), 31–50.

Parrish, Timothy. "Ralph Ellison, Kenneth Burke, and the Form of Democracy." *Arizona Quarterly* 51: 3 (Autumn 1995) 117–48.

Pinckney, Darryl. "The Drama of Ralph Ellison." *New York Review of Books* XLIV: 8 (May 15 1997), 52–60.

Stepto, Robert. "Literary and Hibernations: Ralph Ellison's *Invisible Man*." *The Carleton Miscellany* 18: 3 (Winter 1980), 163–72.

Tate, Claudia. "Notes on the Invisible Woman in Ralph Ellison's *Invisible Man*." In: *Speaking for You: The Vision of Ralph Ellison*. Ed. Kimberly W. Benston (Washington DC: Howard University Press, 1987), 163–72.

Wright, John. "Dedicated Dreamer, Consecrated Acts: Shadowing Ellison." *The Carleton Miscellany* 18: 3 (Winter 1980), 142–99.

INDEX

CAMBRIDGE COMPANIONS TO LITERATURE